CHECKLIST of the BIRDS of
NORTHERN SOUTH AMERICA

CHECKLIST of the BIRDS of
NORTHERN SOUTH AMERICA

*An Annotated Checklist of the Species and Subspecies of
Ecuador, Colombia, Venezuela, Aruba, Curaçao, Bonaire,
Trinidad & Tobago, Guyana, Suriname and French Guiana*

Clemencia Rodner,
Miguel Lentino and Robin Restall

YALE UNIVERSITY PRESS
NEW HAVEN AND LONDON

Published in the United Kingdom by Pica Press (an imprint of Helm Information Ltd) and in the United States by Yale University Press.

ISBN 0-300-08740-3

Library of Congress Catalog Card Number: 00-103554
Printed in Hong Kong.

A catalogue record for this book is available from the British Library.

The paper in this book meets the guidelines for permanence and durability of the Committee on Production Guidelines for Book Longevity of the Council on Library Resources.

10 9 8 7 6 5 4 3 2 1

..."*and what is the use of a book,*"
thought Alice,
"*without pictures or conversation?*"

Lewis Carrol,
Alice in Wonderland

For the joyful hours it has given me, I dedicate this book to Fico, my father; Henry, my husband; and Henry, my son.

With love, tenderness and gratitude

Clemencia Rodner

ACKNOWLEDGEMENTS

We owe a great debt of gratitude to the many friends who helped and encouraged us, discussed mutual points of interest, made constructive suggestions, commented on the text, provided valuable information, and generally answered an enormous number of questions.

This checklist would be poorer indeed if it were not for the gifts of information and wisdom from Alex Aleixo, Richard Banks, Francisco Bisbal, Tom Brown, Steve Cardiff, Mario Cohn-Haft, Paul Coopmans, Jim Dean, Donna Dittman, Carla Dove, Phil Engle, Frank Gill, Gary Graves, Paul Greenfield, Steve Gregory, Steve Hilty, Dan Lane, Manuel Marin, Margarita Martinez, Juan Mazar Barnett, Kasuya Naoki, Storrs Olson, Fernando Ortiz Crespo, Mike Parr, Raymond Paynter, Jorge Pérez, Ramón Rivero, Steve Russell, Tom Ryan, Paul Salaman, Marcos Salcedo, Carlos Sanchez, Chris Sharpe, Karl Schuchmann, Tom Schulenberg, Gary Stiles, Paul Sweet, Kevin Winker, Thomas Züechner and Kevin Zimmer.

The assistance and guidance of Mort and Phyllis Isler, Chris Milensky, John O'Neill and Van Remsen has been fundamental – continuous correspondence with them was a test of their forbearance and their professional generosity, but for us it was a very pleasing experience.

We are particularly grateful to the curators and staff at the museums which opened their doors to us: the Bird Division at the USMNH, LSU-MZ, AMNH, MCZ, MEBRG (Museum of the Rancho Grande Biological Station) and the MHNLS (La Salle Museum of Natural History).

We are also very grateful to the NEOORN Listserver, an inanimate but lively internet tool which seems to have turned the tangled territory of Neotropical ornithology into a landscape of wide panoramas and sunny vistas.

Nevertheless, the contents of this checklist are absolutely our responsibility, and although we do not expect that those who provided help will necessarily agree with our treatments, we hope they will be pleased with the overall result.

A few dear friends have also contributed to our work, though not with bird information. We warmly thank Ruth Norris and John Shores, John and Letty O'Neill, and Phyllis and Mort Isler for their hospitality, unforgettable good food and great times. We also thank Nicla Camerin, Irving Carreño and Carlitos Gonzalez for being there when we needed them.

Clemencia Rodner, Miguel Lentino and Robin Restall

INTRODUCTION

The last two decades of the 20th century seem to have been times of constant taxonomic revision for Neotropical ornithology. Triggered by renewed interest in the documentation of biodiversity, by a worldwide explosion of interest in birding, and by intriguing innovations in the use of genetics and vocalisations in ornithological systematics, revisions at species and subspecies levels have been dramatic.

A major drawback generated by the changing taxonomy is confusion over species names. No two of the recent publications on Neotropical birds has the same list of common English or scientific names. Often, when comparing lists, one will find that even the pairing is changed – i.e. the common name in English does not match the scientific name – and in many cases, no reference or explanation is given.

This checklist arose out of our desire, whilst working on the forthcoming *Field Guide to the Birds of Northern South America* , for a definitive, up-to-date listing of all species and subspecies of birds in the region concerned. As would be expected, we used as our basis the outstanding *Check-list of the Birds of the World* (1931–86), started by J.L. Peters and completed by various other authors. Huge changes in taxonomy have occurred since the completion of this great work, and in updating the list we have been helped very much (especially at the species level) by the works of Sibley & Monroe (1990, 1993), Bock (1994), Stotz *et al.* (1996), and the first five volumes of the *Handbook of the Birds of the World* (del Hoyo *et al.* 1992–99). We have not necessarily followed all the taxonomic treatments given in these works, and indeed they are not always in agreement with each other, but we have chosen what we believe to be the most appropriate decisions, and have inevitably exercised our own judgement in some cases. Most importantly, all recent taxonomic revisions (since Peters *et al.*), as well as some potential future changes, have been fully referenced. Sequence of families and genera follows Bock (1994) or Stotz *et al.* (1996).

The subspecies have proven to be the biggest challenge. There is no complete, up-to-date list of subspecies published for any of the countries we cover, and most world or regional checklists do not list subspecies. This seemed somewhat surprising, given the current interest in biodiversity. Since they are the manifestation of geographic variation, subspecies represent the outer limits of biodiversity. We have used many sources to update the subspecies as listed by Peters *et al.*, in many cases consulting the original type descriptions of the taxa concerned. We have not sought to make judgements on the validity of old or new subspecies and have tended to include them all for the sake of completeness. References are given so that readers may go back to the original sources, but in some cases we highlight that doubt exists. Subspecies which are widely regarded as invalid are usually given as synonyms.

Two major items are lacking and some will say they should have been included. One is Spanish common names. We did not include them simply because there are no names *common* to all the countries. Each one has its own list of Spanish names, some stemming from popular use, some from well-known publications. The other item lacking is the species to be found on islands that belong politically to the countries we cover, and yet, are biogeographically separate. These islands are the Ecuadorian archipelago of Las Galapagos, the Colombian Isla de San Andres, and the Venezuelan Isla de Aves (which is different from the two small archipelagos called Las Aves, located between Bonaire and Los Roques).

This list is bound to be incomplete in many of its smaller details. For example, we know of the ongoing biodiversity project in Guyana by the US National Museum of Natural History and the Guyanese Government. Their list of species new to Guyana has not been published yet, and will undoubtedly include a few species that we have missed. The forthcoming *Birds of Mainland Ecuador* by Ridgely and Greenfield will surely contain species not in *An Annotated List of the Birds of Mainland Ecuador* (Ridgely *et al.* 1998). Around the region, there is a new *Grallaria* antpitta from Ecuador, a new *Synallaxis* spinetail from Venezuela, new records from Colombia, a new flycatcher from somewhere else, and so on, but species awaiting formal description will have to wait for subsequent editions of this Checklist.

Equally inevitably, there will be some relevant papers that we have missed in our searches for taxonomic changes. We apologise for any such omissions and hope that every user of this book will not hesitate to notify us of any errors or omissions. Similarly, we request that researchers notify us of any new discoveries or revisions as they occur. Given the difficulty of accessing some of the local literature, we hope that ornithologists working in the various countries concerned will send us information relating to their regions, thus allowing future editions to be more comprehensive.

Taxonomic revisions in the Neotropics are far from over and there will continue to be a need for a regularly revised and updated list of all the species and subspecies of the region for some time to come. We hope that this list will serve this purpose for the countries of northern South America.

THE CHECKLIST: A USER'S GUIDE

Species Number

Species numbers correspond with those used in the forthcoming *A Field Guide to the Birds of Northern South America* (Restall, Lentino & Rodner, in prep.).

English and Scientific Names

Generally, we have selected the most widely known or most appropriate English names. In a few instances, well-known English names have been modified as a result of taxonomic splits. A few alternative, frequently used English names are given in the References and Comments column. Similarly, scientific names invariably follow the most up-to-date taxonomic opinion. Former generic or specific names are given in the References and Comments column. Family divisions are indicated with a bold rule across the page.

Total Number of Subspecies

The total number of generally accepted subspecies is given. This will give the reader an idea of the complexity of the species over its entire range. Where there is some doubt about the number of valid subspecies, a question mark is added. Where a species is monotypic (i.e. has no regional variation), the letter 'M' is entered in the column.

Subspecies in Northern South America

The subspecies occurring in the countries covered by this checklist are listed in alphabetical order, together with a brief indication of their respective ranges (see below for range abbreviations).

We have only included continental South America, meaning the mainland and islands on the Continental Shelf. Neither the Galapagos Islands (Ecuador), the Isla de San Andres (Colombia) nor the Isla de Aves (Venezuela) are included in the territory covered by this checklist.

Altitude Range

Approximate altitude ranges are given using Chapman's Altitudinal Zones.

The two lowest zones – Tropical and Subtropical – are each divided into two subzones, in order to be more specific for species that have a narrower altitude range, such as those found exclusively in the lowlands or on lower slopes. When a species ranges throughout the entire Tropical or Subtropical zone, only the general abbreviation is used.

O	**Oceanic**	This term is used for coastal and pelagic habitats.
T	**Tropical**	From sea level to approximately 1,400–1,600m.
LT	**Lower Tropical**	From sea level to approx. 800–900m.
UT	**Upper Tropical**	From approx. 800–900 to approx. 1,400–1,600m.
S	**Subtropical**	From approx. 1,400–1,600m. to approx. 2,300–2,600m.
LS	**Lower Subtropical**	From approx. 1,400–1,600m. to approx. 2,000m.
US	**Upper Subtropical**	From approx. 2,000 to approx. 2,300–2,600m.
Te	**Temperate**	From approx. 2,300–2,600 to approx. 3,100–3,400m.
P	**Páramo**	From approx. 3,100–3,400 (tree line) to snow line.

References and Comments

This column contains a variety of information, including alternative or former names, synonyms, vagrancy, endemism and other status data. Potential future taxonomic changes are highlighted.

Important references are also given in this column; these may be type descriptions for taxa described since Peters *et al.*, or other taxonomic revisions. All references are detailed in the Bibliography.

The conservation status comments that appear in this column follow *Birds to Watch 2* (Collar *et al.* 1994).

Country Distribution

Presence in each country is indicated by a shaded column. For the most part, we have followed the country ranges given by Stotz *et al.* (1996), updated with range extensions found in more recent publications.

No indication is given for status, but uncertain occurrence or unconfirmed records (e.g. sight records only) are indicated with a question mark in the column concerned.

Country headings are abbreviated as follows:

Ec	Ecuador
Co	Colombia
Ve	Venezuela
Ar, Cu, Bo	Aruba, Curaçao, Bonaire
Tr, To	Trinidad & Tobago
Gu	Guyana
Su	Suriname
FG	French Guiana

Abbreviations

In addition to the countries listed above, other geographical regions or terms are abbreviated as follows:

N.Am.	North America
C.Am.	Central America
S.Am.	South America
Marg.	Isla Margarita (Venezuela)
NZ	New Zealand
Is	Islands
Arch.	Archipelago
M	monotypic
ssp.	subspecies
sep. sp.	separate species (spp = plural)
poss.	possibly
pers. comm.	personal communication
=	(sometimes) synonymous with
N	North
S	South
E	East
W	West
C	Central

References

Most references are cited in the usual way (by author and year, with full citations given in the Bibliography), but a few frequently used sources are listed simply by the authors' initials. These major works are as follows:

A&S   Altman, A. & Swift, B. 1993. *Checklist of the Birds of South America.* (3rd edn.). Privately published.

AOU 1998 A.O.U. 1998. *Checklist of North American Birds.* (7th edn.) American Ornithologists' Union, Washington, D.C.

F&K   Fjeldså, J. & Krabbe, N. 1990. *Birds of the High Andes.* Mus. Univ. of Copenhagen.

HBW   del Hoyo, J., Elliott, A. & Sargatal. J. 1992-99. *Handbook of the Birds of the World.* Volumes 1–5. Lynx Edicions, Barcelona.

H&B   Hilty, S.L. & Brown, W.L. 1986. *A Guide to the Birds of Colombia.* Princeton Univ. Press, Princeton.

RG&G   Ridgely, R.S., Greenfield, P.J. & Guerrero, M. 1998. *Una Lista Anotada de las Aves de Ecuador Continental Continental.* Fund. Ornitologica del Ecuador, CECIA, Quito.

S&M   Sibley, C.G. & Monroe, B.L. 1990. *Distribution and Taxonomy of Birds of the World.* Yale Univ. Press, New Haven.

S&M 1993 Sibley, C.G. & Monroe, B.L. 1993. *A Supplement to Distribution and Taxonomy of Birds of the World.* Yale Univ. Press, New Haven.

SFP&M   Stotz, D.F., Fitzpatrick, J.W., Parker, T.A. & Moskovitz. 1996. *Neotropical Birds: Ecology and Conservation.* Univ. of Chicago Press, Chicago.

No.	Species	Ssp. Total	Subspecies in Northern South America	Altitude Range	References and Comments	Ec	Co	Ve	Ar Cu Bo	Tr To	Gu	Su	FG
1	**Grey Tinamou** *Tinamus tao*	4	*kleei* (SC Co, E Ec) *larensis* (C Co, NW Ve) *septentrionalis* (NE Ve, NW Gu)	T-LS									
2	**Black Tinamou** *Tinamus osgoodi*	2	*hershkovitzi* (SC Co)	UT-S	The 2 ssp. may be sep. spp.: P. Salaman, pers. comm.								
3	**Great Tinamou** *Tinamus major*	12	*latifrons* (SW Co, W Ec) *major* (E Ve) *peruvianus* (SE Co, E Ec) *saturatus* (NW Co) *zuliensis* (NE Co, N Ve)	LT									
4	**White-throated Tinamou** *Tinamus guttatus*	M		LT									
5	**Highland Tinamou** *Nothocercus bonapartei*	5	*bonapartei* (NC Co, W Ve) *discrepans* (EC Co) *intercedens* (WC Co) *plumbeiceps* (EC Ec)	S									
6	**Tawny-breasted Tinamou** *Nothocercus julius*	M		S-Te									
7	**Berlepsch's Tinamou** *Crypturellus berlepschi*	M		LT									
8	**Cinereous Tinamou** *Crypturellus cinereus*	M		LT									
9	**Little Tinamou** *Crypturellus soui*	14	*andrei* (NE Ve & Tr) *caquetae* (SE Co) *caucae* (NC Co) *harterti* (W Co & W Ec) *mustelinus* (NE & NW Ve) *nigriceps* (E Ec) *soui* (E Co, Ve, Gu, Su, FG)	T									
10	**Tepui Tinamou** *Crypturellus ptaritepui*	M		UT-LS	**Endemic** **Vulnerable**								
11	**Brown Tinamou** *Crypturellus obsoletus*	9	*castaneus* (EC Co to E Ec) *cerviniventris* (N Ve) *knoxi* (NW Ve)	T-US									
12	**Undulated Tinamou** *Crypturellus undulatus*	6	*manapiare* (S Ve) *simplex* (SW Gu) *yapua* (SE Co, E Ec)	LT	Sight records in FG: SFP&M.								?
13	**Pale-browed Tinamou** *Crypturellus transfasciatus*	M		T									
14	**Slaty-breasted Tinamou** *Crypturellus boucardi*	2	Ssp in Co uncertain: *boucardi* or *costaricensis* ?	LT									
15	**Choco Tinamou** *Crypturellus kerriae*	M		LT	**Vulnerable**								
16	**Red-legged Tinamou** *Crypturellus erythropus*	7	*columbianus* (NC Co) *cursitans* (N Co, W Ve) *erythropus* (NE Ve, Gu, Su) *idoneus* (NE Co, NW Ve) *margaritae* (Ve: Marg) *saltuarius* (NC Co) *spencei* (N&W Ve)	T	Races need revision - 3 are almost certainly sep.spp.: *idoneus* (Sta Marta T.), *columbianus* (Colombian T.) & *saltuarius* (Magdalena T., known from a single specimen, is particularly different & critically threatened): S&M. Uncertain in Tr: SFP&M. Listed in RG&G.					?			

No.	Species	Ssp. Total	Subspecies in Northern South America	Altitude Range	References and Comments	Ec	Co	Ve	Ar Cu Bo	Tr To	Gu	Su	FG
17	**Grey-legged Tinamou** *Crypturellus duidae*	M		LT									
18	**Variegated Tinamou** *Crypturellus variegatus*	M		LT									
19	**Rusty Tinamou** *Crypturellus brevirostris*	M		LT									
20	**Bartlett's Tinamou** *Crypturellus bartletti*	M		LT	Listed in RG&G. Perhaps conspecific with *C. brevirostris*.								
21	**Barred Tinamou** *Crypturellus casiquiare*	M		LT									
22	**Tataupa Tinamou** *Crypturellus tataupa*	4	*peruviana* (SE Ec)	T	Listed in RG&G.								
23	**Andean Tinamou** *Nothoprocta pentlandii*	7	*ambigua* (S Ec)	UT-P									
24	**Curve-billed Tinamou** *Nothoprocta curvirostris*	2	*curvirostris* (C Ec)	Te-P									
25	**Least Grebe** *Tachybaptus dominicus*	4	*speciosus* (S Am.)	T-S									
26	**Pied-billed Grebe** *Podilymbus podiceps*	3	*antarticus* (S Am.)	T-Te	Sight records in FG: SFP&M.								?
27	**Colombian Grebe** *Podiceps andinus*	M		Te	Formerly *P. nigricollis andinus*: Fjeldså 1985. **Endemic** **Extinct**: Collar *et al.* 1992								
28	**Silvery Grebe** *Podiceps occipitalis*	2	*juninensis* (Ec, Co: C Andes)	T-P	Vagrant to Ec: RG&G.								
29	**Humboldt Penguin** *Spheniscus humboldti*	M		O	Vagrant to Ec: RG&G.								
30	**Galapagos Penguin** *Spheniscus mendiculus*	M		O	**Vulnerable**	?							
31	**Waved Albatross** *Diomedea irrorata*	M		O	Formerly *Phoebastria*								
32	**Black-footed Albatross** *Diomedea nigripes*	M		O	Sight records in Ec: SFP&M.	?							
33	**Black-browed Albatross** *Diomedea melanophris*	2	Ssp. uncertain: *impavida* or *melanophris* ?	O	Formerly *Thalassarche* Migrant to Ec: RG&G. Vagrant to Co.								
34	**Southern Giant Petrel** *Macronectes giganteus*	M		O	Sight records in Ec: SFP&M.	?							
35	**Southern Fulmar** *Fulmarus glacialoides*	M		O	Vagrant to Ec: SFP&M.								
36	**Cape Petrel** *Daption capense*	2	Ssp. uncertain: *australe* or *capense* ?	O	Vagrant to Co: SFP&M.								
37	**Dark-rumped Petrel** *Pterodroma phaeopygia*	2	*phaeopygia* (Galapagos)	O	**Critically threatened** Listed in RG&G.								
38	**Mottled Petrel** *Pterodroma inexpectata*	M		O	Vagrant to Ec: SFP&M.								
39	**Kermadec Petrel** *Pterodroma neglecta*	2	Ssp. uncertain: *juana* or *neglecta* ?	O	Listed in RG&G.								
40	**Black-capped Petrel** *Pterodroma hasitata*	2	*hasitata* (Caribbean) *caribbaea** (Jamaica)	O	*caribbaea* possibly extinct **Endangered** Sight records in Ar/Cu/Bo: SFP&M.				?				
41	**Antarctic Prion** *Pachyptila desolata*	3	Ssp. uncertain: *banksi* most probable	O	Vagrant to Ec: SFP&M.								
42	**Bulwer's Petrel** *Bulweria bulwerii*	M		O	Vagrant to Ar/Cu/Bo, Tr, FG: SFP&M.								

No.	Species	Ssp. Total	Subspecies in Northern South America	Altitude Range	References and Comments	Ec	Co	Ve	Ar Cu Bo	Tr To	Gu	Su	FG
43	White-chinned Petrel *Procellaria aequinoctialis*	2	Ssp. uncertain: *aequinoctialis* most probable	O	Sight records in Ec: RG&G.	?							
44	Parkinson's (Black) Petrel *Procellaria parkinsoni*	M		O	**Vulnerable**								
45	Cory's Shearwater *Calonectris diomedea*	3	Ssp. uncertain: *borealis* most probable	O	Sight records in FG: SFP&M. Sight record in Ve: C. Sharpe, pers. comm.			?					?
46	Wedge-tailed Shearwater *Puffinus pacificus*	M		O									
47	Flesh-footed Shearwater *Puffinus carneipes*	M		O	Not in N S.Am.: SFP&M & HBW. Migrant to Ec: A&S.								
48	Pink-footed Shearwater *Puffinus creatopus*	M		O	**Vulnerable** Vagrant to Co: SFP&M.								
49	Buller's Shearwater *Puffinus bulleri*	M		O	Uncertain in Ec: SFP&M.	?							
50	Great Shearwater *Puffinus gravis*	M		O	Vagrant to Ar/Cu/Bo: SFP&M.								
51	Sooty Shearwater *Puffinus griseus*	M		O									
52	Manx Shearwater *Puffinus puffinus*	M		O	Uncertain in Ve: SFP&M.			?					
53	Little Shearwater *Puffinus assimilis*	8	Ssp. uncertain: *baroli* or *boydi* most probable	O	Vagrant to FG: SFP&M.								
54	Audubon's Shearwater *Puffinus lherminieri*	10	*loyemilleri* (Caribbean) *subalaris* (E Equatorial Pacific)	O	Sight records in Ec: RG&G. Uncertain in Gu: SFP&M.	?					?		
55	Wilson's Storm-Petrel *Oceanites oceanicus*	2	Ssp. uncertain: *oceanicus* or *exasperatus* ?	O	Vagrant to Tr: SFP&M.								
56	White-vented Storm-Petrel *Oceanites gracilis*	2	*galapagoensis* (Galapagos) *gracilis* (off coast of Ec.)	O									
57	White-faced Storm-Petrel *Pelagodroma marina*	6	*maoriana* (breeds in N.Z., disperses to W S.Am.)	O	Vagrant to Ec: RG&G.								
58	White-bellied Storm-Petrel *Fregetta grallaria*	4	*segethi* (Juan Fernandez Is.)	O									
59	Least Storm-Petrel *Oceanodroma microsoma*	M		O	Formerly *Halocyptena*.								
60	Wedge-rumped Storm-Petrel *Oceanodroma tethys*	2	*kelsalli* (Is. off Peru) *tethys* (Galapagos)	O									
61	Band-rumped Storm-Petrel *Oceanodroma castro*	M		O	Sight records in Ec: RG&G. Vagrant to Co: SFP&M.								
62	Leach's Storm-Petrel *Oceanodroma leucorhoa*	4	*leucorhoa* (Atlantic) *chapmani, cheimomneistes* & *socorroensis* (Pacific)	O	Vagrant to Ar/Cu/Bo: SFP&M.								
63	Markham's Storm-Petrel *Oceanodroma markhami*	M		O	Vagrant to Co: SFP&M.								
64	Black Storm-Petrel *Oceanodroma melania*	M		O									
65	Ashy Storm-Petrel *Oceanodroma homochroa*	M		O	Sight records in Ec: RG&G.	?							
66	Ringed Storm-Petrel *Oceanodroma hornbyi*	M		O									
67	Red-billed Tropicbird *Phaethon aethereus*	3	*mesonauta* (Caribbean & E Pacific)	O									

No.	Species	Ssp. Total	Subspecies in Northern South America	Altitude Range	References and Comments	Ec	Co	Ve	Ar Cu Bo	Tr To	Gu	Su	FG
68	**White-tailed Tropicbird** *Phaethon lepturus*	5	*catesbyi* (Caribbean)	O	Vagrant to Co, sight records in Tr, Ar/Cu/Bo: SFP&M.				?	?			
69	**Magnificent Frigatebird** *Fregata magnificens*	M		O									
70	**Great Frigatebird** *Fregata minor*	5	*ridgwayi* (E Pacific)	O	Sight records in Ec: RG&G.	?							
71	**Blue-footed Booby** *Sula nebouxii*	2	*nebouxii* (E Pacific)	O									
72	**Peruvian Booby** *Sula variegata*	M		O	Vagrant to Ec: RG&G.								
73	**Masked Booby** *Sula dactylatra*	4 ?	*dactylatra* (Caribbean & Atlantic)	O	Vagrant to Tr: SFP&M.								
74	**Nazca Booby** *Sula granti*	M		O	Formerly *S. dactylatra granti*: Pitman & Jehl 1998.								
75	**Red-footed Booby** *Sula sula*	3	*sula* (Caribbean & SW Atlantic) *websteri* (E Pacific)	O	Sight records in FG: SFP&M.								?
76	**Brown Booby** *Sula leucogaster*	4	*etesiaca* (CE Pacific) *leucogaster* (Caribbean & tropical Atlantic)	O	Sight records in Ec: RG&G.	?							
77	**Neotropic Cormorant** *Phalacrocorax brasilianus*	2	*olivaceus* (all S.Am.)	O-Te	Formerly *P. olivaceus*: Browning 1989.								
78	**Double-crested Cormorant** *Phalacrocorax auritus*	4	*floridanus* (N Caribbean)	O	Vagrant to Ar/Cu/Bo: SFP&M.								
79	**Guanay Cormorant** *Phalacrocorax bougainvillii*	M		O	Vagrant to Ec: RG&G.								
80	**Anhinga** *Anhinga anhinga*	2	*anhinga* (all E tropical S.Am.)	T									
81	**Brown Pelican** *Pelecanus occidentalis*	5	*murphyi* (Ec, Co: Pacific coast & islands) *occidentalis* (Co & Ve: Caribbean islands, Ar, Tr, To) *urinator* (Co & Ec: offshore waters)	O									
82	**Peruvian Pelican** *Pelecanus thagus*	M		O	Formerly *P. occidentalis thagus*. Listed in RG&G.								
83	**Horned Screamer** *Anhima cornuta*	M		LT									
84	**Northern Screamer** *Chauna chavaria*	M		T									
85	**Fulvous Whistling-Duck** *Dendrocygna bicolor*	M		T	Vagrant to Ar/Cu/Bo: SFP&M.								
86	**White-faced Whistling-Duck** *Dendrocygna viduata*	M		T	Vagrant to Ar/Cu/Bo, FG: SFP&M.								
87	**Black-bellied Whistling-Duck** *Dendrocygna autumnalis*	2	*discolor* (S.Am.)	T	Vagrant to Ar/Cu/Bo: SFP&M.								
88	**Masked Duck** *Oxyura dominica*	M		LT	Vagrant to Ar/Cu/Bo: SFP&M.								
89	**Andean Duck** *Oxyura ferruginea*	3	*andina* (Co: C&N Andes) *ferruginea* (S Co, Ec)	S-P	Livezy 1995.								
90	**Greater White-fronted Goose** *Anser albifrons*	5	Ssp. uncertain: *elgasi, flavirostris* or *gambeli* ?	LT	Vagrant to Ar/Cu/Bo: SFP&M.								

No.	Species	Ssp. Total	Subspecies in Northern South America	Altitude Range	References and Comments	Ec	Co	Ve	Ar Cu Bo	Tr To	Gu	Su	FG
91	Snow Goose *Anser caerulescens*	2	Ssp. uncertain: *caerulescens* or *atlanticus* ?	LT	Vagrant to Tr: SFP&M.								
92	Orinoco Goose *Neochen jubata*	M		LT	Status uncertain in Ec: SFP&M, RG&G.	?							
93	Muscovy Duck *Cairina moschata*	M		T									
94	Comb Duck *Sarkidiornis melanotos*	2	*sylvicola* (S.Am.)	T	Vagrant to Ar/Cu/Bo, Tr: SFP&M.								
95	Brazilian Teal *Amazonetta brasiliensis*	2	*brasiliensis* (N S.Am.)	T									
96	Torrent Duck *Merganetta armata*	6	*colombiana* (Ve, Co, N Ec) *leucogenis* (C&S Ec)	S-P									
97	American Wigeon *Anas americana*	M		T	Rare transient in Aruba.								
98	Green-winged Teal *Anas crecca*	3	*carolinensis* (migrant from Nearctic: Co, Ve, To)	T-S	Vagrant to Co & Tr: SFP&M. Recorded in Ve: banding recovery.								
99	Merida Speckled Teal *Anas altipetens*	M	(NW Ve, Co: E Andes)	S-P	Formerly *A. flavirostris altipetens*: Livezey 1991.								
100	Andean Teal *Anas andium*	M	(Co, N Ec)		Formerly *A. flavirostris andium*: Livezey 1991.								
101	Mallard *Anas platyrhynchos*	7	Ssp. uncertain: *comboschas* or *platyrhynchos* ?	T	Vagrant to Ar/Cu/Bo: SFP&M.								
102	Northern Pintail *Anas acuta*	3	*acuta* (boreal migrant: winters to Co, Ve, rarely to Gu, Su)	T-S	Vagrant to Gu, Su; sight records in Ar/Cu/Bo: SFP&M.				?				
103	Yellow-billed Pintail *Anas georgica*	3	*niceforoi* (SE Co) *spinicauda* (S Co, Ec)	T-P	*niceforoi* apparently extinct.								
104	White-cheeked Pintail *Anas bahamensis*	3	*bahamensis* (N S.Am.)	LT									
105	Blue-winged Teal *Anas discors*	M		T-S									
106	Cinnamon Teal *Anas cyanoptera*	5	*borreroi* (Co: E Andes) *tropica* (NW Co)	T-P	Vagrant to Ve: SFP&M.								
107	Northern Shoveler *Anas clypeata*	M		T-S	Vagrant to Ar/Cu/Bo: SFP&M.								
108	Southern Pochard *Netta erythrophthalma*	2	*crythrophthalma* (Ve)	T-P	Vagrant to Tr: SFP&M								
109	Ring-necked Duck *Aythya collaris*	M		T-S	Vagrant to Ve, Tr; sight records in Co, Ar/Cu/Bo: SFP&M.		?		?				
110	Lesser Scaup *Aythya affinis*	M		T-S	Vagrant to Su: SFP&M.								
111	Greater Flamingo *Phoenicopterus ruber*	2	*ruber* (Caribbean)	LT	Sight records in Ec: SFP&M.	?							
112	Chilean Flamingo *Phoenicopterus chilensis*	M		T-P									
113	Whistling Heron *Syrigma sibilatrix*	2	*fostersmithi* (E Co, Ve)	T									
114	Reddish Egret *Egretta rufescens*	2	*rufescens* (N Co, N Ve, islands)	LT	Formerly *Hydranassa* Sight records in Tr: SFP&M.					?			
115	Tricolored Heron *Egretta tricolor*	2	*ruficollis* (Co, NW Ve) *tricolor* (Ec, NE Ve, Tr)	LT	Formerly *Hydranassa*								
116	Little Blue Heron *Egretta caerulea*	M		LT	Formerly *Hydranassa*. Straggler to Ar/Cu/Bo: Voous 1982.								

5

No.	Species	Ssp. Total	Subspecies in Northern South America	Altitude Range	References and Comments	Ec	Co	Ve	Ar Cu Bo	Tr To	Gu	Su	FC
117	**Little Egret** *Egretta garzetta*	3 ?	Ssp. uncertain: *garzetta* ?	T	Vagrant to Tr & Su: SFP&M.								
118	**Western Reef-Heron** *Egretta gularis*	2 ?	Ssp. uncertain: *gularis* ?	T	Formerly *E. garzetta gularis*: HBW. Vagrant to Tr: SFP&M.					?			
119	**Snowy Egret** *Egretta thula*	2	*thula* (E Co, Ve)	T									
120	**Capped Heron** *Pilherodius pileatus*	M		LT	Formerly *Nycticorax*.								
121	**Grey Heron** *Ardea cinerea*	4	Ssp. uncertain: *cinerea* ?	T	Vagrant to Tr: SFP&M.								
122	**Great Blue Heron** *Ardea herodias*	5	*occidentalis* (Ve: islands & Caribbean coast)	T-S									
123	**Cocoi Heron** *Ardea cocoi*	M		LT									
124	**Great Egret** *Ardea alba*	4	*egretta* (N.Am. & S.Am.)	T	Formerly *Egretta*, or *Casmerodius*.								
125	**Cattle Egret** *Bubulcus ibis*	3	*ibis* (N.Am. & S.Am.)	T-S	Formerly *Ardeola*								
126	**Striated Heron** *Butorides striatus*	30 ?	*maculatus* * (Ar, Cu, Bo) *striatus* (S.Am.)	T-LS	* Voous 1986.								
127	**Green Heron** *Butorides virescens*	M	(migrant from N.Am.)	T-LS	Formerly *B. striatus virescens*: Monroe & Browning 1992. Vagrant to Ec, Gu & Su.								
128	**Agami Heron** *Agamia agami*	M		LT									
129	**Yellow-crowned Night-Heron** *Nyctanassa violacea*	6	*calignis* (Co, Ec) *cayennensis* (Co, Ve, Gu, Su, FG)	LT	Formerly *Nycticorax*								
130	**Black-crowned Night-Heron** *Nycticorax nycticorax*	4	*hoactli* (N S.Am.)	T-P									
131	**Boat-billed Heron** *Cochlearius cochlearia*	5	*cochlearia* (Co, Ve, Gu, Su, FG)	LT	Straggler to Ar/Cu/Bo: Voous 1982.								
132	**Bare-throated Tiger-Heron** *Tigrisoma mexicanum*	M		LT									
133	**Fasciated Tiger-Heron** *Tigrisoma fasciatum*	3	*salmoni* (Co, Ve, Ec)	T-Te									
134	**Rusfecent Tiger-Heron** *Tigrisoma lineatum*	2	*lineatum* (N S.Am.)	T	= Lineated Tiger-Heron.								
135	**Zigzag Heron** *Zebrilus undulatus*	M		LT									
136	**Stripe-backed Bittern** *Ixobrychus involucris*	M		LT	Sight records in Ec: RG&G.	?							
137	**Least Bittern** *Ixobrychus exilis*	4	*bogotensis* (C Co) *erythromelas* (all N S.Am.)	T-Te									
138	**Pinnated Bittern** *Botaurus pinnatus*	2	*pinnatus* (N S.Am.)	T	Straggler to Ar/Cu/Bo: Voous 1982.								
139	**White Ibis** *Eudocimus albus*	M		LT	Uncertain in Gu: SFP&M. Straggler to Ar/Cu/Bo: Voous 1982.							?	
140	**Scarlet Ibis** *Eudocimus ruber*	M		LT	Uncertain in Ar/Cu/Bo & FG: SFP&M. Sight records in Ec: RG&G.	?				?			?
141	**Bare-faced Ibis** *Phimosus infuscatus*	3	*berlepschi* (NE Co, E Ec, Ve, Gu, Su)	LT	Vagrant to Ec: RG&G.								

6

No.	Species	Ssp. Total	Subspecies in Northern South America	Altitude Range	References and Comments	Ec	Co	Ve	Ar Cu Bo	Tr To	Gu	Su	FG
142	**Glossy Ibis** *Plegadis falcinellus*	M		LT	Sight records in Ec & Tr: SFP&M. Sight records in Ec: RG&G.	?				?			
143	**White-faced Ibis** *Plegadis chihi*	M		T-S	Recorded in Ar/Cu/Bo: Voous 1982.								
144	**Sharp-tailed Ibis** *Cercibis oxycerca*	M		LT									
145	**Buff-necked Ibis** *Theristicus caudatus*	2	*caudatus* (Co, Ve, Gu, Su, FG)	T									
146	**Andean Ibis** *Theristicus branickii*	M		P	= *T. melanopsis* or *T. caudatus*. S&M.								
147	**Green Ibis** *Mesembrinibis cayennensis*	M		T									
148	**Roseate Spoonbill** *Ajaia ajaja*	M		LT									
149	**Wood Stork** *Mycteria americana*	M		LT	Vagrant to Ar/Cu/Bo: SFP&M, Voous 1982.								
150	**Maguari Stork** *Ciconia maguari*	M		LT									
151	**Jabiru** *Jabiru mycteria*	M		LT	Sight records in Ec: RG&G.	?				?			
152	**Black Vulture** *Coragyps atratus*	3	*brasilianus* (N&E S.Am.) *foetens* (W S.Am.)	T-Te									
153	**Turkey Vulture** *Cathartes aura*	4	*jota* (S Ec.) *ruficollis* (lowlands S.Am.) *septentrionalis* & *aura*: migrants from US & Mexico	T-Te									
154	**Lesser Yellow-headed Vulture** *Cathartes burrovianus*	2	*burrovianus* (N&C Co, NW Ve) *urubitinga* (lowlands S.Am.)	T		?							
155	**Greater Yellow-headed Vulture** *Cathartes melambrotus*	M		LT									
156	**Andean Condor** *Vultur gryphus*	M		T-P									
157	**King Vulture** *Sarcoramphus papa*	M		T									
158	**Osprey** *Pandion haliaetus*	4	*carolinensis* (N.Am. & S.Am.)	LT									
159	**Grey-headed Kite** *Leptodon cayanensis*	2	*cayanensis* (N S.Am.)	T									
160	**Hook-billed Kite** *Chondrohierax uncinatus*	3	*uncinatus* (N S.Am.)	T-Te									
161	**Swallow-tailed Kite** *Elanoides forficatus*	2	*yetapa* (N S.Am.)	T-S									
162	**Pearl Kite** *Gampsonyx swainsonii*	3	*leonae* (N Co, Ve, Tr, Gu, Su) *magnus* (W Co, Ec)	T									
163	**White-tailed Kite** *Elanus leucurus*	2	*leucurus* (N S.Am.)	T-Te	Formerly *E. caeruleus leucurus* (Black-winged Kite): Clark & Banks 1992. Sight records in Ar/Cu/Bo: SFP&M.				?				
164	**Snail Kite** *Rostrhamus sociabilis*	3	*sociabilis* (C.Am. & S.Am.)	T									
165	**Slender-billed Kite** *Rostrhamus hamatus*	M		LT	Formerly *Helicolestes*								

No.	Species	Ssp. Total	Subspecies in Northern South America	Altitude Range	References and Comments	Ec	Co	Ve	Ar Cu Bo	Tr To	Gu	Su	FG
166	**Double-toothed Kite** *Harpagus bidentatus*	2	*bidentatus* (S.Am., where *fasciatus* does not occur) *fasciatus* (W Co, W Ec)	T									
167	**Rufous-thighed Kite** *Harpagus diodon*	M		T									
168	**Mississippi Kite** *Ictinia mississippiensis*	M		LT									
169	**Plumbeous Kite** *Ictinia plumbea*	M		T-S									
170	**Long-winged Harrier** *Circus buffoni*	M		LT	*C. (falco) brasiliensis* not valid: Banks & Dove 1992								
171	**Northern Harrier** *Circus cyaneus*	2	*hudsonius* (N Co, N Ve)	LT	Vagrant to Ve: SFP&M.								
172	**Cinereous Harrier** *Circus cinereus*	M		T-P									
173	**Grey-bellied Hawk** *Accipiter poliogaster*	M		LT									
174	**Tiny Hawk** *Accipiter superciliosus*	2	*fontanieri* (W Co, W Ec) *superciliosus* (E Co, Ec, Ve, Gu, Su, FG)	T									
175	**Semicollared Hawk** *Accipiter collaris*	M	(Andes: Ve, Co, Ec)	UT-S									
176	**Plain-breasted Hawk** *Accipiter ventralis*	M		T-Te	Sometimes treated as conspecific with *A. striatus*, *A. chionogaster* & *A. erythronemius*.								
177	**Cooper's Hawk** *Accipiter cooperii*	M		UT-Te	Vagrant to Co: SFP&M.								
178	**Bicolored Hawk** *Accipiter bicolor*	4	*bicolor* (N S.Am.)	T-S									
179	**Crane Hawk** *Geranospiza caerulescens*	6	*balzarensis* (Ec, Co: W Andes) *caerulescens* (Co, Ec, Ve, Gu, Su, FG)	LT	*caerulescens* may be a sep. sp., (Grey Crane Hawk): S&M.								
180	**Plumbeous Hawk** *Leucopternis plumbea*	M	(W Co, W Ec)	LT									
181	**Slate-coloured Hawk** *Leucopternis schistacea*	M		LT									
182	**Barred Hawk** *Leucopternis princeps*	M	(W Co, N Ec)	UT-Te									
183	**Black-faced Hawk** *Leucopternis melanops*	M		T									
184	**Semiplumbeous Hawk** *Leucopternis semiplumbea*	M	(W Co, NW Ec)	T									
185	**White Hawk** *Leucopternis albicollis*	4	*albicollis* (E Ec, E Co, NW Ve, Tr, Gu, Su, FG) *costaricensis* (W Co) *williaminae* (NW Co, NW Ve)	T									
186	**Grey-backed Hawk** *Leucopternis occidentalis*	M	(W Ec)	T	**Endangered**								
187	**Rufous Crab-Hawk** *Buteogallus aequinoctialis*	M		LT	Sight records in Tr: SFP&M.					?			
188	**Common Black-Hawk** *Buteogallus anthracinus*	3	*anthracinus* (N Co, N Ve, Tr, NW Gu)	T-S									
189	**Mangrove Black-Hawk** *Buteogallus subtilis*	3	*subtilis* (W Co, W Ec)	LT									
190	**Great Black-Hawk** *Buteogallus urubitinga*	2	*urubitinga* (all N S.Am.)	T-LS									

No.	Species	Ssp. Total	Subspecies in Northern South America	Altitude Range	References and Comments	Ec	Co	Ve	Ar Cu Bo	Tr To	Gu	Su	FG
191	Savanna Hawk *Buteogallus meridionalis*	M		T	Formerly *Heterospizias*								
192	Harris' Hawk *Parabuteo unicinctus*	2	harrisi (W Co, Ec) unicinctus (NE Co, Ve)	T-S									
193	Black-collared Hawk *Busarellus nigricollis*	2	nigricollis (all N S.Am.)	LT						?			
194	Black-chested Buzzard-Eagle *Geranoaetus melanoleucus*	2	australis (Co, Ve, Ec)	T-P									
195	Solitary Eagle *Harpyhaliaetus solitarius*	2	solitarius (Co, Ve, Ec)	UT-Te									
196	Grey-lined Hawk *Asturina nitida*	4	costaricensis (N Co, W Ec) nitidus (E Co, E Ec, Ve, Gu, Su, FG)	T	Formerly *Buteo nitidus* or Grey Hawk								
197	Roadside Hawk *Buteo magnirostris*	12	magnirostris (N S.Am.)	T-S									
198	Broad-winged Hawk *Buteo platypterus*	6	platypterus (winters all N S.Am.)	T	Sight records in Su, vagrant to FG: SFP&M.							?	
199	White-rumped Hawk *Buteo leucorrhous*	M		S-Te									
200	Short-tailed Hawk *Buteo brachyurus*	2	brachyurus (N S.Am.)	T	Sight records in Tr: SFP&M.					?			
201	White-throated Hawk *Buteo albigula*	M		S-P									
202	Swainson's Hawk *Buteo swainsoni*	M		UT-S	Sight records in Tr: SFP&M.					?			
203	White-tailed Hawk *Buteo albicaudatus*	3	colonus (E Co, E Ve, Gu, Su, Tr, Ar, Bo, Cu, FG) hypospodius (N Co, NW Ve)	T-S	Uncertain in Ec: SFP&M.	?							
204	Red-backed Hawk *Buteo polyosoma*	2	polyosoma (Co, Ec)	T-Te	Considered conspecific with *B. poecilochrous*: Farquhar 1998.								
205	Puna Hawk *Buteo poecilochrous*	M		S-P									
206	Zone-tailed Hawk *Buteo albonotatus*	M		T-Te									
207	Red-tailed Hawk *Buteo jamaicensis*	14	Ssp. uncertain: borealis or kriderii ?	T-Te	Sight record in Ve: Hilty 1999.		?						
208	Crested Eagle *Morphnus guianensis*	M		T									
209	Harpy Eagle *Harpia harpyja*	M		LT									
210	Black-and-white Hawk-Eagle *Spizastur melanoleucus*	M		T									
211	Black Hawk-Eagle *Spizaetus tyrannus*	2	serus (all N S.Am.)	T-S									
212	Ornate Hawk-Eagle *Spizaetus ornatus*	4	ornatus (E Co, E Ec, Ve, Tr, Gu, Su, FG) vicarius (W Co, W Ec)	T									
213	Black-and-chestnut Eagle *Oroaetus isidori*	M		S-Te	Formerly *Spizaetus*								
214	Black Caracara *Daptrius ater*	M		LT									
215	Red-throated Caracara *Daptrius americanus*	M		T									
216	Caruncuated Caracara *Phalcoboenus carunculatus*	M		Te-P									
217	Mountain Caracara *Phalcoboenus magalopterus*	M	(S Ec)	Te-P	Listed in RG&G.								

No.	Species	Ssp. Total	Subspecies in Northern South America	Altitude Range	References and Comments	Ec	Co	Ve	Ar Cu Bo	Tr To	Gu	Su	F
218	**Southern Crested Caracara** *Caracara plancus*	4	*cheriway* (N S.Am.)	T-Te	Formerly *Polyborus*: Banks & Dove 1992. Sight records in Ar/Cu/Bo: SFP&M.					?			
219	**Yellow-headed Caracara** *Milvago chimachima*	2	*cordatus* (N S.Am.)	T-S	Sight records in Ar/Cu/Bo, Tr: SFP&M.				?	?			
220	**Laughing Falcon** *Herpetotheres cachinnans*	2	*cachinnans* (N S.Am.)	T-LS									
221	**Barred Forest-Falcon** *Micrastur ruficollis*	6	*concentricus* (S Ve, Gu, Su, FG) *interstes* (W Co, W Ec) *zonothorax* (E Co, Ve)	T-S									
222	**Plumbeous Forest-Falcon** *Micrastur plumbeus*	M	(Ec, S Co)	LT	Formerly *M. ruficollis plumbeus*: HBW. **Endangered**								
223	**Lined Forest-Falcon** *Micrastur gilvicollis*	M	(E Co, SE Ve, Gu, Su, FG)	LT	Formerly *M. ruficollis gilvicollis*: Schwartz 1972.								
224	**Slaty-backed Forest-Falcon** *Micrastur mirandollei*	M		LT									
225	**Collared Forest-Falcon** *Micrastur semitorquatus*	2	*naso* (N&W Co, Ec) *semitorquatus* (E Co, Ve, Gu, Su, FG)	T									
226	**Buckley's Forest-Falcon** *Micrastur buckleyi*	M		LT									
227	**American Kestrel** *Falco sparverius*	17	*aequatorialis* (N Ec) *brevipennis* (Ar, Cu, Bo) *caucae* (W Co) *isabellinus* (Ve) *ochraceus* (E Co to NW Ve) *peruvianus* (SW Ec)	T-P	Sight records in Tr: SFP&M.					?			
228	**Aplomado Falcon** *Falco femoralis*	3	*femoralis* (N&E Co, Ve, Gu, Su, FG) *pichinchae* (SW Co, Ec)	T-P									
229	**Merlin** *Falco columbarius*	9	(boreal migrants to N S.Am.) Ssp. uncertain: *columbarius* or *richardsoni* ?		Sight records in Gu, FG: SFP&M.						?		?
230	**Bat Falcon** *Falco rufigularis*	3	*petoensis* (W Co, W Ec) *rufigularis* (E Co, Ve, Tr, Gu, Su, FG)	LT									
231	**Peregrine Falcon** *Falco peregrinus*	19	*cassini* = resident in N S.Am. (Ec); *tundrius, anatum, pealei* = boreal migrants, passing through N S.Am.	T-Te									
232	**Orange-breasted Falcon** *Falco deiroleucus*	M		T-S									
233	**Common Kestrel** *Falco tinnunculus*	11	Ssp. uncertain: several are possible	?	Sight records in FG: SFP&M.								?
234	**Grey-headed Chachalaca** *Ortalis cinereiceps*	M		T									
235	**Chestnut-winged Chachalaca** *Ortalis garrula*	M		LT	**Endemic**								
236	**Rufous-vented Chachalaca** *Ortalis ruficauda*	2	*ruficauda* (N Co, N&NE Ve, To) *ruficrissa* (N Co, NW Ve)	T	*ruficrissa* may be a sep. sp. (Rufous-tipped Chachalaca): S&M.								
237	**Rufous-headed Chachalaca** *Ortalis erythroptera*	M	(W Ec)	LT	**Vulnerable**								

No.	Species	Ssp. Total	Subspecies in Northern South America	Altitude Range	References and Comments	Ec	Co	Ve	Ar Cu Bo	Tr To	Gu	Su	FG
238	Speckled Chachalaca *Ortalis guttata*	M	(E Co, E Ec)	T-LS		■	■						
239	Colombian Chachalaca *Ortalis colombiana*	M	(NC Co)		**Endemic** Population threatened.		■						
240	Little Chachalaca *Ortalis motmot*	3	*motmot* (S Ve, Gu, Su, FG)	T-S				■			■	■	■
241	Band-tailed Guan *Penelope argyrotis*	3	*albicauda* (Co & Ve: Perija) *argyrotis* (N Co, NW Ve) *colombiana* (N Co)	UT-S			■	■					
242	Bearded Guan *Penelope barbata*	M		S-Te	Vulnerable	■							
243	Baudo Guan *Penelope ortoni*	M		UI-LS	Vulnerable	■	■						
244	Andean Guan *Penelope montagnii*	5	*atrogularis* (SW Co, W Ec) *brooki* (SE Co, E Ec) *montagni* (NW Ve, NC Co)	S-P		■	■	■					
245	Marail Guan *Penelope marail*	2	*jacupeba* (SE Ve) *marail* (SE Ve, Gu, Su, FG)	LT				■			■	■	■
246	Crested Guan *Penelope purpurascens*	3	*aequatorialis* (NW Co, SE Ec) *brunnescens* (N Co, E Ve)	T-S	Eley 1982	■	■	■					
247	Cauca Guan *Penelope perspicax*	M		UT-S	**Endangered** **Endemic** Eley 1982		■						
248	Spix's Guan *Penelope jacquacu*	5	*granti* (SE Ve) *jacquacu* (E Co, E Ec) *orienticola* (SE Ve)	T	*granti* may be a sep. sp. (Green-backed Guan): S&M. Eley 1982	■	■	■					
249	Trinidad Piping-Guan *Pipile pipile*	M	(Tr)	LT	Possibly conspecific with *P. cumanensis* : S&M 1993. **Critically threatened** **Endemic** James & Hislop 1988.					■			
250	Blue-throated Piping-Guan *Pipile cumanensis*	2	*cumanensis* (E Ec, C&E Co, S Ve, Gu, Su, FG)	LT	Vaurie 1967, 1968.	■	■	■			■	■	■
251	Wattled Guan *Aburria aburri*	M		UT-S		■	■	■					
252	Sickle-winged Guan *Chamaepetes goudotii*	5	*fagani* (SW Co, W Ec) *goudotti* (Co: C&W Andes) *sanctamartae* (Co: Sta. Marta) *tschudii* (SE Co, E Ec)	UT Te		■	■						
253	Nocturnal Curassow *Nothocrax urumutum*	M		LT		■	■	■					
254	Lesser Razor-billed Curassow *Mitu tomentosa*	M		LT			■	■			■		
255	Salvin's Curassow *Mitu salvini*	M		LT		■	■						
256	Razor-billed Curassow *Mitu tuberosa*	M		LT	Endemic		■						
257	Helmeted Curassow *Pauxi pauxi*	2	*gilliardi* (Co & Ve: Perija) *pauxi* (NC&W Ve, E Co)	LT	Formerly *Crax* **Endangered**		■	■					
258	Great Curassow *Crax rubra*	2	*rubra* (W Co, W Ec)	LT		■	■						
259	Blue-billed Curassow *Crax alberti*	M		T	**Endemic** **Critically threatened**		■						
260	Yellow-knobbed Curassow *Crax daubentoni*	M		T			■	■					

11

No.	Species	Ssp. Total	Subspecies in Northern South America	Altitude Range	References and Comments	Ec	Co	Ve	Ar Cu Bo	Tr To	Gu	Su	FG
261	**Black Curassow** *Crax alector*	2	*alector* (E Ve, Gu, Su, FG) *erythrognatha* (E Co, S Ve)	T									
262	**Wattled Curassow** *Crax globulosa*	M		LT	Vulnerable								
263	**Crested Bobwhite** *Colinus cristatus*	13	*badius* (Co: W Andes) *barnesi* (WC Ve) *bogotensis* (NC Co: E Andes) *cristatus* (NE Co, NW Ve, Ar, Cu) *decoratus* (Co: Caribbean coast) *hovarthi* (NW Ve: Merida) *leucotis* (C Co) *littoralis* (NE Co: Sta Marta) *mocquerysi* (NE Ve) *parvicristatus* (C Co, SC Ve) *sonnini* (NC&SE Ve, Gu, Su, FG)	T									
264	**Marbled Wood-Quail** *Odontophorus gujanensis*	8	*buckleyi* (E Co, E Ec) *gujanensis* (SE Ve, Gu, Su, FG) *marmoratus* (N Co, NW Ve) *medius* (S Ve)	LT									
265	**Rufous-fronted Wood-Quail** *Odontophorus erythrops*	2	*erythrops* (SW Ec) *parambae* (W Co, W Ec)	T									
266	**Black-fronted Wood-Quail** *Odontophorus atrifrons*	3	*atrifrons* (Co: Sta. Marta) *navai* (Co & Ve: Perija) *variegatus* (Co: E Andes)	UT-Te									
267	**Chestnut Wood-Quail** *Odontophorus hyperythus*	M		S-Te	Endemic								
268	**Dark-backed Wood-Quail** *Odontophorus melanonotus*	M		UT									
269	**Rufous-breasted Wood-Quail** *Odontophorus speciosus*	3	*sonderstroemii* (E&S Ec)	UT-Te									
270	**Tacarcuna Wood-Quail** *Odontophorus dialeucus*	M		UT									
271	**Gorgeted Wood-Quail** *Odontophorus strophium*	M		S	Endangered Endemic								
272	**Venezuelan Wood-Quail** *Odontophorus columbianus*	M		UT-S	Endemic								
273	**Starred Wood-Quail** *Odontophorus stellatus*	M		T									
274	**Tawny-faced Quail** *Rhynchortyx cinctus*	3	*australis* (W Co, W Ec)	T									
275	**Speckled Crake** *Coturnicops notatus*	M		T									
276	**Ocellated Crake** *Micropygia schomburgkii*	2	*schomburgkii* (Co, Ve, Gu)	T									
277	**Chestnut-headed Crake** *Anurolimnas castaneiceps*	2	*castaneiceps* (E Ec) *coccineipes* (S Co, NE Ec)	LT									
278	**Russet-crowned Crake** *Anurolimnas viridis*	2	*brunnescens* (E Co) *viridis* (E Ec, S Ve, Gu, Su, FG)	T	Formerly *Laterallus*								
279	**Black-banded Crake** *Anurolimnas fasciatus*	M		LT	Formerly *Laterallus*								
280	**Rufous-sided Crake** *Laterallus melanophaius*	2	*melanophaius* (Ve, Gu, Su) *oenops* (SE Co, E Ec)	T									

No.	Species	Ssp. Total	Subspecies in Northern South America	Altitude Range	References and Comments	Ec	Co	Ve	Ar Cu Bo	Tr To	Gu	Su	FG
281	Rusty-flanked Crake *Laterallus levraudi*	M		LT	Vulnerable Endemic								
282	White-throated Crake *Laterallus albigularis*	3	albigularis (N&W Co, W Ec) cerdaleus (E Co)	T									
283	Grey-breasted Crake *Laterallus exilis*	M		T									
284	Black Rail *Laterallus jamaicensis*	4	jamaicensis (N.Am.)	T-P	Occasional to Co: A&S. Uncertain in Co: SFP&M.		?						
285	Clapper Rail *Rallus longirostris*	22	cypereti (SW Co, Ec) dillonripleyi * (NE Ve) longirostris (Gu, Su, FG) margaritae (Marg Is.) pelodramus (Tr) phelpsi (NE Co, NW Ve)	LT	* Phelps & Aveledo 1987								
286	Plain-flanked Rail *Rallus wetmorei*	M		LT	Endangered Endemic								
287	Virginia Rail *Rallus limicola*	3	aequatorialis (SW Co, Ec)	T-Te									
288	Bogota Rail *Rallus semiplumbeus*	2	semiplumbeus (Co: E Andes)	Te	Endangered Endemic								
289	Rufous-necked Wood-Rail *Aramides axillaris*	M		T	Sight records in FG: SFP&M.								?
290	Grey-necked Wood-Rail *Aramides cajanea*	8	cajanea (S.Am.)	T									
291	Brown Wood-Rail *Aramides wolfi*	M		LT	Vulnerable								
292	Red-winged Wood-Rail *Aramides calopterus*	M		LT									
293	Uniform Crake *Amaurolimnas concolor*	2	castaneus (Ve, Gu, Su, FG) guatemalensis (W Co, W Ec)	T	Uncertain in FG: SFP&M.								?
294	Sora *Porzana carolina*	M	Boreal migrant to NE S.Am.	LT									
295	Ash-throated Crake *Porzana albicollis*	2	olivacea (Co, Ve, Tr, Gu, Su, FG)	T									
296	Yellow-breasted Crake *Porzana flaviventer*	5	bangsi (N Co) flaviventer (Co, Ve, Tr, Gu, Su, FG)	LT	Formerly *Poliolimnas*								
297	Colombian Crake *Neocrex colombianus*	2	colombianus (N&W Co, W Ec) ripleyi (NW Co)	T-S									
298	Paint-billed Crake *Neocrex erythrops*	2	olivascens (E Co, Ve, Gu, Su, FG)	T-S	Sight records in FG: SFP&M.								?
299	Spotted Rail *Pardirallus maculatus*	2	maculatus (Co, Ve, Tr, To, Gu, Su, FG)	LT	Formerly *Rallus*								
300	Plumbeous Rail *Pardirallus saguinolentus*	6	Ssp. uncertain: simonsi or tschudii ?	T-P	Formerly *Ortygonax* Listed in RG&G.								
301	Blackish Rail *Pardirallus nigricans*	2	caucae (SW Co) nigricans (E Ec)	T-S	Formerly *Ortygonax*								
302	Purple Gallinule *Porphyrio martinicus*	M		T	Formerly *Porphyrula*								
303	Azure Gallinule *Porphyrio flavirostris*	M		LT	Formerly *Porphyrula* Sight records in Tr: SFP&M.				?				
304	Common Moorhen *Gallinula chloropus*	12	galeata (Tr, Gu, Su, FG) pauxilla (N&W Co, W Ec)	T-P	Formerly Common Gallinule								
305	Spot-flanked Gallinule *Gallinula melanops*	3	bogotensis (Co: E Andes)	T-Te	Formerly *Porphyriops*								
306	American Coot *Fulica americana*	2	columbiana (Co, N Ve)	T-Te	Sight records in Ve: SFP&M.			?					

No.	Species	Ssp. Total	Subspecies in Northern South America	Altitude Range	References and Comments	Ec	Co	Ve	Ar Cu Bo	Tr To	Gu	Su	FG
307	**Caribbean Coot** *Fulica caribaea*	M		LT									
308	**Slate-colored Coot** *Fulica ardesiaca*	2	*atrura* (S Co, Ec)	S-P									
309	**Sunbittern** *Eurypyga helias*	3	*helias* (E Co, Ve, Gu, Su, FG) *major* (W Ec, W Co)	T									
310	**Sungrebe** *Heliornis fulica*	M		LT	Vagrant to Tr: SFP&M.								
311	**Limpkin** *Aramus guarauna*	M		LT									
312	**Grey-winged Trumpeter** *Psophia crepitans*	2	*crepitans* (SE Co, E&S Ve, Gu, Su, FG) *napensis* (SE Co, E Ec)	LT									
313	**Wattled Jacana** *Jacana jacana*	6	*hypomelaena* (N Co) *intermedia* (N&C Ve) *jacana* (SE Co, S Ve, Tr, Gu, Su, FG) *melanopygia* (W Co, W Ve) *scapularis* (W Ec)	LT									
314	**Common Snipe** *Gallinago gallinago*	3	*delicata* (boreal migrant to N S.Am.)	T-Te	*delicata* may be a sep. sp. (Wilson's Snipe). Sight records in Ec: RG&G. Vagrant to Gu: SFP&M.	?							
315	**South American Snipe** *Gallinago paraguaiae*	2 ?	*paraguaiae* (E Co, Ve, Gu, Su, FG)	T									
316	**Noble Snipe** *Gallinago nobilis*	M		Te-P									
317	**Giant Snipe** *Gallinago undulata*	2	*undulata* (W&E Co, Ve; poss. in Gu, Su, FG)	T									
318	**Puna Snipe** *Gallinago andina*	M		Te-P	Sight records in Ec: RG&G.	?							
319	**Andean Snipe** *Gallinago jamesoni*	M		T-P	Formerly *Chubbia*								
320	**Imperial Snipe** *Gallinago imperialis*	M		Te-P									
321	**Hudsonian Godwit** *Limosa haemastica*	M		T	Sight records in Co, Su, FG; vagrant to Ar/Cu/Bo: SFP&M.		?					?	?
322	**Bar-tailed Godwit** *Limosa lapponica*	3	Ssp. uncertain: *lapponica*, *menzbieri* or *baueri* ?	T	Vagrant to Ve: Phelps & Meyer de Schauensee 1994, SFP&M.								
323	**Marbled Godwit** *Limosa fedoa*	2	*fedoa* (boreal migrant to Co & Ve)	LT									
324	**Eskimo Curlew** *Numenius borealis*	M		LT	**Critically threatened** Occasional to Ar/Cu/Bo: A&S. Vagrant to Tr: SFP&M.								
325	**Whimbrel** *Numenius phaeopus*	4	*hudsonicus* (boreal migrant to S.Am.)	LT	*hudsonicus* may be a sep. sp. (Hudsonian Curlew): S&M.								
326	**Long-billed Curlew** *Numenius americanus*	2	Ssp. uncertain: *parvus* or *americanus* ? (boreal migrants)	T	Occasional to Ve: A&S. Sight records in FG: SFP&M.								?
327	**Upland Sandpiper** *Bartramia longicauda*	M		T									

No.	Species	Ssp. Total	Subspecies in Northern South America	Altitude Range	References and Comments	Ec	Co	Ve	Ar Cu Bo	Tr To	Gu	Su	FG
328	**Common Greenshank** *Tringa nebularia*	M		T ?	Occasional to Ar/Cu/Bo: A&S. Vagrant to Tr: SFP&M.								
329	**Greater Yellowlegs** *Tringa melanoleuca*	M		T-P									
330	**Lesser Yellowlegs** *Tringa flavipes*	M		T ?									
331	**Solitary Sandpiper** *Tringa solitaria*	2	*cinnamomea* & *solitaria* (boreal migrants to S.Am.)	T									
332	**Spotted Redshank** *Tringa erythropus*	M		T ?	Fisher 1998. Vagrant to Tr: SFP&M.								
333	**Spotted Sandpiper** *Actitis macularia*	M		T-S	Formerly *Tringa*								
334	**Wandering Tattler** *Heteroscelus incanus*	M		LT	Formerly *Tringa* Vagrant to Co: SFP&M, A&S.								
335	**Willet** *Catoptrophorus semipalmatus*	2	*inornatus* & *semipalmatus* (boreal migrants to S.Am.)	T									
336	**Ruddy Turnstone** *Arenaria interpres*	2	*morinella* (boreal migrant to S.Am.)	LT									
337	**Black Turnstone** *Arenaria melanocephala*	M		LT	Vagrant to Ec: SFP&M								
338	**Short-billed Dowitcher** *Limnodromus griseus*	3	*caurinus* (Co & Ec: Pacific coast) *griseus* (Co, Ve, Tr, Gu, Su, FG) *hendersoni* (possible in NW Co?)	LT									
339	**Long-billed Dowitcher** *Limnodromus scolopaceus*	M		LT	Recorded in Ar/Cu/Bo: A&S. Uncertain in Co: SFP&M.		?						
340	**Surfbird** *Aphriza virgata*	M		LT	Sight records in Co		?						
341	**Red Knot** *Calidris canutus*	5	*roselaari* (N Ve) *rufa* (NE & S S.Am.) (boreal migrants)	LT	Sight records in Co, FG: SFP&M.		?						?
342	**Sanderling** *Calidris alba*	M		LT									
343	**Semipalmated Sandpiper** *Calidris pusilla*	M		LT									
344	**Western Sandpiper** *Calidris mauri*	M		T-S									
345	**Least Sandpiper** *Calidris minutilla*	M		T-S									
346	**White-rumped Sandpiper** *Calidris fuscicollis*	M		T									
347	**Baird's Sandpiper** *Calidris bairdii*	M		T-P	Sight records in Ar/Cu/Bo, Tr, Su, FG: SFP&M.				?	?		?	?
348	**Pectoral Sandpiper** *Calidris melanotos*	M		T-P	Sight records in FG: SFP&M.								?
349	**Dunlin** *Calidris alpina*	9	Ssp. uncertain: *artica*, *schinzii*, *articola*, *pacifica* or *hudsonia* ?	LT	Vagrant to FG: SFP&M. Sight record in Ve: A&S. Sight records in Ec: RG&G.	?	?	?					
350	**Curlew Sandpiper** *Calidris ferruginea*	M		LT	Not in N S.Am.: SFP&M & HBW. Occasional in Co: A&S.								

15

No.	Species	Ssp. Total	Subspecies in Northern South America	Altitude Range	References and Comments	Ec	Co	Ve	Ar Cu Bo	Tr To	Gu	Su	FG
351	**Stilt Sandpiper** *Calidris himantopus*	M		T ?	Formerly *Micropalama* Sight records in Gu, FG: SFP&M.						?		?
352	**Buff-breasted Sandpiper** *Tryngites subruficollis*	M		LT	Vagrant to Ar/Cu/Bo; sight records in Gu; uncertain in FG: SFP&M.						?		?
353	**Ruff** *Philomachus pugnax*	M		LT	Vagrant to Co, Tr; sight records in Ve: SFP&M.			?					
354	**Wilson's Phalarope** *Phalaropus tricolor*	M		T-P	Formerly *Steganopus* Sight records in Ve, Su: SFP&M.			?				?	
355	**Red-necked Phalarope** *Phalaropus lobatus*	M		O	Vagrant to Ar/Cu/Bo: SFP&M.								
356	**Red Phalarope** *Phalaropus fulicaria*	M		O									
357	**Rufous-bellied Seedsnipe** *Attagis gayi*	3	*latreillii* (N Ec)	P									
358	**Least Seedsnipe** *Thinocorus rumicivorus*	4	*pallidus* (SW Ec)	T-Te									
359	**Double-striped Thick-knee** *Burhinus bistriatus*	4	*pediacu* (N Co) *vocifer* (Ve, Gu)	LT	Vagrant to Ar/Cu/Bo; sight records in Tr: SFP&M.								
360	**Peruvian Thick-knee** *Burhinus superciliaris*	M		LT									
361	**American Oystercatcher** *Haematopus palliatus*	2	*palliatus* (N S.Am.)	LT	Vagrant to Tr; sight records in FG: SFP&M.								
362	**Black-necked Stilt** *Himantopus mexicanus*	M		T	Sometimes treated as *H. himantopus mexicanus* (Common or Black-winged S.). Sight records in Tr: SFP&M.								
363	**American Avocet** *Recurvirostra americana*	M		T-S	Vagrant to Ec & Tr; sight records in Ar/Cu/Bo: SFP&M.								
364	**American Golden Plover** *Pluvialis dominica*	M		LT									
365	**Pacific Golden Plover** *Pluvialis fulva*	M		LT	Listed in RG&G.	?							
366	**Black-bellied Plover** *Pluvialis squatarola*	M		LT									
367	**Common Ringed Plover** *Charadrius hiaticula*	2	Ssp. uncertain: *hiaticula* ?	T ?	Vagrant to Tr: SFP&M.								
368	**Semipalmated Plover** *Charadrius semipalmatus*	M		LT	Formerly *Catopthrophorus*								
369	**Wilson's Plover** *Charadrius wilsonius*	3	*beldingi* (Co & Ec: Pacific coast) *cinnamominus* (N S.Am.: Caribbean & Atlantic coasts) *wilsonius* (boreal migrant to Co, Ve)	LT	Sight records in FG: SFP&M.								?
370	**Killdeer** *Charadrius vociferus*	3	*vociferus* (boreal migrant to Ec, Co, Ar, Cu, Bo, Ve, Tr, FG)	T-S	Sight records in Tr & Gu: SFP&M.					?	?		
371	**Piping Plover** *Charadrius melodus*	M		LT	**Vulnerable** Vagrant to Ec: SFP&M.								

No.	Species	Ssp. Total	Subspecies in Northern South America	Altitude Range	References and Comments	Ec	Co	Ve	Ar Cu Bo	Tr To	Gu	Su	FG
372	**Snowy Plover** *Charadrius alexandrinus*	5	*nivosus* (Co, Ve, Ar, Cu, Bo, Tr) *occidentalis* (Ec, poss. in Co?)	LT	Sight records in Tr: SFP&M.					?			
373	**Collared Plover** *Charadrius collaris*	M		LT									
374	**Tawny-throated Dotterel** *Oreopholus ruficollis*	2	*pallidus* (Ec)	T-P	Formerly *Eudromias*								
375	**Pied Lapwing** *Hoploxypterus cayanus*	M		LT	Formerly *Vanellus* Vagrant to Ec: SFP&M.								
376	**Southern Lapwing** *Vanellus chilensis*	4	*cayennensis* (N S.Am.)	T-Te	Formerly *Belenopterus*. *cayennensis* may be a sep. sp. (Cayenne Lapwing): S&M. Vagrant To Ar/Cu/Bo: SFP&M.								
377	**Andean Lapwing** *Vanellus resplendens*	M		Te-P									
378	**Band-tailed Gull** *Larus belcheri*	M		O	Not in N S.Am.: SFP&M. Migrant to Co: A&S.								
379	**Grey Gull** *Larus modestus*	M		O	Vagrant to Co: SFP&M.								
380	**Ring-billed Gull** *Larus delawarensis*	M		O	Vagrant to Ar/Cu/Bo; sight records in Ec, Co, Tr: SFP&M.	?	?	?		?			
381	**California Gull** *Larus californicus*	2	Ssp. uncertain: *albertaensis* or *californicus*?	O	Sight records in Ec: RG&G.	?							
382	**Great Black-backed Gull** *Larus marinus*	M		O	Sight records in Ve: Casler 1996. Vagrant to Ar/Cu/Bo: SFP&M				?				
383	**Kelp Gull** *Larus dominicanus*	M		O									
384	**Herring Gull** *Larus argentatus*	4	*smithsonianus* (Co, Ve, Tr)	O	Vagrant to Tr; sight records in Co: SFP&M. Sight records in Ec: RG&G.	?	?						
385	**Lesser Black-backed Gull** *Larus fuscus*	4	Ssp. uncertain: *graellsii* or *intermedius*?	O	Sight records in Ve & Tr: SFP&M. Listed in RG&G (rare).				?				?
386	**Grey-hooded Gull** *Larus cirrocephalus*	2	*cirrocephalus* (Ec)	T									
387	**Brown-hooded Gull** *Larus maculipennis*	M		T	Vagrant to Ar/Cu/Bo: A&S. Not in N S.Am.: SFP&M.								
388	**Black-headed Gull** *Larus ridibundus*	M		O	Vagrant to Ar/Cu/Bo; sight records in Co, Su, FG: SFP&M.		?					?	?
389	**Bonaparte's Gull** *Larus philadelphia*	M		O	Sight records in Ar/Cu/Bo: SFP&M.				?				
390	**Andean Gull** *Larus serranus*	M		Te-P	Sight record in Co: P. Salaman pers. comm.		?						
391	**Laughing Gull** *Larus atricilla*	2	*atricilla* (Tr, Ve) *megalopterus* (winters on Pacific coast)	O									
392	**Franklin's Gull** *Larus pipixcan*	M		O	Sight records in Ve and Ar/Cu/Bo, FG: SFP&M.				?	?			?
393	**Little Gull** *Larus minutus*	M		O	Vagrant to Co: SFP&M.								

No.	Species	Ssp. Total	Subspecies in Northern South America	Altitude Range	References and Comments	Ec	Co	Ve	Ar Cu Bo	Tr To	Gu	Su	FG
394	**Sabine's Gull** *Xema sabini*	4	*paleartica* ? *tschuktschorum* ? *woznesenskii* ? (all winter on Pacific coast)	O	Formerly *Larus*. Vagrant to Tr: SFP&M.								
395	**Swallow-tailed Gull** *Creagrus furcatus*	M		LT									
396	**Black Tern** *Chlidonias niger*	2	*surinamensis* (winters all coasts N S.Am.)	O	Sight records in Ar/Cu/Bo, FG: SFP&M.				?				?
397	**Large-billed Tern** *Phaetusa simplex*	2	*simplex* (all coasts N S.Am.)	O-T	Vagrant to Ar/Cu/Bo: SFP&M.								
398	**Gull-billed Tern** *Sterna nilotica*	6	*aranea* (winters all N S.Am. coasts) *groenvoldi* (FG, poss. Ec?) *vanrossemi* (winters Pacific coast)	O-T	Formerly *Geochelidon* Sight records in FG: SFP&M.								?
399	**Caspian Tern** *Sterna caspia*	M		O	Formerly *Hydroprogne* Vagrant to Tr, sight records in FG: SFP&M. Recorded nesting on Pacific coast of Co: L.F. Castillo, pers. comm.								?
400	**South American Tern** *Sterna hirundinacea*	M		O	Listed in RG&G.								
401	**Royal Tern** *Sterna maxima*	2	*maximus* (all N S.Am. coasts)	O	Formerly *Thalasseus* Sight records in Gu: SFP&M.						?		
402	**Sandwich Tern** *Sterna sandvicensis*	3	*acuflavidus* (winters N S.Am.) *eurygnatha* (breeds Ve, FG, Ar)	O	Formerly *Thalasseus*. *eurygnatha* sometimes considered a sep. sp. (Cayenne Tern).								
403	**Elegant Tern** *Sterna elegans*	M		O	Formerly *Thalasseus* Sight records in FG: SFP&M.								?
404	**Roseate Tern** *Sterna dougallii*	5	*dougallii* (all N S.Am. coasts)	O	Vagrant to FG: SFP&M.								
405	**Common Tern** *Sterna hirundo*	4	*hirundo* (all N S.Am. coasts)	O									
406	**Arctic Tern** *Sterna paradisaea*	M		O	Vagrant to Co: SFP&M.								
407	**Bridled Tern** *Sterna anaethetus*	6	*nelsoni* (migrant possible on Pacific coast) *recognita* (migrant to Caribbean & Atlantic coasts)	O									
408	**Sooty Tern** *Sterna fuscata*	8	*crissalis* (Pacific coast) *fuscata* (Caribbean & Atlantic coasts)	O									
409	**Least Tern** *Sterna antillarum*	3	*antillarum* (winters Caribbean & Atlantic) *athalassos* (winters Caribbean & Atlantic)	O	Sight records in Ec: SFP&M.	?							
410	**Yellow-billed Tern** *Sterna superciliaris*	M		O-LT									
411	**Peruvian Tern** *Sterna lorata*	M		O									
412	**Inca Tern** *Larosterna inca*	M		O	Vagrant to Ec: RG&G. Sight records in Co: SFP&M.		?						

18

No.	Species	Ssp. Total	Subspecies in Northern South America	Altitude Range	References and Comments	Ec	Co	Ve	Ar Cu Bo	Tr To	Gu	Su	FG
413	**Brown Noddy** *Anous stolidus*	5	*galapagoensis* & *ridgwayi* (Pacific coast) *stolidus* (Caribbean & Atlantic coasts)	O									
414	**Black Noddy** *Anous minutus*	7	*americanus* (C.Am.)	O	Recorded on Ve islands: HBW. Vagrant to Ar/Cu/Bo: SFP&M.								
415	**Common White Tern** *Gygis alba*	4	*alba* (Co, Ec, Tr)	O	Vagrant to Tr, Ec; sight records in Co: SFP&M.		?						
416	**Great Skua** *Catharacta skua*	M		O	Vagrant to Gu; sight records in Ar/Cu/Bo, FG; uncertain in Co: SFP&M.		?	?					?
417	**Chilean Skua** *Catharacta chilensis*	M		O	Sight records in Ec: RG&G.	?							
418	**South Polar Skua** *Catharacta maccormicki*	M		O	Sight records in Ec: RG&G. Vagrant to Tr, FG; uncertain in Su: SFP&M.	?						?	
419	**Pomarine Skua or Jaeger** *Stercorarius pomarinus*	M		O	Sight records in Co, Tr, Su, FG: SFP&M.		?			?		?	?
420	**Arctic Skua or Parasitic Jaeger** *Stercorarius parasiticus*	M		O	Vagrant to Ve; sight records in Co, Tr, FG: SFP&M.		?			?			?
421	**Long-tailed Skua or Jaeger** *Stercorarius longicaudus*	2	Ssp. uncertain: *longicaudus* or *pallescens* ?	O	Sight records in Ec: RG&G.	?							
422	**Black Skimmer** *Rynchops niger*	3	*cinerascens* (N S.Am.)	LT									
423	**Scaled Pigeon** *Columba speciosa*	M	(N S.Am.)	T									
424	**White-crowned Pigeon** *Columba leucocephala*	M	(Ve: Aves Is.)	T-S	Sight records in Ve: Hilty 1999. Recorded in Co: SFP&M.		?						
425	**Scaly-naped Pigeon** *Columba squamosa*	M	(Cu, Bo, Ve: Los Testigos Is.)	T-Te									
426	**Bare-eyed Pigeon** *Columba corensis*	M	(Ar, Cu, Bo; Ve: coast + Marg & Blanquilla Is.; Co: N coast)	LT									
427	**Band-tailed Pigeon** *Columba fasciata*	7	*albilinea* (Co, Ve, Ec, Tr) *roraimae* (Ve: Roraima)	UT-Te	*albilinea* may be a sep. sp. (White-necked Pigeon): S&M.								
428	**Pale-vented Pigeon** *Columba cayennensis*	5	*andersoni* (SE Co, E Ec, Ve) *cayennensis* (Gu, Su, FG) *pallidicrissa* (N Co) *tobagensis* (Tr, To)	LT									
429	**Plumbeous Pigeon** *Columba plumbea*	5	*chapmani* (NW Ec) *delicata* (E Co, W&S Ve, Gu, Su, FG)	T-S									
430	**Ruddy Pigeon** *Columba subvinacea*	6	*berlepschi* (W Co, W Ec) *bogotensis* (C Co) *peninsularis* (Ve: Paria) *purpureotincta* (SE Co, S Ve, Gu, Su, FG) *zuliae* (NE Co, W Ve)	T-LS	*berlepschi* and *purpureotincta* may be sep. spp. (Berlepsch's and Purple-tinted Pigeons): S&M								
431	**Short-billed Pigeon** *Columba nigrirostris*	M	(NW Co)	T									
432	**Peruvian Pigeon** *Columba oenops*	M	(SW Ec)	UT-S	Sometimes called Marañon Pigeon. **Vulnerable** Recorded in Ec: RG&G.								

No.	Species	Ssp. Total	Subspecies in Northern South America	Altitude Range	References and Comments	Ec	Co	Ve	Ar Cu Bo	Tr To	Gu	Su	FC
433	**Dusky Pigeon** *Columba goodsoni*	M	(W Co, NW Ec)	T									
434	**Mourning Dove** *Zenaida macroura*	5	Ssp. uncertain: *marginella* or *carolinensis* ?	T-Te	Vagrant to Co: SFP&M.								
435	**Eared Dove** *Zenaida auriculata*	11	*antioquiae* (Co: NC Andes) *caucae* (Co) *hypoleuca* (W Ec) *rubripes* (C Co, Ve, Tr, Gu) *ruficauda* (Ve, Co: E Andes) *vinaceorufa* (Ar, Cu, Bo)	T-Te	Sight records in FG: SFP&M.								?
436	**White-winged Dove** *Zenaida asiatica*	3	Ssp. uncertain: *asiatica* or *australis* ? (Boreal migrant)	T-S	Vagrant to Ar/Cu/Bo: SFP&M. Sight records in Co: S. Russell pers.comm.		?						
437	**Pacific Dove** *Zenaida meloda*	M	(SW Ec)	T-S	Sometimes treated as a race of *asiatica,* but song very different: HBW.								
438	**Scaled Dove** *Columbina squammata*	M	*ridgwayi* (N Co, N Ve, Marg, Gu, Su, FG)	. T	Formerly *Scardafella* Vagrant to Tr: SFP&M.								
439	**Common Ground-Dove** *Columbina passerina*	19	*albivitta* (N Co, Ar, N Ve, Marg, Tr) *griseola* (S Ve, Gu, Su, FG) *nana* (W Co) *parvula* (C Co) *quitensis* (C Ec) *tortugensis* (Ve: Tortuga Is.)	T-S									
440	**Plain-breasted Ground-Dove** *Columbina minuta*	4	*amazilia* (SW Ec) *elaeodes* (WC Co) *minuta* (Ve, Tr, Gu, Su, FG, SE Co)	T									
441	**Ruddy Ground-Dove** *Columbina talpacoti*	4	*caucae* (W Co) *rufipennis* (Co, Ve: N & Marg, Tr, To) *talpacoti* (E Ec)	T	Vagrant to Ar/Cu/Bo: SFP&M.								
442	**Ecuadorean Ground-Dove** *Columbina buckleyi*	M	(W Ec, Co)	LT	Ortiz-Von Halle 1990.								
443	**Picui Ground-Dove** *Columbina picui*	2	Ssp. uncertain: *picui* ?	T	Vagrant to Co: SFP&M.								
444	**Croaking Ground-Dove** *Columbina cruziana*	M		T-S	Ortiz-Von Halle 1990.								
445	**Blue Ground-Dove** *Claravis pretiosa*	M		T									
446	**Maroon-chested Ground-Dove** *Claravis mondetoura*	6	*mondetoura* (N&W Ve, C Co, E Ec)	UT-Te									
447	**Black-winged Ground-Dove** *Metriopelia melanoptera*	2	*melanoptera* (SW Co, Ec)	US-P									
448	**White-tipped Dove** *Leptotila verreauxi*	15	*brasiliensis* (Gu, Su, FG) *decolor* (W Co, W&C Ec) *hernandezi** (SW Co) *tobagensis* (To) *verreauxi* (N Co, N Ve, Ar, Cu, Bo, Marg) *zapluta* (Tr)	T-Te	*Ssp. nov.: Romero & Morales 1981.								
449	**Grey-headed Dove** *Leptotila plumbeiceps*	2	*plumbeiceps* (W Co)	T									

No.	Species	Ssp. Total	Subspecies in Northern South America	Altitude Range	References and Comments	Ec	Co	Ve	Ar Cu Bo	Tr To	Gu	Su	FG
450	**Grey-fronted Dove** *Leptotila rufaxilla*	6	*dubusi* (SE Co, SC Ve, E Ec) *hellmayri* (NE Ve, Tr) *pallidipectus* (E Co, W Ve) *rufaxilla* (E Ve, Gu, Su, FG)	T-LS									
451	**Pallid Dove** *Leptotila pallida*	M		LT									
452	**Caribbean Dove** *Leptotila jamaicensis*	4	Ssp. uncertain: *guameri* or *neoxena* ?	LT	Not in N S.Am.: HBW. Recorded in Co: SFP&M.								
453	**Grey-chested Dove** *Leptotila cassini*	3	*cassini* (NW Co.)	T									
454	**Ochre-bellied Dove** *Leptotila ochraceiventris*	M	(SW Ec)	Ul-LS	Vulnerable								
455	**Tolima Dove** *Leptotila conoveri*	M	(Co: C Andes)	S	**Endangered Endemic**								
456	**Sapphire Quail-Dove** *Geotrygon saphirina*	3	*saphirina* (E Ec, SE Co) *purpurata* (W Co, NW Ec)	UT	*purpurata* may be a sep. sp. (Indigo-crowned Quail-Dove): RG&G.								
457	**Olive-backed Quail-Dove** *Geotrygon veraguensis*	M	(W Co, NW Ec)	LT									
458	**Russet-crowned Quail-Dove** *Geotrygon goldmani*	2	*goldmani* (NW Co)	UT									
459	**Lined Quail-Dove** *Geotrygon linearis*	3	*linearis* (Ve, Co) *trinitatis* (E Ve, Tr, To) *infusca* (C&NE Co, NW Ve)	T-S									
460	**White-throated Quail-Dove** *Geotrygon frenata*	4	*bourcieri* (W Co, W Ec) *erythropareia* (E Ec)	UT-Te	*bourcieri* and *erythropareia* may be sep. spp. (Bourcier's and Dark Quail-Doves): S&M.								
461	**Violaceous Quail-Dove** *Geotrygon violacea*	2	*albiventer* (Co: Sta Marta; Ve) *violacea* (Su)	T									
462	**Ruddy Quail-Dove** *Geotrygon montana*	2	*montana* (C.Am. & S.Am.)	T	Population in Tr. intermediate between this and *martinica* (Lesser Antilles).								
463	**Rose-ringed Parakeet** *Psittacula krameri*	4	*manillensis* (Ve, Cu)	T	**Introduced**								
464	**Blue-and-yellow Macaw** *Ara ararauna*	M		LT									
465	**Military Macaw** *Ara militaris*	3	*militaris* (NW Ve, Co, E Ec)	UT-S	Vulnerable								
466	**Great Green Macaw** *Ara ambigua*	2	*ambigua* (NW Co) *guayaquilensis* (W Ec)	LT									
467	**Scarlet Macaw** *Ara macao*	2	*macao* (N S.Am.)	LT	Sight records in Tr: SFP&M.					?			
468	**Red-and-green Macaw** *Ara chloroptera*	M	(E Ec, Co, S Ve, S Gu, S Su, S FG)	T									
469	**Chestnut-fronted Macaw** *Ara severa*	M		T									
470	**Red-bellied Macaw** *Ara manilata*	M		T	Formerly *Orthopsittaca*								
471	**Red-shouldered Macaw** *Ara nobilis*	3	*nobilis* (E Ve, Gu, Su, FG)	I	Formerly *Diopsittaca*								
472	**Blue-crowned Parakeet** *Aratinga acuticaudata*	5	*haemarrhous* * (NE Co, N Ve) *neoxena* (Ve: Marg)	T-LS	* Arndt 1996, described part of *haemarrhous* as a ssp. nov. *koenigi*, based on disjunct distribution and plumage differences.								

No.	Species	Ssp. Total	Subspecies in Northern South America	Altitude Range	References and Comments	Ec	Co	Ve	Ar Cu Bo	Tr To	Gu	Su	F
473	**Scarlet-fronted Parakeet** *Aratinga wagleri*	4	*frontata* (SW Ec) *transilis* (E Co, N Ve) *wagleri* (W&N Co, NW Ve)	UT-Te	*frontata* may be a sep. sp. (Cordilleran Parakeet): S&M.								
474	**Red-masked Parakeet** *Aratinga erythrogenys*	M	(W Ec)	LT									
475	**White-eyed Parakeet** *Aratinga leucophthalmus*	3	*callogenys* (SE Co, E Ec) *leucophthalmus* (E Ve, Gu, Su, FG) *nicefori* (E Co)	T									
476	**Sun Parakeet** *Aratinga solstitialis*	M	(Ve: Roraima; S Gu, S Su, S FG)	T	Has not been recorded in Ve for many years.								
477	**Dusky-headed Parakeet** *Aratinga weddellii*	M	(E Ec, S Co)	LT									
478	**Peach-fronted Parakeet** *Aratinga aurea*	M	(S Su)	T									
479	**Brown-throated Parakeet** *Aratinga pertinax*	14	*aeruginosa* (N Co, NW Ve) *arubensis* (Ar) *chrysophrys* (SE Ve) *griseipecta* (NE Co) *lehmanni* (E Co, W Ve) *margaritensis* (Ve: Marg) *pertinax* (Cu) *surinama* (NE Ve, Gu) *tortugensis* (Ve: Tortuga Is.) *venezuelae* (NE & SE Ve) *xanthogenia* (Bo)	T									
480	**Golden-plumed Parakeet** *Leptosittaca branickii*	M	(S&N Ec, SW&CW Co)	Te-P	Vulnerable								
481	**Yellow-eared Parakeet** *Ognorhynchus icterotis*	M	(CNE Ec, SWC Co)	US-Te	Critically threatened (but 2 flocks recently found in C Co, P. Salaman, pers. comm.)								
482	**Painted Parakeet** *Pyrrhura picta*	9	*caeruleiceps* (N Co: E Andes) *lucianii* (SE Ec) *pantchenkoi* (Co & Ve: Perija) *picta* (Ve, Gu, Su, FG) *subandina* (NW Co)	T-S	*patchenkoi* treated as a sep. sp.: Hilty in prep. *caeruleiceps* may be a sep. sp.: P. Salaman pers. comm. Sight records in Ec: RG&G, SFP&M.	?							
483	**Maroon-faced Parakeet** *Pyrrhura leucotis*	5	*auricularis* (NE Ve) *emma* (NW Ve)	T									
484	**Santa Marta Parakeet** *Pyrrhura viridicata*	M	(Co: Sta Marta)	S-Te	Vulnerable Endemic								
485	**Fiery-shouldered Parakeet** *Pyrrhura egregia*	2	*egregia* (SE Ve, SW Gu) *obscura* (S Ve)	UT-LS									
486	**Maroon-tailed Parakeet** *Pyrrhura melanura*	5	*berlepschi* (SE Ec) *chapmani* (Co: E slope - C Andes) *melanura* (S Ve, SE Co, E Ec) *pacifica* (SW Co, NW Ec) *souancei* (SC Co)	T	3 ssp. may be sep. sp.: *chapmani* (Magdalena Parakeet), *pacifica* (Pacific Parakeet), *souancei* (East Andean Parakeet) *souancei = berlepschi* ?: Juniper & Parr 1998.								
487	**El Oro Parakeet** *Pyrrhura orcesi*	M	(SW Ec)	UT	Vulnerable Endemic								
488	**White-breasted Parakeet** *Pyrrhura albipectus*	M	(SE Co)	S-Te	Vulnerable Endemic								
489	**Flame-winged Parakeet** *Pyrrhura calliptera*	M	(Co: E Andes)	S-Te	Vulnerable Endemic								

No.	Species	Ssp. Total	Subspecies in Northern South America	Altitude Range	References and Comments	Ec	Co	Ve	Ar Cu Bo	Tr To	Gu	Su	FG
490	**Blood-eared Parakeet** *Pyrrhura hoematotis*	2	*hoematotis* (N Ve) *immarginata* (NW Ve)	UT-S	Endemic								
491	**Rose-headed Parakeet** *Pyrrhura rhodocephala*	M	(W Ve)	UT-Te	Endemic								
492	**Barred Parakeet** *Bolborhynchus lineola*	2	*tigrinus* (W Co, N&W Ve)	UT-Te	Sight records in Ec: SFP&M.	?							
493	**Rufous-fronted Parakeet** *Bolborhynchus ferrugineifrons*	M	(Co: C Andes)	Te-P	Endangered Endemic								
494	**Green-rumped Parrotlet** *Forpus passerinus*	5	*cyanophanes* (N Co) *passerinus* (Gu, Su, FG) *viridissimis* (N Ve, NE Co, Tr, Cu)	LT									
495	**Blue-winged Parrotlet** *Forpus crassirostris*	5	*crassirostris* (SE Co, E Ec) *spengeli* (N Co)	T	Formerly *F. xanthopterygius*: SFP&M.								
496	**Spectacled Parrotlet** *Forpus conspicillatus*	3	*caucae* (SW Co) *conspicillatus* (NC Co) *metae* (C Co to W Ve)	T-LS									
497	**Dusky-billed Parrotlet** *Forpus sclateri*	2	*eidos* (E Co, S&SE Ve, Gu, S FG) *sclateri* (SE Co, NE Ec)	LT	Sight records in FG: SFP&M.								?
498	**Pacific Parrotlet** *Forpus coelestis*	M	(SW Ec)	T									
499	**Canary-winged Parakeet** *Brotogeris versicolurus*	M	(W Ec, S Co, W FG)	T									
500	**Grey-cheeked Parakeet** *Brotogeris pyrrhopterus*	M	(SW Ec)	LT									
501	**Orange-chinned Parakeet** *Brotogeris jugularis*	2	*exsul* (E Co, W Ve) *jugularis* (N Co, NW Ve)	T									
502	**Cobalt-winged Parakeet** *Brotogeris cyanoptera*	23	*cyanoptera* (SE Co, S Ve, E Ec)	LT									
503	**Golden-winged Parakeet** *Brotogeris chrysopterus*	5	*chrysopterus* (NE Ve, Gu, Su, FG)	T									
504	**Tui Parakeet** *Brotogeris sanctithomae*	2	*sanctithomae* (SE Co)	LT	Sight records in Ec: RG&G.	?							
505	**Tepui Parrotlet** *Nannopsittaca panychlora*	M		UT-LS									
506	**Lilac-tailed Parrotlet** *Touit batavica*	M		T-LS	Sight records in FG: SFP&M.								?
507	**Scarlet-shouldered Parrotlet** *Touit huetii*	M		LT									
508	**Red-winged Parrotlet** *Touit dilectissima*	M		UT-LS									
509	**Sapphire-rumped Parrotlet** *Touit purpurata*	2	*purpurata* (S Ve, Gu, Su, FG) *viridiceps* (SE Co, S Ve, E Ec)	T									
510	**Spot-winged Parrotlet** *Touit stictoptera*	M		UT-S	Vulnerable								
511	**Black-headed Parrot** *Pionites melanocephala*	2	*melanocephala* (SE Co, NE Ve, Gu, Su, FG) *pallida* (S Co, E Ec)	LT									
512	**Brown-hooded Parrot** *Pionites haematotis*	2	*coccinicollaris* (NW Co)	T	Formerly *Pionopsitta*								
513	**Rose-faced Parrot** *Pionites pulchra*	M		T	Formerly *Pionopsitta*								
514	**Orange-cheeked Parrot** *Pionites barrabandi*	2	*aurantiigena* (E Ec) *barrabandi* (SW Co, SW Ve)	LT	Formerly *Pionopsitta*								

No.	Species	Ssp. Total	Subspecies in Northern South America	Altitude Range	References and Comments	Ec	Co	Ve	Ar Cu Bo	Tr To	Gu	Su	F
515	Saffron-headed Parrot *Pionites pyrilia*	M		T	Formerly *Pionopsitta*								
516	Caica Parrot *Pionites caica*	M		T	Formerly *Pionopsitta*								
517	Rusty-faced Parrot *Hapalopsittaca amazonina*	3	*amazonina* (Co: E Andes, W Ve) *theresae* (E Co, NW Ve) *velezi* (Co: C Andes)	S-Te	**Endangered**								
518	Indigo-winged Parrot *Hapalopsittaca fuertesi*	M	(WC Co)	Te-P	Formerly *H. amazonina fuertesi*: Graves & Uribe 1989. **Critically threatened Endemic**								
519	Red-faced Parrot *Hapalopsittaca pyrrhops*	M	(SE Ec)	Te-P	**Endangered**								
520	Short-tailed Parrot *Graydidascalus brachyurus*	M	(NE Ec, CS Co, E FG)	LT									
521	Blue-headed Parrot *Pionus menstruus*	3	*menstruus* (E Ec, E Co, Ve, Gu, Su, FG) *rubrigularis* (W Co, W Ec)	T									
522	Red-billed Parrot *Pionus sordidus*	3	*antelius* (NE Ve) *corallinus* (S Co, E Ec) *mindoensis* (W Ec) *ponsi* (N Co, NW Ve) *saturatus* (N Co) *sordidus* (N Ve)	UT-LS									
523	White-capped Parrot *Pionus seniloides*	2	*seniloides* (W Ve, CE Co, N Ec)	S-Te	Formerly *P. tumultuosus*: O'Neill & Parker 1977								
524	Bronze-winged Parrot *Pionus chalcopterus*	2	*chalcopterus* (N&C Co: Andes, NW Ve) *cyanescens* (Ec, SW Co)	UT-S									
525	Dusky Parrot *Pionus fuscus*	M		T									
526	Red-lored Parrot *Amazona autumnalis*	4	*lilacina* (W Ec) *salvini* (SW Co, NW Ve)	T									
527	Blue-cheeked Parrot *Amazona dufresniana*	M	(SE Ve, Gu, Su, FG)	UT-LS	Formerly *A. brasiliensis dufresniana*, but often treated as a sep. sp.: HBW.								
528	Festive Parrot *Amazona festiva*	2	*bodini* (E Co, S Ve, NW Gu) *festiva* (SE Co, E Ec)	LT									
529	Yellow-shouldered Parrot *Amazona barbadensis*	M		LT	Vulnerable								
530	Yellow-crowned Parrot *Amazona ochrocephala*	10	*ochrocephala* (E Co, Ve, Tr, Gu, Su, FG) *panamensis* (NW Co)	LT									
531	Orange-winged Parrot *Amazona amazonica*	M		LT									
532	Scaly-naped Parrot *Amazona mercenaria*	2	*canipalliata* (Andes: Ve, Co & Ec)	UT-Te									
533	Mealy Parrot *Amazona farinosa*	3	*farinosa* (N&W Co, SC Ve, Gu, Su, FG)	T									
534	Red-fan Parrot *Deroptyus accipitrinus*	2	*accipitrinus* (SE Co, E Ec, S Ve, Gu, Su, FG)	LT									
535	Hoatzin *Opisthocomus hoazin*	M		LT									
536	Dwarf Cuckoo *Coccyzus pumilus*	M		T-S									

No.	Species	Ssp. Total	Subspecies in Northern South America	Altitude Range	References and Comments	Ec	Co	Ve	Ar Cu Bo	Tr To	Gu	Su	FG
537	**Ash-coloured Cuckoo** *Coccyzus cinereus*	M	(Co: S Amazonas)	LT	Vagrant to Co: SFP&M, A&S.		■						
538	**Black-billed Cuckoo** *Coccyzus erythropthalmus*	M	(Boreal migrant, rare transient to N S.Am.)		Vagrant to Tr: SFP&M.					■			
539	**Yellow-billed Cuckoo** *Coccyzus americanus*	M	(Boreal migrant)	T									
540	**Pearly-breasted Cuckoo** *Coccyzus euleri*	M		LT	Vagrant to Ec: RG&G. Sight records in FG: SFP&M.								?
541	**Mangrove Cuckoo** *Coccyzus minor*	13?	*maynardi* (Ar) *minor* (N coast of S.Am.)	T	Sometimes considered to be monotypic: HBW. Sight records in Bo & Cu: Voous 1982.				?				
542	**Dark-billed Cuckoo** *Coccyzus melacoryphus*	M	(Resident and austral migrant populations)	T									
543	**Grey-capped Cuckoo** *Coccyzus lansbergi*	M	(Co, Ve; intertropical migrant to SE Ec *)	LT	* Marchant 1960								
544	**Squirrel Cuckoo** *Piaya cayana*	14	*cayana* (E&S Ve, Gu, Su, FG) *circe* (W Ve) *insulana* (Tr) *mehleri* (NE Co, NW Ve) *mesura* (E Ec, E Co) *nigricrissa* (W Co, W Ec) *thermophila* (NW Co)	T-S									
545	**Black-bellied Cuckoo** *Piaya melanogaster*	M		LT									
546	**Little Cuckoo** *Piaya minuta*	4	*barinensis* * (CW Ve) *gracilis* (W Co, W Ec) *minuta* (E Co, Ve, Gu, Su, FG) *panamensis* (N Co)	LT	* Aveledo & Perez 1994								
547	**Greater Ani** *Crotophaga major*	M		LT									
548	**Smooth-billed Ani** *Crotophaga ani*	M		T-S									
549	**Groove-billed Ani** *Crotophaga sulcirostris*	M		T-S									
550	**Guira Cuckoo** *Guira guira*	M		T	Vagrant to Ar/Cu/Bo: SFP&M.								
551	**Striped Cuckoo** *Tapera naevia*	2	*naevia* (N S.Am.)	T									
552	**Pheasant Cuckoo** *Dromococcyx phasianellus*	M		T									
553	**Pavonine Cuckoo** *Dromococcyx pavoninus*	2	*pavoninus* (Ve, Gu, E Ec) *perijanus* (W Ve)	T	Probably monotypic: HBW.								
554	**Rufous-vented Ground-Cuckoo** *Neomorphus geoffroyi*	7	*aequatorialis* (SE Co, Ec) *salvini* (Co: W coast)	T									
555	**Banded Ground-Cuckoo** *Neomorphus radiolosus*	M	(SW Co, NW Ec)	UT	**Endangered**								
556	**Rufous-winged Ground-Cuckoo** *Neomorphus rufipennis*	M	(S Ve, Gu)	T	Present in Co: G. Stiles pers comm.								
557	**Red-billed Ground-Cuckoo** *Neomorphus pucheranii*	2	Ssp. uncertain: *pucheranii* ?	LT	Sight records in Co.: SFP&M. Sight records in Ec: RG&G.	?	?						

No.	Species	Ssp. Total	Subspecies in Northern South America	Altitude Range	References and Comments	Ec	Co	Ve	Ar Cu Bo	Tr To	Gu	Su	FC
558	Barn Owl *Tyto alba*	30	*bargei* (Cu) *contempta* (Co, Ec, W Ve) *hellmayri* (Ve: E & Marg; Tr, To, Gu, Su, FG)) *subandeana* (Ec, Co)	T-P	*subandeana* sometimes merged with extralimital *guatemalae*. *contempta* includes *stictica*: HBW.								
559	Tropical Screech-Owl *Otus choliba*	9	*alticola* (C Co) *crucigerus* (SE Co, S Ve, Tr, Gu, Su, FG) *duidae* (S Ve) *luctisomus* (NW Co) *margaritae* (N Co, Ve: N & Marg)	T-Te	*alticola* not recognised by König *et al.* 1999.								
560	Peruvian Screech-Owl *Otus roboratus*	2	*pacificus* (SW Ec) *roboratus* (extreme S Ec)	T-LS	*pacificus* is likely to be a sep. sp. (Tumbes Screech-Owl): König *et al.* 1999.								
561	Bare-shanked Screech-Owl *Otus clarkii*	M	(extreme NW Co)	UT-Te									
562	Rufescent Screech-Owl *Otus ingens*	3	*ingens* (E Ec, C&E Co) *venezuelanus* (N&W Ve, N Co)	UT-S									
563	Colombian Screech-Owl *Otus colombianus*	M	(NW Ec, CW & SW Co)	S	Formerly included in *Otus ingens*								
564	Cinnamon Screech-Owl *Otus petersoni*	M	(S Ec)	S Te	Sometimes treated as conspecific with *O. ingens* or *O. colombianus*. Possibly forms superspecies with extralimital *O. marshalli*; both formerly included under invalid name *O. huberi*: HBW, König *et al.* 1999. Sp. nov.: Fitzpatrick & O'Neill 1986.								
565	Northern Tawny-bellied Screech-Owl *Otus watsonii*	M	(E Ec, SE Co, NW&S Ve, Gu, Su, FG)	LT									
566	Southern Tawny-bellied Screech-Owl *Otus usta*	M	(SE Co)	LT	Formerly included in *Otus watsonii*: König *et al.* 1999.								
567	Vermiculated Screech-Owl *Otus vermiculatus*	M	(N Co, N Ve)	T-S	Formerly included in *O. guatemalae*: König *et al.* 1999.								
568	Roraima Screech-Owl *Otus roraimae*	M	(S Ve, Gu?)	T-S	Formerly included in *O. vermiculatus*: König *et al.* 1999.						?		
569	Rio Napo Screech-Owl *Otus napensis*	3	(E Ec, E Co)	T-S	Formerly included in *O. vermiculatus*: König *et al.* 1999.								
570	White-throated Screech-Owl *Otus albogularis*	6	*aequatorialis* (E Ec) *albogularis* (N Ec, Co: E Andes) *macabrum* (W Ec, Co: W & C Andes) *meridensis* (W Ve) *obscurus* (NW Ve)	US-Te	*aequatorialis* and *obscurus* not recognised by König *et al.* 1999.								

No.	Species	Ssp. Total	Subspecies in Northern South America	Altitude Range	References and Comments	Ec	Co	Ve	Ar Cu Bo	Tr To	Gu	Su	FG
571	**Great Horned Owl** *Bubo virginianus*	15?	*elutus* (E Co) *colombianus* (C Co) *nacurutu* (E Co, Ve, Gu, Su, FG) *nigrescens* (Ec, Co) *scotinus* (E Ve)	T-P	*elutus, colombianus* and *scotinus* not recognised by König *et al.* 1999. Sight records in Ec, FG: SFP&M.	?							?
572	**Mottled Owl** *Ciccaba virgata*	7	*macconnelli* (Ve, Gu, Su, FG) *virgata* (Ec, Co, Ve, Tr)	T-S	Sometimes placed in *Strix*								
573	**Black-and-white Owl** *Ciccaba nigrolineata*	M		T	Sometimes placed in *Strix*								
574	**Black-banded Owl** *Ciccaba huhula*	2	*huhula* (E Co, S Ve, Gu, Su, FG)	LT	Sometimes placed in *Strix*								
575	**Rufous-banded Owl** *Ciccaba albitarsus*	M		S-Te	Sometimes placed in *Strix*								
576	**Crested Owl** *Lophostrix cristata*	3	*cristata* (E Ec, SW Co, S Ve, Gu, Su, FG) *stricklandi* (W Co) *wedeli* (NE Co, N Ve)	T	Sight records in FG: SFP&M. *stricklandi* may be a sep. sp.: König *et al.* 1999.								?
577	**Spectacled Owl** *Pulsatrix perspicillata*	6	*chapmani* (W Co, W Ec) *perspicillata* (E Co, Ve, Gu, Su, FG) *trinitatis* (Tr)	T									
578	**Band-bellied Owl** *Pulsatrix melanota*	2?	*melanota* (E Ec, SE Co)	UT									
579	**Peruvian Pygmy-Owl** *Glaucidium peruanum*	M	(W & SW Ec)	T-P	S&M 1993								
580	**Central American Pygmy-Owl** *Glaucidium griseiceps*	3	*rarum* (extreme NW Co)	T	Formerly included in extralimital Least Pygmy-Owl *G. minutissimum*: Howell & Robbins 1995. Sometimes considered to be monotypic.								
581	**Subtropical Pygmy-Owl** *Glaucidium parkeri*	M	(SE Ec)	S	Sp. nov.: Robbins & Howell 1995								
582	**Amazonian Pygmy-Owl** *Glaucidium hardyi*	M	(Ve, Gu, FG - Amazon basin)	LT	Sp. nov.: Vielliard 1989								
583	**Ferruginous Pygmy-Owl** *Glaucidium brasilianum*	12	*duidae* (S Ve) *margaritae* (Ve: Marg) *medianum* (N Co, N Ve, Gu, Su, FG?) *olivaceum* (SE Ve) *phaloenoides* (Tr, Marg, N Ve) *ucayalae* (SE Co, S Ve)	T-S	*ucayalae* may be a sep. sp.: König *et al.* 1999.								?
584	**Ridgway's Pygmy-Owl** *Glaucidium ridgwayi*	2	*ridgwayi* (extreme NW Co)	T	= *G. brasilianum*: Heidrich *et al.* 1995.								
585	**Andean Pygmy-Owl** *Glaucidium jardinii*	M	(Co, Ve, Ec)	S-P									
586	**Cloud-forest Pygmy-Owl** *Glaucidium nubicola*	M	(NW Ec, W Co)	S-Te	Sp. nov.: Robbins & Stiles 1999								
587	**Burrowing Owl** *Athene cunicularia*	19	*apurensis** (SE Ve) *arubensis** (Ar) *brachyptera* (Ve: N & Marg) *carrikeri* (Co: E Andes) *minor* (S Gu, S Su) *pichinchae* (W Ec) *punensis** (SW Ec) *tolimae* (W Co)	T-P	Formerly *Speotyto*. * not recognised by König *et al.* 1999.								

No.	Species	Ssp. Total	Subspecies in Northern South America	Altitude Range	References and Comments	Ec	Co	Ve	Ar Cu Bo	Tr To	Gu	Su	F(
588	**Buff-fronted Owl** *Aegolius harrisii*	3	*harrisii* (Ec, Co, NW Ve)	UT-Te									
589	**Stygian Owl** *Asio stygius*	6	*robustus* (Ec, Co, NEW Ve)	T-Te									
590	**Striped Owl** *Asio clamator*	3	*clamator* (Co, Ve, Gu, Su, FG) *oberi* (To)	T	Formerly *Rhinoptynx*. *Oberi* not recognised by König *et al.* 1999.								
591	**Short-eared Owl** *Asio flammeus*	9	*bogotensis* (Co, Ec, Ve, Gu) *pallidicaudus* (Ve, Gu)	T-P	*pallidicaudus* not recognised by König *et al.* 1999. Sight records in FG: SFP&M.								?
592	**Oilbird** *Steatornis caripensis*	M		T-S	Vagrant to Ar/Cu/Bo: SFP&M.								
593	**Great Potoo** *Nyctibius grandis*	M		LT									
594	**Long-tailed Potoo** *Nyctibius aethereus*	3	*chocoensis* (W Co) *longicaudatus* (E Ec, Gu, Ve)	T									
595	**Common Potoo** *Nyctibius griseus*	3	*griseus* (Ec, Co, Ve, Tr, To, Gu, Su, FG)	T-LS	Formerly Grey Potoo AOU 1998								
596	**Andean Potoo** *Nyctibius maculosus*	M	(C Ec, W Co, W Ve)	S-Te									
597	**White-winged Potoo** *Nyctibius leucopterus*	M		LT	Cohn-Haft 1993								
598	**Rufous Potoo** *Nyctibius bracteatus*	M		LT	Uncertain in Co: SFP&M.		?						
599	**Short-tailed Nighthawk** *Lurocalis semitorquatus*	5	*nattereri* (C Co, W Ve) *noctivagus* (W Co, NW Ec) *schaeferi* (NC Ve) *semitorquatus* (NE Co; W, C&S Ve; Tr, To, Gu, Su, FG)	T-LS	*nattereri* may be a sep. sp. (Chestnut-banded or Chestnut-bellied Nighthawk): H&B, S&M.								
600	**Rufous-bellied Nighthawk** *Lurocalis rufiventris*	M		S-Te	Formerly included in *L. semitorquatus*								
601	**Least Nighthawk** *Chordeiles pusillus*	6	*esmeraldae* (S Ve, E Co) *septentrionalis* (NE Co, C&E Ve, Gu, W Su)	LT									
602	**Sand-colored Nighthawk** *Chordeiles rupestris*	2	*rupestris* (E Ec, SE Co, S Ve) *xyostictus* (C Co)	LT									
603	**Lesser Nighthawk** *Chordeiles acutipennis*	8	*acutipennis* (Co, Ve, Marg, Tr, To, Gu, Su, FG) *aequatorialis* (W Co, W Ec) *crissalis* (SW Co) *texenis* (W Co)	T-S	Sight records in Ar/Cu/Bo: SFP&M.				?				
604	**Common Nighthawk** *Chordeiles minor*	9	Migrants: *minor* recorded wintering in N S.Am.; *aserriensis, henryi, hesperis, howelli, neotropicalis, panamensis* & *sennetti* possibly winter in N S.Am.	T-S	Uncertain in Tr: SFP&M.					?			
605	**Antillean Nighthawk** *Chordeiles gundlachii*	2	*gundlachii* & *vicinus* (migrants – winter in S.Am.)	LT									
606	**Band-tailed Nighthawk** *Nyctiprogne leucopyga*	5	*exigua* (S Ve, E Co) *latifasciata* (S Ve) *leucopyga* (E Ve?, Gu, Su, FG) *pallida* (C&W Ve, NE Co)	LT									

No.	Species	Ssp. Total	Subspecies in Northern South America	Altitude Range	References and Comments	Ec	Co	Ve	Ar Cu Bo	Tr To	Gu	Su	FG
607	**Nacunda Nighthawk** *Podager nacunda*	2	*minor* (N&C Co, Ve, Tr, To, Gu, Su) (partial migrant to austral S.Am.)	T									
608	**Pauraque** *Nyctidromus albicollis*	7	*albicollis* (E&S Ve, Tr, Gu, Su, FG) *gilvus* (N Co)	T-LS									
609	**Ocellated Poorwill** *Nyctiphrynus ocellatus*	2	*ocellatus* (E Ec, S Co)	T									
610	**Choco Poorwill** *Nyctiphrynus rosenbergi*	M	(W Co, NW Ec)	LT	Formerly *N. ocellatus rosenbergi*: Robbins & Ridgely 1992								
611	**Chuck-wills-widow** *Caprimulgus carolinensis*	M	(migrant – winters N Co, N Ve, N Gu, N Su)	?	Vagrant to Ve: SFP&M.								
612	**Rufous Nightjar** *Caprimulgus rufus*	6	*minimus* (N Co, W&N Ve, NW Tr) *rufus* (S Ve, Gu, Su, FG) *rutilus* (migrant from S S.Am. – reaches S Ve?)	LT	*otiosus* (St. Lucia Nightjar) conspecific with *rufus* – Ve records erroneous; *noctivagulus* = *rufus*: Robbins & Parker 1997. *minimus* may be a sep. sp. (Ruddy Nightjar): Cleere & Nurney 1998. Recorded in Gu: Robbins & Parker 1997.							?	
613	**Silky-tailed Nightjar** *Caprimulgus sericocaudatus*	2	*mengeli* (poss. in extreme E Ec)	LT	Cleere & Nurney 1998	?							
614	**Band-winged Nightjar** *Caprimulgus longirostris*	7	*roraimae* (Ve: Pantepui) *ruficervix* (W&N Ve, Co, Ec)	T-P									
615	**White-tailed Nightjar** *Caprimulgus cayennensis*	6	*albicauda* (NW Co) *apertus* (W Co, N Ec) *cayennensis* (C&NE Co, Ve, Gu, Su, FG) *insularis* (NE Co, NW Ve, Marg, Ar, Cu, Bo) *leopetes* (Tr, To)	T									
616	**Spot-tailed Nightjar** *Caprimulgus maculicaudus*	M		T	Uncertain in Ec: RG&G.	?							
617	**Little Nightjar** *Caprimulgus parvulus*	2	*heterurus* (E Co, NW&SE Ve) *parvulus* (extreme SE Co?)	T									
618	**Scrub Nightjar** *Caprimulgus anthonyi*	M	(W Ec)	LT	= Anthony's Nightjar								
619	**Cayenne Nightjar** *Caprimulgus maculosus*	M		LT	**Endemic** Known only from type collected in FG.								
620	**Blackish Nightjar** *Caprimulgus nigrescens*	M	(E Co, E Ec, C&S Ve, Gu, Su, FG)	T									
621	**Roraiman Nightjar** *Caprimulgus whitelyi*	M	(Ve: Pantepui)	S	**Endemic**								
622	**Ladder-tailed Nightjar** *Hydropsalis climacocerca*	5	*climacocerca* (E Ec, E&SE Co; S Ve?) *schomburgki* (E Ve, Gu, Su, FG)	LT									
623	**Scissor-tailed Nightjar** *Hydropsalis brasiliana*	2	*brasiliana* (S Su)	T	Cleere & Nurney 1998.								
624	**Swallow-tailed Nightjar** *Uropsalis segmentata*	2	*segmentata* (Co & Ec)	US-Te									

No.	Species	Ssp. Total	Subspecies in Northern South America	Altitude Range	References and Comments	Ec	Co	Ve	Ar Cu Bo	Tr To	Gu	Su	FG
625	**Lyre-tailed Nightjar** *Uropsalis lyra*	3	*lyra* (Ve, Co, C Ec)	UT-S									
626	**Tepui Swift** *Cypseloides phelpsi*	M	(Ve: Pantepui)	UT	Formerly *Streptoprocne:* Marin & Stiles 1992.								
627	**Black Swift** *Cypseloides niger*	3	*niger* (sedentary in Tr) *borealis* & *costaricensis* (migrants – perhaps reach N S.Am.)	UT-Te	Formerly *Nephoecetes.* Sight records in Tr; vagrant to Gu: SFP&M.					?			
628	**White-chested Swift** *Cypseloides lemosi*	M	(SW Co)	UT	**Vulnerable** Endemic to Co: SFP&M. Sight records in Ec: RG&G.	?							
629	**Spot-fronted Swift** *Cypseloides cherriei*	M		UT-S									
630	**White-chinned Swift** *Cypseloides cryptus*	M		T-Te									
631	**Chestnut-collared Swift** *Cypseloides rutilus*	3	*brunnitorques* (Co & Ec – Andes) *rutilus* (Ve, Tr, Gu, Su, FG)	UT-Te	May be included in *Streptoprocne:* Marin & Stiles 1992.								
632	**White-collared Swift** *Streptoprocne zonaris*	9	*albicincta* (Ve, Gu) *altissima* (Co, Ec) *minor* (N Ve ?, Tr) *subtropicalis* (E Co, W Ve ?)	T-Te	Sight records in FG: SFP&M.								?
633	**Band-rumped Swift** *Chaetura spinicauda*	5	*aetherodroma* (W Co, W Ec) *fumosa* (NW Co: Panama border) *latirostris* (SE Ve) *spinicauda* (E Ve, Gu, Su, FG)	T									
634	**Grey-rumped Swift** *Chaetura cinereiventris*	7	*guianensis* (E Ve, W Gu) *lawrenci* (N Ve, Marg, Tr, To) *schistacea* (E Co, W Ve) *sclateri* (S Ve, S Co)	T-S									
635	**Pale-rumped Swift** *Chaetura egregia*	M	(E Ec)	T	Formerly *C. cinereiventris egregia :* Parker & Remsen 1987.								
636	**Chimney Swift** *Chaetura pelagica*	M	(migrant from N Am. to W Ec, Co, Ve)	?									
637	**Vaux's Swift** *Chaetura vauxi*	6	*aphanes* (N Ve)	T-Te	*aphanes* = *C. andrei:* Marin 1997.								
638	**Ashy-tailed Swift** *Chaetura andrei*	M	(C&N Ve)	T	May be conspecific with *vauxi:* Marin 1997.								
639	**Chapman's Swift** *Chaetura chapmani*	M		T									
640	**Amazonian Swift** *Chaetura viridipennis*	M	(migrates from S S.Am. to N Co & Ve ?)		Formerly *C. chapmani viridipennis:* Marin 1997. Sight records in Ec, as listed in RG&G, are tentatively ascribed here to this taxon.	?							
641	**Sick's Swift** *Chaetura meridionalis*	M	(migrates from S S.Am. to Ve, Gu, Su, Co)	T	Formerly *C. andrei meridionalis* Marin 1997. Sight records in FG: SFP&M.								?
642	**Short-tailed Swift** *Chaetura brachyura*	4	*brachyura* (Ec, Co, Ve, Tr, Gu, Su, FG) *ocypetes* (SW Ec) *praevelox* (To)	T									

No.	Species	Ssp. Total	Subspecies in Northern South America	Altitude Range	References and Comments	Ec	Co	Ve	Ar Cu Bo	Tr To	Gu	Su	FG
643	**White-tipped Swift** *Aeronautes montivagus*	2	*montivagus* (Co, N&W Ve, Ec) *tatei* (S Ve: Pantepui)	UT-S	Sight records in Gu: SFP&M.						?		
644	**Pygmy Swift** *Tachornis furcata*	2	*furcata* (NE Co, NW Ve) *nigrodorsalis* (W Ve)	LT	Formerly *Micropanyptila*. *nigrodorsalis* synonymous with *furcata*: Phelps 1973.								
645	**Fork-tailed Palm-Swift** *Tachornis squamata*	2	*semota* (Tr, Gu, Su, FG) *squamata* (Ve, Co)	LT	Formerly *Reinarda*								
646	**Lesser Swallow-tailed Swift** *Panyptyla cayennensis*	2	*cayennensis* (Ec, Co, Ve, Gu, Su, FG)	T									
647	**Bronzy Hermit** *Glaucis aenea*	M		LT									
648	**Rufous-breasted Hermit** *Glaucis hirsuta*	3	*affinis* (Co: C & Sta. Marta, W Ve, E Ec) *hirsuta* (N&E Ve, Gu, Su, FG) *insularum* (Tr, To)	T									
649	**Sooty Barbthroat** *Threnetes niger*	M		LT	Synonymised with *T. leucurus* by Hinkelmann & Schuchmann 1997.								
650	**White-tailed Barbthroat** *Threnetes leucurus*	5	*cervinicauda* (E Co, E Ec) *leucurus* (S Ve, Gu, Su)	T									
651	**Band-tailed Barbthroat** *Threnetes ruckeri*	4	*darienensis* (N Co) *ruckeri* (W Co, W Ec) *venezuelensis* (W Ve)	T									
652	**White-whiskered Hermit** *Phaethornis yaruqui*	2	*sancti-johannis** (W Co) *yaruqui* (W Ec)	T	* possibly an invalid ssp.								
653	**Green Hermit** *Phaethornis guy*	4	*apicalis* (E Ec, Co: E Andes, W Ve) *coruscus* (NW Co) *emiliae* (N&C Co) *guy* (NE Ve, Tr)	UT-S									
654	**Tawny-bellied Hermit** *Phaethornis syrmatophorus*	2	*columbianus* (SE Co, E Ec) *syrmatophorus* (W Co, W Ec)	UT-S									
655	**Western Long-tailed Hermit** *Phaethornis longirostris*	6?	*baroni* (W Ec) *cassini* (=*cephalus* ?) (NW Co) *cephalus* (NW Co) *sussurus* (Co: Sta. Marta)	T-S	Hinkelmann 1996, AOU 1998. Formerly all considered ssp. of *P. superciliosus*: Hinkelmann & Schuchmann 1997.								
656	**Eastern Long-tailed Hermit** *Phaethornis superciliosus*	3?	*saturior* (= *superciliosus* ?) (SE Ve) *superciliosus* (Gu, Su, FG)	T	Rusty-breasted Hermit: S&M.								
657	**Great-billed Hermit** *Phaethornis malaris*	6	*insolitus* (E Co, SW Ve) *malaris* (Su, FG) *moorei* (E Ec, E Co)	LT	Hinkelmann 1996.								
658	**White-bearded Hermit** *Phaethornis hispidus*	M	(E Ec, SE Co, S Ve)	LT									
659	**Pale-bellied Hermit** *Phaethornis anthophilus*	4	*anthophilus* (N Co) *fuliqinosus* (SE&C Co) *fuscicapillus* (E Co, Ve)	LT	*fuliginosus* = *anthophilus*: Stiles 1995.								
660	**Straight-billed Hermit** *Phaethornis bourcieri*	3 ?	*bourcieri* (E Ec, SE Co, Ve: Amazonas) *whitelyi* (SE Co, Ve: Bolivar, Gu, Su, FG)	T	*whitelyi* possibly synonymous with *bourcieri*								

31

No.	Species	Ssp. Total	Subspecies in Northern South America	Altitude Range	References and Comments	Ec	Co	Ve	Ar Cu Bo	Tr To	Gu	Su	FG
661	**Streak-throated Hermit** *Phaethornis rupurumii*	2	rupurumii (Co, Ve, Gu)	T	Formerly *P. squalidus rupurumii*: S&M, Hinkelmann & Schuchmann 1997		█	█			█		
662	**Sooty-capped Hermit** *Phaethornis augusti*	3	augusti (E Co, W&N Ve) curiosus (Co: Sta Marta) incanescens (SE Ve, Gu)	T			█	█			█		
663	**Reddish Hermit** *Phaethornis ruber*	4	episcopus (E&S Ve, Gu) nigricinctus (E Ec, E Co, SW Ve) ruber (Su, FG)	T		█	█	█			█	█	█
664	**Grey-chinned Hermit** *Phaethornis griseogularis*	3	griseogularis (Co: Andes, S&SE Ve) porcullae (SW Ec)	UT-S		█	█	█					
665	**Little Hermit** *Phaethornis longuemareus*	4 ?	imatacae* (Ve, Gu) longuemareus (Tr, Su, FG)	T	*Ssp. possibly invalid; considered monotypic by recent authors.			█		█	█	█	█
666	**Stripe-throated Hermit** *Phaethornis striigularis*	4	ignobilis (NW Ve) saturatus (NW Co) striigularis (N Co, NW Ve) subrufescens (W Co, W Ec)	T	All ssp. formerly included in *P. longuemareus*: Hinkelmann & Schuchmann 1997.	█	█	█					
667	**Black-throated Hermit** *Phaethornis atrimentalis*	2	atrimentalis (E Ec, Co: E Andes)	T	Formerly *P. longuemareus atrimentalis*: Hinkelmann & Schuchmann 1997.	█	█						
668	**White-tipped Sicklebill** *Eutoxeres aquila*	4 ?	aquila (E Co, E Ec) heterura (W Ec, W Co) munda (W Co) salvini (NW Co)	T-S		█	█						
669	**Buff-tailed Sicklebill** *Eutoxeres condamini*	2	condamini (SE Co, E Ec)	T-Te		█	█						
670	**Tooth-billed Hummingbird** *Androdon aequatorialis*	M		UT-S		█	█						
671	**Blue-fronted Lancebill** *Doryfera johannae*	2	guianensis (S Ve, Gu) johannae (E&C Co, E Ec)	UT-S		█	█	█			█		
672	**Green-fronted Lancebill** *Doryfera ludovicae*	4	ludovicae (Ve & Co: Andes) rectirostris (Ec: Andes)	UT-Te	*rectirostris* synonymous with *ludovicae*: HBW.	█	█	█					
673	**Scaly-breasted Hummingbird** *Phaeochroa cuvierii*	5	berlepschi (N Co)	T			█						
674	**Gray-breasted Sabrewing** *Campylopterus largipennis*	3	aequatorialis (E Co, E Ec) largipennis (E Ve, Gu, Su, FG)	LT		█	█	█			█	█	█
675	**Rufous-breasted Sabrewing** *Campylopterus hyperythrus*	M		UT-S				█					
676	**Buff-breasted Sabrewing** *Campylopterus duidae*	2	duidae (S Ve: Amazonas) guaiquinimae (S Ve: Bolivar)	UT-S	Formerly *C. hyperythrus duidae* **Endemic**			█					
677	**White-tailed Sabrewing** *Campylopterus ensipennis*	M		UT-LS	**Vulnerable**			█		█			
678	**Lazuline Sabrewing** *Campylopterus falcatus*	M		UT-Te		█	█	█					
679	**Santa Marta Sabrewing** *Campylopterus phainopeplus*	M		UT-Te	**Endemic**		█						
680	**Napo Sabrewing** *Campylopterus villaviscensio*	M		UT-LS		█							

32

No.	Species	Ssp. Total	Subspecies in Northern South America	Altitude Range	References and Comments	Ec	Co	Ve	Ar Cu Bo	Tr To	Gu	Su	FG
681	**Swallow-tailed Hummingbird** *Eupetomena macroura*	3	*macroura* (Gu, Su, FG)	T							▓	▓	▓
682	**White-necked Jacobin** *Florisuga mellivora*	2	*flabellifera* (To) *mellivora* (all N S.Am., Tr)	LT	Vagrant to Ar/Cu/Bo: SFP&M. Ssp. *flabellifera* possibly not valid: Peters.	▓	▓	▓	▓	▓	▓	▓	▓
683	**Brown Violetear** *Colibri delphinae*	M		UT-S		▓	▓	▓		▓	▓	▓	▓
684	**Green Violetear** *Colibri thalassinus*	5	*cyanotus* (Ec, Co, Ve) *kerdeli* (E Ve)	S-Te	*cyanotus* may be a sep. sp. (Mountain Violetear): Monroe & Sibley 1993.	▓	▓	▓					
685	**Sparkling Violetear** *Colibri coruscans*	3	*coruscans* (Ec, Co, Ve) *germanus* (S Ve, Gu?) *rostratus* (S Ve)	UT-Te	Uncertain in Gu: SFP&M.	▓	▓	▓			?		
686	**Green-throated Mango** *Anthracothorax viridigula*	M		LT				▓		▓	▓	▓	▓
687	**Green-breasted Mango** *Anthracothorax prevostii*	5	*viridicordatus* (N Co, NW Ve)	T			▓	▓					
688	**Black-throated Mango** *Anthracothorax nigricollis*	2	*iridescens* (W Co, W Ec) *nigricollis* (Tr, To, all continental N S.Am.)	T	*iridescens* often a ssp. of *A. prevostii*, but may be a sep. sp.: S&M.	▓	▓	▓		▓	▓	▓	▓
689	**Fiery-tailed Awlbill** *Avocettula recurvirostris*	M		LT		▓		▓			▓	▓	▓
690	**Ruby-topaz Hummingbird** *Chrysolampis mosquitus*	M		T			▓	▓	▓	▓	▓	▓	▓
691	**Violet-headed Hummingbird** *Klais guimeti*	2	*guimeti* (Co, E Ec, W Ve)	UT		▓	▓	▓					
692	**Tufted Coquette** *Lophornis ornatus*	M		LT				▓		▓	▓	▓	▓
693	**Rufous-crested Coquette** *Lophornis delattrei*	2	*lessoni* (C&E Co)	T-S			▓						
694	**Spangled Coquette** *Lophornis stictolophus*	M		UT		▓	▓	▓					
695	**Festive Coquette** *Lophornis chalybeus*	3	*klagesi* (E Ve) *verreauxii* (Ec, E Co, S Ve)	LT	*verreauxii* may be a sep. sp. (Buttery Coquette): Monroe & Sibley 1993.	▓	▓	▓					
696	**Peacock Coquette** *Lophornis pavoninus*	3	*duidae* (S Ve) *pavoninus* (SE Vc, Gu) *punctigula* (SE Ve)	UT-S				▓			▓		
697	**Wire-crested Thorntail** *Popelaria popelarii*	M		UT		▓	▓						
698	**Black-bellied Thorntail** *Popelaria langsdorffi*	2	*malanosteron* (E Ec, S Co, SW Ve)	LT		▓	▓	▓					
699	**Green Thorntail** *Popelaria conversii*	M		UT		▓	▓						
700	**Racket-tailed Coquette** *Discosura longicauda*	M		LT				▓			▓	▓	▓
701	**Blue-chinned Sapphire** *Chlorestes notatus*	2	*notatus* (Ec, SE Co, N&E Ve, Tr, To, Gu, Su, FG)	T		▓	▓	▓		▓	▓	▓	▓
702	**Blue-tailed Emerald** *Chlorostilbon mellisugus*	6	*caribaeus* (N,NE&C Ve) *duidae* (S Ve) *mellisugus* (Su, FG) *napensis* (E Ec, SC & SE Co) *subfurcatus* (SE Ve, Gu)	T-S	Formerly *C. prasinus*: Stiles 1996	▓	▓	▓			▓	▓	▓
703	**Chiribiquete Emerald** *Chlorostilbon olivaresi*	M	(SC Co)		Sp. nov.: Stiles 1996 **Endemic**		▓						

No.	Species	Ssp. Total	Subspecies in Northern South America	Altitude Range	References and Comments	Ec	Co	Ve	Ar Cu Bo	Tr To	Gu	Su	F
704	Red-billed Emerald *Chlorostilbon gibsoni*	3	*chrysogaster* (N Co: coast, Ve) *gibsoni* (C Co) *nitens* (Co & Ve: Guajira, Ve: Falcon)	T-S	Stiles 1996								
705	West Andean Emerald *Chlorostilbon melanorhynchus*	2	*melanorhynchus* (NC Ec, extreme SW Co) *pumilus* (W Co)	?	Formerly conspecific with *C. gibsoni*: Stiles 1996.								
706	Coppery Emerald *Chlorostilbon russatus*	M	(N Co, NW Ve)	UT-Te									
707	Narrow-tailed Emerald *Chlorostilbon stenura*	2	*ignota* (N&NW Ve) *stenura* (Ve, Co, Ec)	UT-Te									
708	Green-tailed Emerald *Chlorostilbon alice*	M	(NC Ve)	UT-LS	Endemic								
709	Short-tailed Emerald *Chlorostilbon poortmani*	2	*euchloris* (Co) *poortmani* (E Co, W Ve)	UT-Te									
710	Fork-tailed Wood-Nymph *Thalurania furcata*	13 ?	*fissilis* (SE Ve) *furcata* (Gu, Su, FG) *nigrofasciata* (E Co, E Ec) *orenocensis* (S Ve) *refulgens* (NE Ve)	T-LS	*orenocenois* may be synonymous with *fissilis*.								
711	Violet-crowned Wood-Nymph *Thalurania colombica*	4	*colombica* (N Co: C Andes & Sta Marta, W Ve) *rostrifera* (W Ve)	T-LS	Formerly included in *T. furcata*: Escalante & Peterson 1992.								
712	Green-crowned Wood-Nymph *Thalurania fannyi*	4	*fannyi* (W Co: Pacific slope) *hypochlora* (W Ec) *subtropicalis* (W Co) *verticeps* (S Co: W Andes, N Ec)	T&S	Escalante & Peterson 1992 All ssp. formerly included in *T. furcata*. *hypochlora* may be a sep. sp. (Emerald-bellied Wood-Nymph): S&M.								
713	Violet-bellied Hummingbird *Damophila julie*	3	*feliciana* (W Ec) *julie* (N Co)	LT									
714	Sapphire-throated Hummingbird *Lepidopyga coeruleogularis*	3	*coelina* (NE Co) *confinis* (NW Co)	LT									
715	Sapphire-bellied Hummingbird *Lepidopyga lilliae*	M	(N Co)	LT	Critically threatened Endemic								
716	Shining-green Hummingbird *Lepidopyga goudoti*	3	*goudoti* (C Co) *phaeochroa* (W Ve) *zuliae* (NW Ve)	T									
717	Blue-throated Sapphire *Hylocharis eliceae*	M	(NW Co)	T									
718	Rufous-throated Sapphire *Hylocharis sapphirina*	M	(S Ve, Gu, Su, FG)	LT									
719	White-chinned Sapphire *Hylocharis cyanus*	3	*viridiventris* (N Co, Ve, Gu, Su, FG)	T									
720	Blue-headed Sapphire *Hylocharis grayi*	M	(WC Co, N Ec)	T-S									
721	Humboldt's Sapphire *Hylocharis humboldti*	M	(W Co, NW Ec)	T-S	Formerly *H. grayi humboldti*								
722	Golden-tailed Sapphire *Chrysuronia oenone*	3	*longirostris* (E&C Co) *oenone* (Tr, N&W Ve, E&C Ec)	T-LS									
723	Violet-capped Hummingbird *Goldmania violiceps*	M	(Extreme NW Co)	UT	H&B								

34

No.	Species	Ssp. Total	Subspecies in Northern South America	Altitude Range	References and Comments	Ec	Co	Ve	Ar Cu Bo	Tr To	Gu	Su	FG
724	Rufous-cheeked Hummingbird *Goethalsia bella*	M	(Extreme NW Co)	UT-S	H&B		▓						
725	White-tailed Goldenthroat *Polytmus guainumbi*	3	doctus (Co) guainumbi (Ve, Tr, Gu, Su, FG)	LT			▓	▓		▓	▓	▓	▓
726	Tepui Goldenthroat *Polytmus milleri*	M		S	Formerly *Waldronia*			▓					
727	Green-tailed Goldenthroat *Polytmus theresiae*	2	leucorrhous (S Co, S Ve, Gu, Su) theresiae (Ve, Gu, Su, FG)	LT	Formerly *Smaragdites*		▓	▓			▓	▓	▓
728	Buffy Hummingbird *Leucippus fallax*	3	cervina (NE Cu, NW) fallax (NC Ve) richmondi (NW Ve, Marg, To)	LT			▓	▓	▓				
729	Tumbes Hummingbird *Leucippus baeri*	M		LT		▓							
730	Olive-spotted Hummingbird *Leucippus chlorocercus*	M	(E Ec, extreme SE Co)	LT	Formerly *Talaphorus*	▓	▓						
731	Many-spotted Hummingbird *Taphrospilus hypostictus*	2	hypostictus (E Ec)	UT	Formerly *Talaphorus*	▓							
732	White-chested Emerald *Amazilia chionopectus*	5	chionopectus (E Ve, Tr, Gu, Su) orienticola (FG) whitelyi (Gu)	LT	Treated as *Agyrtria brevirostris* in HBW.			▓		▓	▓	▓	▓
733	Versicolored Emerald *Amazilia versicolor*	4	hollandi (S Ve) millerii (E Co, Ve)	LT	Included in *Agyrtria*: HBW.		▓	▓					
734	Glittering-throated Emerald *Amazilia fimbriata*	8	apicalis (E Co) elegantissima (N Ve) fimbriata (FG) fluviatilis (SE Co, E Ec) maculicauda (E Ve, Gu, Su) obscuricauda (Ve)	LT	Included in *Polyerata*: HBW.	▓	▓	▓			▓	▓	▓
735	Tachira Emerald *Amazilia distans*	M	(Ve: Tachira)	T	Endangered Endemic Known from a single specimen; several sight reports in recent years.			▓					
736	Sapphire-spangled Emerald *Amazilia lactea*	3	zimmeri (SE Ve: Auyan-tepui)	LT	Included in *Polyerata*: HBW. Sight records in Ec: RG&G.	?		▓					
737	Blue-chested Hummingbird *Amazilia amabilis*	3	amabilis (W Co, W Ec)	LT	Included in *Polyerata*: HBW.	▓	▓						
738	Purple-chested Hummingbird *Amazilia rosenbergi*	M	(W Co, NW Ec)	LT	Included in *Polyerata*: HBW.	▓	▓						
739	Andean Emerald *Amazilia franciae*	3	franciae (Co: Andes) viridiceps (SW Co, W Ec)	UT-S	Included in *Agyrtria*: HBW.	▓	▓						
740	Plain-bellied Emerald *Amazilia leucogaster*	2	leucogaster (Ve, Gu, Su, FG)	LT	Included in *Agyrtria*: HBW.			▓			▓	▓	▓
741	Indigo-capped Hummingbird *Amazilia cyanifrons*	2	cyanifrons (N Co)	UT-S	Included in *Saucerrottia*: HBW. Endemic		▓						
742	Steely-vented Hummingbird *Amazilia saucerrottei*	4	braccata (W Ve) saucerrottei (W Co) warscewiczi (Co: N & E Andes, Ve)	T-S	Included in *Saucerrottia*: HBW.		▓	▓					

No.	Species	Ssp. Total	Subspecies in Northern South America	Altitude Range	References and Comments	Ec	Co	Ve	Ar Cu Bo	Tr To	Gu	Su	FG
743	Copper-rumped Hummingbird *Amazilia tobaci*	7	*aliciae* (Ve: Marg) *caudata* (NE Ve) *caurensis* (SE Ve) *erythronotus* (Tr) *feliciae* (Ve: N range) *monticola* (NW Ve) *tobaci* (To)	T-LS	Included in *Saucerrottia*: HBW.								
744	Green-bellied Hummingbird *Amazilia viridigaster*	3	*cupreicauda* (SE Ve, W Gu) *duidae* (S Ve) *viridigaster* (Ve, Co: E Andes)	T-S	Included in *Saucerrottia*: HBW. *cupreicauda* & *duidae* may be a sep. sp.: HBW.								
745	Rufous-tailed Hummingbird *Amazilia tzacatl*	3	*jucunda* (SW Co, W Ec) *tzacatl* (E Co, W Ve) *brehmi* * (Co: SW Nariño)	T-LS	*Ssp. nov.: Weller & Schuchmann 1999.						?		
746	Chesnut-bellied Hummingbird *Amazilia castaneiventris*	M	(Co: E Andes)	UT-S	**Endangered Endemic**								
747	Amazilia Hummingbird *Amazilia amazilia*	5	*alticola* (SE Ec) *dumerilii* (SW Ec)	T									
748	White-vented Plumeleteer *Chalybura buffonii*	5	*aeneicauda* (NW Ve, Co: Sta. Marta) *buffoni* (C Co, NW Ve) *caeruleogaster* (Co: E Andes) *intermedia* (SW Ec) *micans* (NW Co)	LT	*intermedia* may be a sep. sp.: Peters, HBW; assigned to *C. urochrysia* in HBW.								
749	Bronze-tailed Plumeleteer *Chalybura urochrysia*	4	*isaurae* (extreme NW Co) *urochrysia* (W Co, NW Ec)	LT									
750	Speckled Hummingbird *Adelomyias melanogenys*	8	*aeneosticta* (NC Ve) *cervina* (Co: W&C Andes) *connectens* (S Co) *debellardiana* * (W Ve) *maculata* (Ec) *melanogenys* (Ve, E Co)	S	*Aveledo & Perez 1994								
751	Blossomcrown *Anthocephala floriceps*	2	*berlepschi* (Co: C Andes) *floriceps* (Co: Sta. Marta)	S	**Endemic**								
752	Ecuadorean Piedtail *Phlogophilus hemileucurus*	M	(E Ec, S Co)	UT-LS	Fitzpatrick & Willard 1982								
753	Gould's Jewelfront *Polyplancta aurescens*	M	(E Ec, Co, S Ve)	T	Formerly *Heliodoxa*								
754	Fawn-breasted Brilliant *Heliodoxa rubinoides*	3	*aequatorialis* (W Co, W Ec) *cervinigularis* (E Ec) *rubinoides* (Co: E Andes)	S									
755	Violet-fronted Brilliant *Heliodoxa leadbeateri*	3	*leadbeateri* (E Ec, Co, Ve) *parvula* (Co, Ve) *sagitta* (S Co, E Ec)	UT-S									
756	Green-crowned Brilliant *Heliodoxa jacula*	3	*jacula* (Co: E Andes) *jamesoni* (W Ec)	UT-S									
757	Velvet-browed Brilliant *Heliodoxa xanthogonys*	M	(S Ve, SW Gu)	UT-S									
758	Black-throated Brilliant *Heliodoxa schreibersii*	2	*schreibersii* (E Ec, Co)	T	Formerly *Ionolaima*								
759	Pink-throated Brilliant *Heliodoxa gularis*	M	(E Ec, Co)	UT	Formerly *Agapeta*								
760	Empress Brilliant *Heliodoxa imperatrix*	M	(W Ec, Co)	UT-LS	Formerly *Eugenia*								
761	Scissor-tailed Hummingbird *Hylonympha macrocerca*	M	(NE Ve)	UT-LS	**Endangered Endemic**								

No.	Species	Ssp. Total	Subspecies in Northern South America	Altitude Range	References and Comments	Ec	Co	Ve	Ar Cu Bo	Tr To	Gu	Su	FG
762	Violet-chested Hummingbird *Sternoclyta cyanopectus*	M		UT-S	Endemic			▓					
763	Fiery Topaz *Topaza pyra*	M	(E Ec, S Co, S Ve)	LT		▓	▓	▓					
764	Crimson Topaz *Topaza pella*	4	pamprepta (E Ec) pella (Ve, Gu, Su) smaragdula (FG)	LT		▓		▓			▓	▓	▓
765	Chimborazo Hillstar *Oreotrochilus chimborazo*	3	chimborazo (C Ec: Mt. Chimborazo) jamesoni (N Ec, extreme S Co) soderstroemi (C Ec: Mt. Quillota)	P		▓	▓						
766	Andean Hillstar *Oreotrochilus estella*	2	stolzmanni (extreme S Ec)	P	Carpenter 1976. *stolzmanni* may be a sep. sp.: S&M.	▓							
767	White-tailed Hillstar *Urochroa bougueri*	2	bougueri (SW Co, NW Ec) leucura (E Ec)	UT-Te		▓	▓						
768	Giant Hummingbird *Patagona gigas*	2	peruviana (Ec)	S-P	Sight records in Co: SFP&M.	▓	?						
769	Shining Sunbeam *Aglaeactis cupripennis*	4	cupripennis (Co, N&C Ve) parvulus (S Ec)	Te-P		▓	▓	▓					
770	Mountain Velvetbreast *Lafresnaya lafresnayi*	5	greenewalti (Ve) lafresnayi (E Co) liriope (Co: Sta Marta) saul (Ec, Co: W Andes) tamae (Ve: Tamá)	S-Te		▓	▓	▓					
771	Great Sapphirewing *Pterophanes cyanopterus*	2	cyanopterus (SC Co)	Te-P		▓	▓						
772	Bronzy Inca *Coeligena coeligena*	10 ?	coeligena (Ve: N Range) columbiana (NE Ve, Ec, Co: C&E Andes) ferruginea (Co: W&C Andes) obscura (Ec, S Co) zuliana (NW Ve: Perijá) zuloagae (N Ve: Falcon)	UT-Te		▓	▓	▓					
773	Brown Inca *Coeligena wilsoni*	M	(W Ec, W Co)	UT-S		▓	▓						
774	Black Inca *Coeligena prunellei*	M	(Co: E Andes)	S	Endangered Endemic		▓						
775	Collared Inca *Coeligena torquata*	7 ?	conradii (NW Ve, NE Co) fulgidigula (W Ec) insectivora (Ec?) torquata (Ec, Co, Ve: Tamá)	S-Te	Weske 1985	▓	▓	▓					
776	White-tailed Starfrontlet *Coeligena phalerata*	M	(Co: Sta. Marta)	S	Endemic		▓						
777	Dusky Starfrontlet *Coeligena orina*	M		?	Endemic Known from a single specimen: Carriker 1954.		▓						
778	Golden-bellied Starfrontlet *Coeligena bonapartei*	3	bonapartei (Co: E Andes) consita (NW Ve: Perijá) eos (W Ve)	S-Te	eos may be a sep. sp.: HBW.		▓	▓					
779	Blue-fronted Starfrontlet *Coeligena helianthea*	2	helianthea (Co) tamae (W Ve)	S-Te			▓	▓					
780	Buff-winged Starfrontlet *Coeligena lutetiae*	M	(Ec, Co: C Andes)	Te-P		▓	▓						
781	Rainbow Starfrontlet *Coeligena iris*	6	aurora (S Ec) hesperus (SC Ec) iris (S Ec)	S-P		▓							

No.	Species	Ssp. Total	Subspecies in Northern South America	Altitude Range	References and Comments	Ec	Co	Ve	Ar Cu Bo	Tr To	Gu	Su	FG
782	**Sword-billed Hummingbird** *Ensifera ensifera*	M	(Andes: Ve, Co, Ec)	S-Te									
783	**Buff-tailed Coronet** *Boissonneaua flavescens*	2	flavescens (Ve, Co) tinochlora (W Ec)	S-Te									
784	**Chestnut-breasted Coronet** *Boissonneaua matthewsii*	M		S-Te									
785	**Velvet-purple Coronet** *Boissonneaua jardini*	M	(W Ec, Co: W Andes)	UT-S									
786	**Orange-throated Sunangel** *Heliangelus mavors*	M	(NE Co, W Ve)	S-Te									
787	**Merida Sunangel** *Heliangelus spencei*	M	(Ve: Merida Andes)	S-P	Endemic								
788	**Amethyst-throated Sunangel** *Heliangelus amethysticollis*	5	clarisse (Co) laticlavius (S Ec) verdiscutatus (NE Co, Ve: Tamá) violiceps (Ve: Perija)	S-Te	verdiscutatus & clarisse may be sep. spp.: H&B.								
789	**Gorgeted Sunangel** *Heliangelus strophianus*	M		UT-Te									
790	**Tourmaline Sunangel** *Heliangelus exortis*	M	(E Ec, Co)	Te									
791	**Flame-throated Sunangel** *Heliangelus micraster*	2	micraster (S Ec)	Te									
792	**Purple-throated Sunangel** *Heliangelus viola*	M	(W Ec)	US-Te									
793	**Bogota Sunangel** *Heliangelus zusii*	M	(C Co)	?	Extinct ? Known from a single "Bogota" specimen: Graves 1993.								
794	**Black-breasted Puffleg** *Eriocnemis nigrivestris*	M	(NW Ec)	Te-P	Critically threatened Endemic								
795	**Glowing Puffleg** *Eriocnemis vestitus*	3	paramillo (Co: W Andes) smaragdinipectus (E Ec, Co: C Andes) vestitus (Ve, Co: E Andes)	Te-P									
796	**Turquoise-throated Puffleg** *Eriocnemis godini*	M		US-Te	Critically threatened Uncertain in Co: SFP&M.		?						
797	**Sapphire-vented Puffleg** *Eriocnemis luciani*	3	luciani (Ec, S Co)	Te-P									
798	**Coppery-bellied Puffleg** *Eriocnemis cupreoventris*	M	(Ve, Co: E Andes)	Te									
799	**Golden-breasted Puffleg** *Eriocnemis mosquera*	M	(Co, N Ec)	Te									
800	**Colorful Puffleg** *Eriocnemis mirabilis*	M		US-Te	Vulnerable Endemic Meyer de Schauensee 1967								
801	**Emerald-bellied Puffleg** *Eriocnemis alinae*	2	alinae (SE Ec, Co)	S-Te									
802	**Black-thighed Puffleg** *Eriocnemis derbyi*	2	derbyi (S Co, N Ec) longirostris (N Co: C Andes)	Te-P									
803	**Greenish Puffleg** *Haplophaedia aureliae*	5	aureliae (Co: C&E Andes) bernali (N Co: E Andes) caucensis (Co: W&C Andes) russata (E Ec)	S									
804	**Hoary Puffleg** *Haplophaedia lugens*	M	(N Ec, Co)	UT-S									
805	**Purple-bibbed Whitetip** *Urosticte benjamini*	3	benjamini (Ec, SW Co) rostrata (W Co)	UT-S									

No.	Species	Ssp. Total	Subspecies in Northern South America	Altitude Range	References and Comments	Ec	Co	Ve	Ar Cu Bo	Tr To	Gu	Su	FG
806	**Rufous-vented Whitetip** *Urosticte ruficrissa*	M	(E Ec, Co)	S		●	●						
807	**Booted Racket-tail** *Ocreatus underwoodii*	8 ?	*addae* (S Co, Ec?) *ambiguus* (CW Co) *discifer* (W Ve) *melanantherus* (W Ec) *peruanus* (E Ec) *polystictus* (N Ve) *underwoodii* (Co)	UT-S	*addae* may be a sep. sp. (Buff-booted Racket-tail), reported from Nariño, Co: Salaman 1999. Zimmer 1951.	●	●	●					
808	**Black-tailed Trainbearer** *Losbia victoriao*	5	*aequatorialis* (Ec) *victoriao* (S&E Co)	Te-P	Ssp. *eucharis* formerly believed to come from Co, now known to be from C Peru.	●	●						
809	**Green-tailed Trainbearer** *Lesbia nuna*	6	*gouldii* * (NE & SC Co, Ve: Merida) *gracilis* (Ec)	S-Te	* One record only for Ve	●	●	?					
810	**Purple-backed Thornbill** *Ramphomicron microrhynchum*	3	*andicolum* (W Ve) *microrhynchum* (Ec, Co)	Te-P		●	●	●					
811	**Black-backed Thornbill** *Ramphomicron dorsale*	M	(Co: Sta. Marta)	S-P	**Endemic**		●						
812	**Viridian Metaltail** *Metallura williami*	4	*atrigularis* (S Ec) *primolina* (NE Ec) *recisa* * (NW Co) *williami* (Co: C Andes)	Te-P	* Wetmore 1970. *primolina* may be a sep. sp. (Ecuadorian Metaltail): S&M.	●	●						
813	**Violet-throated Metaltail** *Metallura baroni*	M	(C Ec)	Te-P	**Vulnerable Endemic**	●							
814	**Neblina Metaltail** *Metallura odomae*	M	(S Ec)	Te-P	**Endemic** Sp. nov.: Graves 1980	●							
815	**Tyrian Metaltail** *Metallura tyrianthina*	8	*chloropogon* (N Ve) *districta* (Co: Sta. Marta, Ve: Perijá) *oreopola* (Ve) *quitensis* (NW Ec) *tyrianthina* (E&S Ec, Co, Ve: Tamá)	Te-P	*districta* may be a sep. sp. (Santa Marta Metaltail): P. Salaman pers. comm.	●	●	●					
816	**Perijá Metaltail** *Metallura iracunda*	M ?	(Ve, Co)	Te	Sp. nov.: Wetmore 1946		●	●					
817	**Rufous-capped Thornbill** *Chalcostigma ruficeps*	2	*aureofastigata* (S Ec)	Te		●							
818	**Blue-mantled Thornbill** *Chalcostigma stanleyi*	3	*stanleyi* (Ec)	Te-P		●							
819	**Bronze-tailed Thornbill** *Chalcostigma heteropogon*	M	(W Ve, Co: E Andes)	Te			●	●					
820	**Rainbow-bearded Thornbill** *Chalcostigma herrani*	2	*herrani* (S Co, N Ec) *tolimae* (Co: W Andes)	Te		●	●						
821	**Bearded Helmetcrest** *Oxypogon guerinii*	4	*cyanolemus* (Co: Sta. Marta) *guerinii* (Co: E Andes) *lindenii* (Ve) *stubelii* (Co: C Andes)	Te-P			●	●					
822	**Mountain Avocetbill** *Opisthoprora euryptera*	M	(S Co, NE Ec)	Te-P		●	●						
823	**Berlepsch's Sylph** *Aglaiocercus berlepschi*	M	(NE Ve)	S	Formerly *A. kingi berlepschi*: Schuchmann & Duffner 1993. **Endemic**			●					

No.	Species	Ssp. Total	Subspecies in Northern South America	Altitude Range	References and Comments	Ec	Co	Ve	Ar Cu Bo	Tr To	Gu	Su	FG
824	**Long-tailed Sylph** *Aglaiocercus kingi*	6	*caudata* (Ve, Co: E Andes) *emmae* (Co: W&C Andes) *kingi* (Co: E Andes) *margarethae* (NC Ve) *mocoa* (Ec, Co: C&E Andes)	S-Te	*emmae*, with *caudata* and *mocoa*, may be a sep. sp.: Schuchmann & Duffner 1993. *kingi*, with *margaretha*, may be a sep. sp.: S&M.								
825	**Violet-tailed Sylph** *Aglaiocercus coelestis*	2	*aethereus* (SW Ec) *coelestis* (NW Ec, Co: W Andes)	UT-S									
826	**Wedge-billed Hummingbird** *Schistes geoffroyi*	3	*albogularis* (W Ec, Co: W&C Andes) *geoffroyi* (E Ec, E Co, N Ve)	UT-S	Formerly *Augastes*								
827	**Purple-crowned Fairy** *Heliothryx barroti*	M	(W Ec, W Co, NE Ve)	T									
828	**Black-eared Fairy** *Heliothryx aurita*	4	*aurita* (E Ec, N&E Co, Ve, Gu, Su, FG) *major* (Ec)	T									
829	**Horned Sungem** *Heliactin cornuta*	M		T	= *Heliactin bilopha* (nomen nudum)								
830	**Marvelous Spatuletail** *Loddigesia mirabilis*	M	(Extreme S Ec)	S-Te	**Vulnerable** Records for Ec doubtful; sight reports only. Does not occur N of the Marañon River: G. Graves, pers. comm.	?							
831	**Long-billed Starthroat** *Heliomaster longirostris*	4	*albicrissa* (W Ec) *longirostris* (N Co, Ve, Tr, Gu, Su, FG) *stuartae* (S Co)	T									
832	**Blue-tufted Starthroat** *Heliomaster furcifer*	M		T	Sight record in Ec: RG&G. Possibly austral migrant to Co: H&B.	?							
833	**Peruvian Sheartail** *Thaumastura cora*	M	(Extreme S Ec)	T-Te	Records for Ec doubtful; sight reports only. Does not occur N of the Marañon River: G. Graves, pers. comm.	?							
834	**Purple-throated Woodstar** *Philodice mitchellii*	M	(W Ec, W Co)	UT-S									
835	**Amethyst Woodstar** *Calliphlox amethystina*	M	(E Ec, E Ve, Gu, Su, FG)	T									
836	**Purple-collared Woodstar** *Myrtis fanny*	M		T-Te									
837	**Short-tailed Woodstar** *Myrmia micrura*	M	(W Ec)	LT									
838	**White-bellied Woodstar** *Acestrura mulsant*	M	(Ec, Co, W Ve)	UT-Te									
839	**Little Woodstar** *Acestrura bombus*	M		T-S	**Endangered**								
840	**Gorgeted Woodstar** *Acestrura heliodor*	2	*cleavesi* (NE Ec) *heliodor* (Ec, Co, Ve)	UT-Te	*meridae* (Zimmer & Phelps 1950) synonymous with *heliodor*: Graves 1986.								
841	**Santa Marta Woodstar** *Acestrura astreans*	M	(Co: Sta. Marta)	UT-Te	**Endemic**								
842	**Esmeraldas Woodstar** *Acestrura berlepschi*	M	(W Ec)	LT	**Endangered Endemic**								

No.	Species	Ssp. Total	Subspecies in Northern South America	Altitude Range	References and Comments	Ec	Co	Ve	Ar Cu Bo	Tr To	Gu	Su	FG
843	**Rufous-shafted Woodstar** *Chaetocercus jourdanii*	3	*andinus* (NW &N Ve) *jourdanii* (NE Ve, Tr) *rosae* (N&W Ve, Co: C Andes)	UT-S									
844	**Crested Quetzal** *Pharomachrus antisianus*	M	(Ec, Co, W Ve)	UT-Te									
845	**White-tipped Quetzal** *Pharomachrus fulgidus*	2	*festatus* (Co: Sta Marta) *fulgidus* (NE & NC Ve)	S-Te	Uncertain in Gu: SFP&M.						?		
846	**Golden-headed Quetzal** *Pharomachrus auriceps*	3	*auriceps* (Co, Ec) *hargitti* (Ve, Co) *heliactin* (W Ec)	UT-Te	Formerly *P. pavoninus auriceps*, *P. pavoninus heliactin* and *P. calurus hargitti*: (Meyer de Schauensee, 1966).								
847	**Pavonine Quetzal** *Pharomachrus pavoninus*	2	*pavoninus* (SE Co, E Ec)	T									
848	**Slaty-tailed Trogon** *Trogon massena*	3	*australis* (Ec, W Co) *hoffmani* (extreme NW Co)	T									
849	**Black-tailed Trogon** *Trogon melanurus*	4	*eumorphus* * (SE Co, Ec) *macroura* (N Co) *melanurus* (E Ec, E Co, S Ve, Gu, Su) *mesurus* (W Ec)	T	* Zimmer 1948. *macroura* may be a sep. sp. (Large-tailed Trogon). S&M.								
850	**Blue-tailed Trogon** *Trogon comptus*	M	(NW Ec, W Co)	T-LS	Zimmer 1948.								
851	**White-tailed Trogon** *Trogon viridis*	5 ?	*chionurus* (W&C Co, W Ec) *viridis* (E Co, Ve, Gu, Su, FG)	T	Formerly *T. strigilatus*								
852	**Collared Trogon** *Trogon collaris*	7	*castaneus* (extreme S Co) *collaris* (E Ec, E Co, S Ve, Su) *exoptatus* (N Co, N Ve, Tr, To) *subtropicalis* * (C Co) *virginalis* (W Ec, W Co)	T-S	* Zimmer 1948.								
853	**Masked Trogon** *Trogon personatus*	8 ?	*assimilis* (W Ec, W Co) *duidae* (S Ve) *personatus* (E Ec, W Ve, Co: C&E Andes) *roraimae* (SE Ve, W Gu) *sanctamartae* (Co: Sta. Marta) *temperatus* (Co, Ec)	S-Te	*temperatus* may be a sep. sp. (Highland Trogon): S&M.								
854	**Black-throated Trogon** *Trogon rufus*	6	*amazonicus* (S Ve) *cupreicauda* (W Co, W Ec) *ptaritepui* (SE Ve) *rufus* (E Ve, Gu, Su, FG) *sulphureus* (Ec, extreme S Co, S Ve) *tenellus* (NW Co)	LT									
855	**Blue-crowned Trogon** *Trogon curucui*	3	*peruvianus* (Ec, S Co)	T	*bolivianus* (in Peters) = *peruvianus*: Zimmer 1948.								
856	**Violaceous Trogon** *Trogon violaceus*	6	*caligatus* (N Co, W Ve) *concinnus* (W Ec, W Co) *crissalis* (Ec, S Co, S Ve) *ramonianus* (E Ec, SE Co) *violaceus* (Ve, Tr, Gu, Su, FG)	T	*caligatus* and *ramonianus* may be sep. spp. (Gartered and Amazonian Trogons): S&M.								

No.	Species	Ssp. Total	Subspecies in Northern South America	Altitude Range	References and Comments	Ec	Co	Ve	Ar Cu Bo	Tr To	Gu	Su	F
857	**Belted Kingfisher** *Megaceryle alcyon*	M	(Migrant to Ec, N Co, N Ve, N Gu, Tr)	T?	Formerly *Ceryle*. Sight records in Gu: SFP&M. Recorded for Ar/Cu/Bo: A&S.						?		
858	**Ringed Kingfisher** *Megaceryle torquata*	3	*torquata* (N S.Am., Tr, Ve: Marg)	T-S	Formerly *Ceryle*								
859	**Amazon Kingfisher** *Chloroceryle amazona*	M		T	Sight records in Ar/Cu/Bo: SFP&M.				?				
860	**Green Kingfisher** *Chloroceryle americana*	7 ?	*americana* (E Ec, E Co, C&E Ve, Gu, Su, FG) *bottomeiana* * (N Ve) *cabanisii* (W Co, W Ec) *croteta* (Tr, To) *septentrionalis* (Co, W Ve)	T-S	* Aveledo & Perez 1994.								
861	**Green-and-rufous Kingfisher** *Chloroceryle inda*	2	*chocoensis* (W Ec, W Co) *inda* (Ec, Co, Ve, Tr, To)	LT	Considered monotypic in Fry *et al.* 1992.								
862	**American Pygmy Kingfisher** *Chloroceryle aenea*	2	*aenea* (W Ec, Co, Ve, Tr, To, Gu, Su, FG)	LT	Recorded for Ar/Cu/Bo: A&S.								
863	**Tody Motmot** *Hylomanes momotula*	3	*obscurus* (NW Co)	T									
864	**Broad-billed Motmot** *Electron platyrhynchum*	5	*minor* (C Co) *platyrhynchum* (W Ec, W Co) *pyrrholaemum* (E Ec, E Co)	T	*pyrrholaemum* may be a sep. sp. (Plain-tailed Motmot): S&M.								
865	**Rufous Motmot** *Baryphthengus martii*	M	(E Co, E Ec)	T	Formerly *B. ruficapillus martii*								
866	**Blue-crowned Motmot** *Momotus momota*	19 ?	*argenticintus* (W Ec, Co?) *bahamensis* (Tr, To) *conexus* (N Co) *microstephanus* (E Ec, E Co) *momota* (E Co, C&S Ve, Gu, Su, FG) *osgoodi* (W Ve, E Co) *spatha* * (Co: Guajira) *subrufescens* (Co & Ve: N coast)	T	* Wetmore 1946. *reconditus* synonymous with *conexus*: Wetmore 1968.								
867	**Highland Motmot** *Momotus aequatorialis*	2	*aequatorialis* (Ec, Co)	S	Formerly *M. momota aequatorialis*: Parker *et al.* 1982.								
868	**Chestnut Jacamar** *Galbalcyrhynchus leucotis*	2	*leucotis* (Ec, Co)	LT	Haffer 1974								
869	**Dusky-backed Jacamar** *Brachygalba salmoni*	M	(NW Co)	LT									
870	**Pale-headed Jacamar** *Brachygalba goeringi*	M	(E Co, N Ve)	LT									
871	**Brown Jacamar** *Brachygalba lugubris*	6	*caquetae* (C Co, E Ec) *fulviventris* (E Co, SW Ve) *lugubris* (E&S Ve, Gu, Su, Fg) *obscuriceps* (SE Ve)	LT									
872	**Yellow-billed Jacamar** *Galbula albirostris*	3	*albirostris* (SE Co, E Ve, Gu, Su, FG) *chalcocephala* (Ve, Co & Ec: Amazonia)	LT									
873	**Bluish-fronted Jacamar** *Galbula cyanescens*	M	(Co: Amazonia)	LT	Sight records in Co: P. Salaman, pers.comm.		?						

42

No.	Species	Ssp. Total	Subspecies in Northern South America	Altitude Range	References and Comments	Ec	Co	Ve	Ar Cu Bo	Tr To	Gu	Su	FG
874	**Rufous-tailed Jacamar** *Galbula ruficauda*	6	*brevirostris* (NW Ve) *melanogenia* (W Co, W Ec) *pallens* (Co: N & Sta. Marta, W Ve) *ruficauda* (C Co, Ve, Tr, To, Gu, Su, FG)	LT	*melanogenia* may be a sep. sp. (Black-chinned Jacamar): Monroe & Sibley 1993.								
875	**Green-tailed Jacamar** *Galbula galbula*	M	(E Co, Ve, Gu, Su, FG)	LT									
876	**Coppery-chested Jacamar** *Galbula pastazae*	M	(E Ec)	UT-S	Vulnerable								
877	**White-chinned Jacamar** *Galbula tombacea*	2	*tombacea* (Co & Ec: Amazonia)	T									
878	**Purplish Jacamar** *Galbula chalcothorax*	M	(E Ec)	LT	Formerly *G. leucogastra chalcothorax*: Parker & Remsen 1997.								
879	**Bronzy Jacamar** *Galbula leucogastra*	2 ?	*leucogastra* (Co, S Ve, Gu, Su, FG)	LT									
880	**Paradise Jacamar** *Galbula dea*	4	*brunneiceps* (Co: Amazonia) *dea* (Ve, Gu, Su, FG)	LT									
881	**Great Jacamar** *Jacamerops aurea*	4	*aurea* (E Co, Ve, Gu, Su, FG) *penardi* (W Co) *ridgwayi* (S Ve)	T									
882	**White-necked Puffbird** *Notharchus macrorhynchus*	4	*hyperrhynchus* (S Ve)* (N&NE Co) *macrorhynchus* (SE Ve, Gu, Su, FG)	LT	* Eisenmann 1958								
883	**Black-breasted Puffbird** *Notharchus pectoralis*	M	(C&S Co, NW Ec)	T									
884	**Brown-banded Puffbird** *Notharchus ordii*	M	(SE Co, S Ve: Amazonas)	LT									
885	**Pied Puffbird** *Notharchus tectus*	3	*picatus* (E Ec, S Co) *subtectus* (W Co, SW Ec) *tectus* (S Ve, Gu, Su, FG)	T									
886	**Chestnut-capped Puffbird** *Bucco macrodactylus*	2	*caurensis* (SE Ve) *macrodactylus* (E Ec, E Co, S Ve)	LT	Sometimes treated as monotypic.								
887	**Spotted Puffbird** *Bucco tamatia*	6	*pulmentum* (E Ec, E Co) *tamatia* (E Co, E Ve, Gu, Su, FG)	LT									
888	**Sooty-capped Puffbird** *Bucco noanamae*	M	(W Co)	LT	**Endemic.**								
889	**Collared Puffbird** *Bucco capensis*	2	*capensis* (SE Ve, Gu, Su, FG) *dugandi* (E Ec, SE Co, S Ve)	T	Sometimes treated as monotypic.								
890	**Barred Puffbird** *Nystalus radiatus*	M	(W Co)	LT									
891	**Striolated Puffbird** *Nystalus striolatus*	2	*striolatus* (E Ec)	T									
892	**Russet-throated Puffbird** *Hypnelus ruficollis*	5	*bicinctus* (EC Co, S Ve) *coloratus* (NW Ve) *decolor* (NE Co, NW Ve) *ruficollis* (N&NE Co, NW Ve) *stoicus* (Margarita Is.) *striaticollis* (NW Ve)	T	*bicinctus* may be a sep. sp. (Two-banded Puffbird): S&M, but rejected by H&B.								
893	**White-chested Puffbird** *Malacoptila fusca*	3	*fusca* (E Ec, SE Co, Gu, Su, FG) *venezuelae* (S Ve)	LT									

No.	Species	Ssp. Total	Subspecies in Northern South America	Altitude Range	References and Comments	Ec	Co	Ve	Ar Cu Bo	Tr To	Gu	Su	FG
894	**Black-streaked Puffbird** *Malacoptila fulvogularis*	3	fulvogularis (E Ec) huilae (C Co) substriata (Co)	UT-S		■	■						
895	**White-whiskered Puffbird** *Malacoptila panamensis*	6	chocoana (W Co) magdalenae (C Co) panamensis (NW Co) poliolipis (SW Co, W Ec)	T		■	■						
896	**Moustached Puffbird** *Malacoptila mystacalis*	2	mystacalis (Co: Sta Marta, W Ve) pacifica (SW Co)	UT-S			■	■					
897	**Lanceolated Monklet** *Micromonacha lanceolata*	2	lanceolata (W Co, E Ec)	UT-S		■	■						
898	**Rusty-breasted Nunlet** *Nonnula rubecula*	5 ?	cineracea (Co?) duidae (S Ve, Co?) tapanahoniensis (Su)	LT	Ssp in Co uncertain. Sight records in FG: SFP&M.		■	■				■	?
899	**Brown Nunlet** *Nonnula brunnea*	M	(Co, E Ec)	LT		■	■						
900	**Grey-cheeked Nunlet** *Nonnula frontalis*	3 ?	frontalis (N Co) pallescens (NE Co) stulta * (W Co)	T	Formerly *N. ruficapilla frontalis*: Wetmore 1968. * Wetmore 1953.		■						
901	**White-faced Nunbird** *Hapaloptila castanea*	M	(W Co, W Ec)	UT-Te		■	■						
902	**Black Nunbird** *Monasa atra*	M	(S Ve, Gu, Su, FG)	LT				■			■	■	■
903	**Black-fronted Nunbird** *Monasa nigrifrons*	2	nigrifrons (SE Co, E Ec)	LT		■	■						
904	**White-fronted Nunbird** *Monasa morphoeus*	7	pallescens (NW Co) peruana (E Ec, SE Co, S Ve) sclateri (N Co)	T	*pallescens* may be a sep. sp. (Pale-winged Nunbird): S&M.	■	■	■					
905	**Yellow-billed Nunbird** *Monasa flavirostris*	M	(E Co, E Ec)	T		■	■						
906	**Swallow-wing** *Chelidoptera tenebrosa*	2	tenebrosa (E Ec, E Co, Ve, Gu, Su, FG)	T		■	■	■			■	■	■
907	**Scarlet-crowned Barbet** *Capito aurovirens*	M	(Co & Ec: Amazonia)	LT		■	■						
908	**Spot-crowned Barbet** *Capito maculicoronatus*	4	pirrensis (NW Co) rubrilateralis (W Co)	T	*pirrensis* synonymous with *rubrilateralis*: Wetmore 1968. **Endemic**		■						
909	**Orange-fronted Barbet** *Capito squamatus*	M	(SW Co, W Ec)	T		■	■						
910	**White-mantled Barbet** *Capito hypoleucus*	3	carrikeri* (Co: Antioquia) extinctus (C Co: Caldas) hypoleucus (NC Co)	UT	*Known from a single specimen. *extinctus* (Graves 1986a) considered extinct, but several recent records: Lane 1999. **Endangered Endemic**		■						
911	**Five-colored Barbet** *Capito quinticolor*	M	(W Co, W Ec)	LT	**Vulnerable Endemic**	■	■						
912	**Black-spotted Barbet** *Capito niger*	M	(E Ve, Gu, Su, FG)	T	Haffer 1997, Lane 1999.			■			■	■	■

No.	Species	Ssp. Total	Subspecies in Northern South America	Altitude Range	References and Comments	Ec	Co	Ve	Ar Cu Bo	Tr To	Gu	Su	FG
913	Gilded Barbet *Capito auratus*	13	*aurantiicinctus* (S Ve) *macintyrei* (SC Co) *auratus** (extreme SE Ec) *nitidior* (SE Co) *punctatus* (Ec, Co) *transileus* (SE Co, SW Ve)	T	Formerly, all ssp. included in *C. niger*: Haffer 1997, Lane 1999. *macintyrei* synonymous with *punctatus*: Lane 1999. *Recorded in Ec: RG&G.								
914	Lemon-throated Barbet *Eubucco richardsoni*	5	*richardsoni* (E Co, E Ec)	LT									
915	Red-headed Barbet *Eubucco bourcierii*	6	*aequatorialis* (W Ec) *bourcierii* (Co: C & E Andes, N Ve) *occidentalis* (Co: W Andes) *orientalis* (E Ec)	UT-S	Lane 1999.								
916	Toucan Barbet *Semnornis ramphastinus*	2	*caucae* (Co: W Andes) *ramphastinus* (Ec)	UT-S									
917	Emerald Toucanet *Aulacorhynchus prasinus*	8	*albivitta* (E Ec, Co: C&E Andes, Ve) *cyanolaemus* (SE Ec) *griseigularis* (Co: W Andes) *lautus* (Co: Sta Marta) *phaeolaemus* (Co: W Andes)	T-Te									
918	Groove-billed Toucanet *Aulacorhynchus sulcatus*	2	*erythrognathus* (NE Ve) *sulcatus* (NC Ve)	UT-S	**Endemic**								
919	Yellow-billed Toucanet *Aulacorhynchus calorhynchus*	M	(N Co, NW Ve)	UT-S	Formerly *A. sulcatus calorhynchus*: Schwartz 1972								
920	Chestnut-tipped Toucanet *Aulacorhynchus derbianus*	5	*derbianus* (E Ec, E Co) *duidae* (S Ve) *osgoodi* (Gu, Su) *whitelianus* (SE Ve, SW Gu)	UT-S									
921	Crimson-rumped Toucanet *Aulacorhynchus haematopygus*	2	*haematopygus* (Co: Andes, Ve: Perijá) *sexnotatus* (SW Co, W Ec)	UT-S									
922	Lettered Aracari *Pteroglossus inscriptus*	2	*humboldti* (SE Co, E Ec)	LT	Formerly *P. viridis inscriptus*: Haffer 1974.								
923	Green Aracari *Pteroglossus viridis*	M	(SE Ve, Gu, Su, FG)	LT									
924	Ivory-billed Aracari *Pteroglossus azara*	3	*flavirostris* (E Ec, SE Co, S Ve)	LT	Treated as *P. flavirostris* in Peters, but *azara* is the older name.								
925	Chestnut-eared Aracari *Pteroglossus castanotis*	2	*castanotis* (E Ec, E Co)	LT									
926	Black-necked Aracari *Pteroglossus aracari*	2	*atricollis* (S&E Ve, Gu, Su, FG)	LT									
927	Collared Aracari *Pteroglossus torquatus*	4	*nuchalis* (N Co, N Ve) *torquatus* (NW Co)	T	In Haffer 1974 *nuchalis* includes *pectoralis*.								
928	Stripe-billed Aracari *Pteroglossus sanguineus*	M	(W Co, NW Ec)	T	Formerly *P. torquatus sanguineus*: Haffer 1974. Not treated as a sep. sp. in SFP&M.								
929	Pale-mandibled Aracari *Pteroglossus erythropygius*	M	(W Ec)	T	Formerly *P. torquatus erythropigius*: Haffer 1974. Not treated as a sep. sp. in SFP&M.								
930	Many-banded Aracari *Pteroglossus pluricinctus*	M	(E Ec, E Co, S Ve)	LT									

No.	Species	Ssp. Total	Subspecies in Northern South America	Altitude Range	References and Comments	Ec	Co	Ve	Ar Cu Bo	Tr To	Gu	Su	FG
931	Plate-billed Mountain-Toucan *Andigena laminirostris*	M	(SW Co, W Ec)	UT-P									
932	Grey-breasted Mountain-Toucan *Andigena hypoglauca*	2	*hypoglauca* (Co: C Andes) *lateralis* (E Ec)	Te-P									
933	Black-billed Mountain-Toucan *Andigena nigrirostris*	3	*nigrirostris* (Ve, Co: E Andes) *occidentalis* (Co: W Andes) *spilorhynchus* (NE Ec, Co: C Andes)	S-P									
934	Yellow-eared Toucanet *Selenidera spectabilis*	M	(Ec, NW Co)	T									
935	Golden-collared Toucanet *Selenidera reinwardtii*	2	*reinwardtii* (E Co, E Ec)	T									
936	Tawny-tufted Toucanet *Selenidera nattereri*	M	(S Co, S Ve, Gu, FG)	LT	Sight records in FG: SFP&M.								?
937	Guianan Toucanet *Selenidera culik*	M	(SE Ve, Gu, Su, FG)	LT									
938	Keel-billed Toucan *Ramphastos sulfuratus*	2	*brevicarinatus* (N Co, Ve)	T									
939	Choco Toucan *Ramphastos brevis*	M	(NW Ec, W Co)	T									
940	Citron-throated Toucan *Ramphastos citreolaemus*	M	(C Co)	T	Formerly *R. vitellinus citrolaemus*: Haffer 1974. Treated as a sep. sp. in H&B., but not so in SFP&M. **Endemic**								
941	Yellow-ridged Toucan *Ramphastos culminatus*	M		T	Formerly *R. vitellinus culminatus*: Haffer 1974.Treated as a sep. sp. in H&B., but not so in SFP&M.								
942	Channel-billed Toucan *Ramphastos vitellinus*	3 ?	*vitellinus* (Ve, Tr, Gu, Su, FG)	T									
943	Black-mandibled Toucan *Ramphastos ambiguus*	3	*abbreviatus* (W Ve, Co: C Andes) *ambiguus* (E Co, E Ec) *swainsonii* (W Co, Ec)	T-S	*swainsonii* may be a sep. sp. (Chestnut-mandibled Toucan): RG&G.								
944	Red-billed Toucan *Ramphastos tucanus*	M	(E Ec, E Co, Ve, Gu, Su, FG)	T									
945	Cuvier's Toucan *Ramphastos cuvieri*	M	(E Ec, E Co, S Ve)	T	Formerly *R. tucanus cuvieri:* Haffer 1974								
946	Toco Toucan *Ramphastos toco*	2	*toco* (Gu, Su, FG)	T									
947	Bar-breasted Piculet *Picumnus aurifrons*	7 ?	*aurifrons* (SW Co) *flavifrons* (SE Co, E Ec)	T									
948	Orinoco Piculet *Picumnus pumilus*	M	(SE Co)	T									
949	Lafresnaye's Piculet *Picumnus lafresnayi*	4 ?	*lafresnayi* (E Ec, SE Co)	T									
950	Ecuadorean Piculet *Picumnus sclateri*	3	*parvistriatus* (W Ec) *sclateri* (SW Ec)	T									
951	Golden-spangled Piculet *Picumnus exilis*	7 ?	*buffoni* (E Gu, Su, FG) *salvini* (NE Ve) *clarus* (SE Ve) *undulatus* (E Co, S Ve, Gu)	T-LS	Sight records in Co: SFP&M.		?						

No.	Species	Ssp. Total	Subspecies in Northern South America	Altitude Range	References and Comments	Ec	Co	Ve	Ar Cu Bo	Tr To	Gu	Su	FG
952	Black-dotted Piculet *Picumnus nigropunctatus*	M	(E Ve)	LT	Phelps & Phelps 1958. Synonymisation with *P. exilis salvini* (Short 1982) is probably not valid: Lentino & Restall, in prep. **Endemic**			■					
953	Chestnut Piculet *Picumnus cinnamomeus*	4	cinnamomeus (N Co, NW Ve) larensis (Ve: Lara) perijanus (NW Ve) persaturatus (N Co) venezuelensis (W Ve)	LT	*larensis* (Aveledo 1998) is probably synonymous with *perijanus*.		■	■					
954	Guianan Piculet *Picumnus minutissimus*	M		LT							■	■	■
955	White-barred Piculet *Picumnus cirratus*	6	confusus (Gu, FG)	T-S							■		■
956	Olivaceous Piculet *Picumnus olivaceus*	8	eisenmanni (Co & Ve: Perijá) harterti (SW Co, W Ec) malleolus * (NW Co) olivaceus (Co) panamensis * (extreme NW Co) tachirensis (W Ve, E Co)	T	* Wetmore 1965	■	■	■					
957	Rufous-breasted Piculet *Picumnus rufiventris*	3	rufiventris (Ec, Co)	LT		■	■						
958	Plain-breasted Piculet *Picumnus castelnau*	M	(E Ec, SE Co)	LT	Sight records in Ec: RG&G.	?	■						
959	Scaled Piculet *Picumnus squamulatus*	5	apurensis (N Ve) lovejoyi (NW Ve) obsoletus (NE Ve) rohli (N Ve) squamulatus (Co)	T-LS	*P. salvini*, known from a single specimen of unknown origin, is synonymous with *P. s. obsoletus*: Lentino & Restall, in prep.		■	■					
960	Greyish Piculet *Picumnus granadensis*	2	antioquensis (WS Co) granadensis (WC Co)	UT-S	**Endemic**		■						
961	White-bellied Piculet *Picumnus spilogaster*	3	orinocensis (E Ve) spilogaster (Gu, Su, FG)	LT	Phelps & Phelps 1958.			■			■	■	■
962	White Woodpecker *Melanerpes candidus*	M		T	Sight records in FG: SFP&M.								?
963	Acorn Woodpecker *Melanerpes formicivorus*	7 ?	flavigula (Co)	T-Te			■						
964	Black-cheeked Woodpecker *Melanerpes pucherani*	M	(W Ec, W Co)	LT		■	■						
965	Golden-naped Woodpecker *Melanerpes chrysauchen*	2	pulcher (Co)	T	*pulcher* may be a sep. sp. (Beautiful Woodpecker) S&M.		■						
966	Yellow-tufted Woodpecker *Melanerpes cruentatus*	M	(E Ec, E Co, Ve, Gu, Su, FG)	T		■	■	■			■	■	■
967	Red-crowned Woodpecker *Melanerpes rubricapillus*	5	paraguanae (N Ve) rubricapillus (Co, Ve, To, Gu, Su)	T-LS			■	■		■	■	■	
968	Yellow-bellied Sapsucker *Sphyrapicus varius*	M	(Boreal migrant, winter range reaches NW Co)	?			■						
969	Scarlet-backed Woodpecker *Veniliornis callonotus*	2	callonotus (W Ec, SW Co) major (S Ec)	T		■	■						
970	Yellow-vented Woodpecker *Veniliornis dignus*	3	abdominalis (W Ve: Tamá) baezae (Ec) dignus (Co)	UT-S		■	■	■					

No.	Species	Ssp. Total	Subspecies in Northern South America	Altitude Range	References and Comments	Ec	Co	Ve	Ar Cu Bo	Tr To	Gu	Su	FG
971	**Bar-bellied Woodpecker** *Veniliornis nigriceps*	3	equifasciatus (Ec, Co) pectoralis (S Ec)	S-P									
972	**Smoky-brown Woodpecker** *Veniliornis fumigatus*	5	reichenbachi (N Co, N Ve)	T-Te									
973	**Little Woodpecker** *Veniliornis passerinus*	9	agilis (E Ec) fidelis (E Co, W Ve) modestus (NE Ve) passerinus (Gu, Su, FG)	T								?	
974	**Blood-coloured Woodpecker** *Veniliornis sanguineus*	M		LT									
975	**Red-rumped Woodpecker** *Veniliornis kirkii*	5	cecilii (W Ec, W Co) continentalis (N&W Ve) kirkii (Tr, To, NE Ve) monticola (SE Ve: Roraima)	T-S									
976	**Choco Woodpecker** *Veniliornis chocoensis*	M	(W Co, NW Ec)	T	Formerly *V. affinis chocoensis*: S&M. **Endemic**								
977	**Golden-collared Woodpecker** *Veniliornis cassini*	M	(S&SE Ve, Gu, Su, FG)	T									
978	**Red-stained Woodpecker** *Veniliornis affinis*	4	hilaris (E Ec) orenocensis (E Co, S Ve)	T									
979	**Lita Woodpecker** *Piculus litae*	M	(NW Ec, W Co)	T	Formerly *P. leucolaemus litae*: S&M								
980	**White-throated Woodpecker** *Piculus leucolaemus*	M	(NW Co)	T									
981	**Yellow-throated Woodpecker** *Piculus flavigula*	3	flavigula (Co, Ve, Gu, Su, FG) magnus (SE Co)	LT									
982	**Golden-green Woodpecker** *Piculus chrysochlorus*	9	capistratus (Ec, C Co, S Ve) guianensis (FG) xanthochlorus (NE Co, NW Ve)	LT									
983	**Golden-olive Woodpecker** *Piculus rubiginosus*	19	allei (Co: Sta Marta) buenavistae (E Ec, E Co) deltanus (E Ve) guianae (S Ve) gularis (S Co) meridensis (W Ve) nigriceps (Gu, Su) rubiginosus (NC&NE Ve) rubripileus (SW Co) tobagensis (Tr) trinitatis (Tr) viridissimus (SE Ve: Auyantepui)	T-S									
984	**Crimson-mantled Woodpecker** *Piculus rivolii*	6	brevirostris (Ec, SW Co) meridae (W Ve) quindiuna (NC Co) rivolii (W Ve, EC Co) zuliae (W Ve: Perijá)	S-Te									

No.	Species	Ssp. Total	Subspecies in Northern South America	Altitude Range	References and Comments	Ec	Co	Ve	Ar Cu Bo	Tr To	Gu	Su	FG
985	Spot-breasted Woodpecker *Colaptes punctigula*	7	punctigula (Gu, Su, FG) punctitectus (Ve) speciosus (Ec, SE Co) striatigularis (WC Co) ujhelyii (N Co) zuliensis (NW Ve)	LT									
986	Andean Flicker *Colaptes rupicola*	3	cinereicapillus (extreme SE Ec)	Te-P	Recorded in Ec: RG&G.								
987	Campo Flicker *Colaptes campestris*	2	campestris (Su)	T-S									
988	Cinnamon Woodpecker *Celeus loricatus*	4	innotatus (N Co) loricatus (W Ec, W Co) mentalis (NW Co)	LT									
989	Scale-breasted Woodpecker *Celeus grammicus*	4	grammicus (S Co, S Ve) verreauxi (E Ec)	LT	Uncertain in FG: SFP&M								?
990	Waved Woodpecker *Celeus undulatus*	3	amacurensis (NE Ve) undulatus (E Ve, Gu, Su, FG)	LT									
991	Chestnut Woodpecker *Celeus elegans*	6	citreopygius (E Ec) deltanus (NE Ve) elegans (Su, FG) hellmayri (E Ve, Gu, Su) jumana (SW Ve, E Co) leotaudi (Tr)	LT									
992	Cream-colored Woodpecker *Celeus flavus*	5 ?	flavus (E Co, S Ve, Gu, Su, FG) semicinnamomeus (E Ve)	LT									
993	Rufous-headed Woodpecker *Celeus spectabilis*	3	spectabilis (E Ec)	LT									
994	Ringed Woodpecker *Celeus torquatus*	3	occidentalis (E Ec, Co, S Ve) torquatus (E Ve, Gu, Su, FG)	LT									
995	Lineated Woodpecker *Dryocopus lineatus*	6	fuscipennis (W Ec) lineatus (W Co, Ve, Tr, Gu, Su, FG) nuperus (N Co, N Ve)	T									
996	Powerful Woodpecker *Campephilus pollens*	2	pollens (Ec, Co, Ve)	S-Te									
997	Crimson-bellied Woodpecker *Campephilus haematogaster*	2	haematogaster (E Ec, E Co) splendens (W Ec, W Co)	T-S	splendens may be a sep. sp. (Splendid Woodpecker): P. Salaman pers. comm.								
998	Red-necked Woodpecker *Campephilus rubricollis*	3	rubricollis (E Co, S Ve, Gu, Su, FG) trachelopyrus (S Ec)	T									
999	Crimson-crested Woodpecker *Campephilus melanoleucos*	3	malherbii (N&W Co, W Ve) melanoleucos (E Ec, E Co, Ve, Tr, Gu, Su, FG)	T-S									
1000	Guayaquil Woodpecker *Campephilus gayaquilensis*	M	(W Ec, SW Co)	T									
1001	Tyrannine Woodcreeper *Dendrocincla tyrannina*	3	hellmayri (Co & Ve: Tachira) macrorhyncha (E Ec: Pun) tyrannina (Co, W Ec)	T-S	macrorhyncha is known from 2 specimens only.								

No.	Species	Ssp. Total	Subspecies in Northern South America	Altitude Range	References and Comments	Ec	Co	Ve	Ar Cu Bo	Tr To	Gu	Su	FC
1002	Plain-brown Woodcreeper *Dendrocincla fuliginosa*	11	*barinensis* (WC Ve) *deltana* * (NE Ve: Delta) *fuliginosa* (Se Ve, Gu) *lafresnayei* (N&E Co, NW Ve) *meruloides* (N Ve, Tr, To) *neglecta* (E Ec) *phaeochroa* (E Ec, E Co, S Ve) *ridgwayi* (W Ec, W Co)	T	* Phelps & Phelps 1963								
1003	White-chinned Woodcreeper *Dendrocincla merula*	7	*bartletti* (S Ve) *merula* (Gu, Su, FG)	LT									
1004	Ruddy Woodcreeper *Dendrocincla homochroa*	3	*meridionalis* * (W Ve) *ruficeps* (NE Co)	T	*Phelps & Phelps 1963								
1005	Long-tailed Woodcreeper *Deconychura longicauda*	6	*connectens* (SE Ec) *longicauda* (SE Co, Ve, Gu, Su, FG) *minor* (N Co) *typica* (NW Co)	T									
1006	Spot-throated Woodcreeper *Deconychura stictolaema*	3	*clarior* (FG) *secunda* (E Ec, S Ve)	LT									
1007	Olivaceous Woodcreeper *Sittasomus griseicapillus*	19 ?	*aequatorialis* (W Ec) *enochrus* * (N Co) *amazonus* (E Ec, SE Co, S Ve) *axillaris* (S Ve, Gu) *griseus* (N Ve, To) *perijanus** (NW Ve) *tachirensis** (NC & NE Co, W Ve)	T	* Wetmore 1970 ** Phelps & Phelps 1963 Sight records in Su: SFP&M.							?	
1008	Wedge-billed Woodcreeper *Glyphorynchus spirurus*	10	*amacurensis** (NE Ve: Delta) *castelnaudii* (E Ec) *integratus* (NE Co) *pallidus* * (NW Co) *rufigularis* (E Ec, Co: E Andes, S Ve) *spirurus* (E Ve, Gu, Su, FG) *sublestus* (W Ec, W&C Co, W Ve) *subrufescens* (W Co)	T	** Phelps & Phelps 1963 * Wetmore 1970								
1009	Long-billed Woodcreeper *Nasica longirostris*	M	(E Ec, S Co, S Ve, FG)	LT									
1010	Cinnamon-throated Woodcreeper *Dendrexetastes rufigula*	4	*devillei* (E Ec, SE Co) *rufigula* (Ve, Gu, Su, FG)	LT									
1011	Red-billed Woodcreeper *Hylexetastes perrotii*	2	*perrotii* (E Ve, Gu, FG)	LT									

No.	Species	Ssp. Total	Subspecies in Northern South America	Altitude Range	References and Comments	Ec	Co	Ve	Ar Cu Bo	Tr To	Gu	Su	FG
1012	**Strong-billed Woodcreeper** *Xiphocolaptes promeropirhynchus*	22	*crassirostris* (SW Ec) *ignotus* (Ec) *neblinae** (S Ve: Neblina, Amazonas) *orenocensis* (E Ec, S Ve: Amazonas) *procerus* (N&C Ve) *promeropirhynchus* (Co: C&E Andes, W Ve) *rostratus* (N Co) *sanctaemartae* (NE Co, NW Ve) *tenebrosus* (SE Ve: Amazonas & Bolivar, Gu, FG) *virgatus* (C Co)	T-Te	* Known from a single specimen: Phelps & Phelps 1963. Ve: Amazonas ssp. separated altitudinally: *neblinae* = S, *orenocensis* = LT, *tenebrosus* = UT.								
1013	**Northern Barred Woodcreeper** *Dendrocolaptes sanctithomae*	5	*punctipectus* (Perija: Co & Ve) *sanctithomae* (NW Ec, N&W Co)	T-S	Formerly *D. certhia sanctithomae*: Willis 1992. *nigrirostris* and *colombianus* synonymous with *sanctithomae*; *hyleorus* synonymous with *punctipectus*: Marantz 1997.								
1014	**Southern Barred Woodcreeper** *Dendrocolaptes certhia*	6	*certhia* (SE Ve, Gu, Su) *radiolatus* (E Ec, SE Co)	T	Marantz 1997								
1015	**Black-banded Woodcreeper** *Dendrocolaptes picumnus*	10	*multistrigatus* (Co, W Ve) *picumnus* (E Ve, Gu, Su, FG) *seilerni* (NE Co, N Ve) *validus* (E Ec, SE Co)	T-Te	Marantz 1997								
1016	**Straight-billed Woodcreeper** *Xiphorhynchus picus*	14	*altirostris* (Tr) *choicus* (N Ve) *deltanus* (NE Ve: Delta) *dugandi* (N Co) *duidae* (S Ve) *longirostris* (Ve: Marg Is.) *paraguanae* (NW Ve) *phalara* (C Ve) *picirostris* (N Co, NW Ve) *picus* (E Co, S Ve) *saturatior* (E Co, W Ve) *caicarae* (SC Ve)	LT	Phelps & Phelps 1952 Phelps & Phelps 1962 Zimmer & Phelps 1955								
1017	**Striped Woodcreeper** *Xiphorhynchus obsoletus*	3	*notatus* (E Co, W&S Ve) *obsoletus* (E Ve, Gu, FG) *palliatus* (E Ec, SE Co)	LT									
1018	**Ocellated Woodcreeper** *Xiphorhynchus ocellatus*	6	*lineatocapillus** (S Ve) *napensis* (E Ec, S Co) *ocellatus* (S Ve)	T	* Known from a single specimen.								
1019	**Spix's Woodcreeper** *Xiphorhynchus spixii*	4	*buenavistae* (E Co)	LT									
1020	**Elegant Woodcreeper** *Xiphorhynchus elegans*	2	*ornatus* (E Ec, SE Co)	LT	Formerly *X. spixi elegans*: R&T								
1021	**Chestnut-rumped Woodcreeper** *Xiphorhynchus pardalotus*	2	*caurensis* (S Ve, Gu) *pardalotus* (FG)	T-S									

51

No.	Species	Ssp. Total	Subspecies in Northern South America	Altitude Range	References and Comments	Ec	Co	Ve	Ar Cu Bo	Tr To	Gu	Su	F(
1022	**Buff-throated Woodcreeper** *Xiphorhynchus guttatus*	3	guttatoides (E Ec, SE Co, S Ve) polystictus (E Co, S Ve, Gu, Su, FG) rosenbergi (W Co)	T									
1023	**Cocoa Woodcreeper** *Xiphorhynchus susurrans*	4	jardinei (NE Ve) margaritae (Ve: Marg Is.) nanus (N&E Co, N&W Ve) susurrans (NE Ve, Tr, To)		demonstratus synonymous with nanus.								
1024	**Black-striped Woodcreeper** *Xiphorhynchus lachrymosus*	2	alarum (N Co) lachrymosus (NW Ec, W Co)	T									
1025	**Spotted Woodcreeper** *Xiphorhynchus erythropygius*	5	aequatorialis (W Ec, W Co) insolitus (NW Co)	T-S									
1026	**Olive-backed Woodcreeper** *Xiphorhynchus triangularis*	4	hylodromus (N Ve) triangularis (E Ec, Co, W Ve)	S									
1027	**Streak-headed Woodcreeper** *Lepidocolaptes souleyetii*	8	esmeraldae (W Ec, SW Co) lineaticeps (N Co, W Ve) littoralis (N Co, N Ve, Tr, Gu) souleyetii (SW Ec) uaireni (SE Ve)	T									
1028	**Narrow-billed Woodcreeper** *Lepidocolaptes angustirostris*	8	griseiceps (Su)	T	Mees 1974								
1029	**Spot-crowned Woodcreeper** *Lepidocolaptes affinis*	11	aequatorialis (W Ec, SW Co) lacrymiger (E Co, W Ve) lafresnayi (N Ve) sanctaemartae (N Co) sneiderni (C Co)	S-Te									
1030	**Lineated Woodcreeper** *Lepidocolaptes albolineatus*	5	albolineatus (E Ve, Gu, Su, FG) duidae (S Ve) fuscicapillus (E Ec)	T	Sight records in Co: SFP&M.		?						
1031	**Greater Scythebill** *Campylorhamphus pucherani*	M	(E Ec, W Co)	S-Te									
1032	**Red-billed Scythebill** *Campylorhamphus trochilirostris*	14	brevipennis (W Co) napensis (E Ec) thoracicus (W Ec, SW Co) venezuelensis (N Co, N Ve)	T									
1033	**Brown-billed Scythebill** *Campylorhamphus pusillus*	3	guapiensis* (SW Co) pusillus (W Ec, Co) tachirensis** (Ve: Tachira)	T-S	* Ssp. nov.: Romero 1980. ** Phelps & Phelps 1956								
1034	**Curve-billed Scythebill** *Campylorhamphus procurvoides*	4	procurvoides (Su, FG) sanus (E Co, S Ve, W Gu)	LT									
1035	**Slender-billed Miner** *Geositta tenuirostris*	2	tenuirostris (SW Ec) kalimayae * (N Ec)	Te-P	* Ssp. nov.: Krabbe 1992.								
1036	**Bar-winged Cinclodes** *Cinclodes fuscus*	8 ?	albidiventris (Ec) heterurus (W Ve) oreobates (Co: Sta Marta + E&C Andes, Ve) paramo (SW Co)	T-P									
1037	**Stout-billed Cinclodes** *Cinclodes excelsior*	3	columbiana (Co: C Andes) excelsior (Ec)	Te-P	Formerly Geositta. Vaurie 1980.								
1038	**Lesser Hornero** *Furnarius minor*	M	(E Ec, SE Co)	LT									
1039	**Pale-billed Hornero** *Furnarius torridus*	M	(SE Ec Co)	LT	Sight records in Ec: RG&G.	?							

No.	Species	Ssp. Total	Subspecies in Northern South America	Altitude Range	References and Comments	Ec	Co	Ve	Ar Cu Bo	Tr To	Gu	Su	FG
1040	**Pale-legged Hornero** *Furnarius leucopus*	6?	*cinnamomeus* (SW Ec) *endoecus* (N Co, NW Ve) *leucopus* (Co, Ve, Gu) *longirostris* (N Co, NW Ve)	T-Te	*cinnamomeus* may be a sep. sp. (Pacific Hornero): R&T 1994.								
1041	**Andean Tit-Spinetail** *Leptasthenura andicola*	5	*andicola* (Ec, Co: C Andes) *certhia* (W Ve) *exterior* (Co: E Andes) *extima* (Co: Sta Marta)	Te-P									
1042	**Perijá Thistletail** *Schizoeaca perijana*	M	(Co, Ve: Perijá)	Te-P	Sp. nov.: Phelps 1977b **Endemic**								
1043	**Ochre-browed Thistletail** *Schizoeaca coryi*	M	(Ve: Andes)	Te-P	**Endemic**								
1044	**White-chinned Thistletail** *Schizoeaca fuliginosa*	6	*fuliginosa* (N Ec, Co: C&E Andes, W Ve)	Te-P	Vaurie 1980								
1045	**Mouse-colored Thistletail** *Schizoeaca griseomurina*	M	(S Ec)	Te-P	**Endemic**								
1046	**Sooty-fronted Spinetail** *Synallaxis frontalis*	2	*frontalis* ? (Gu?, FG?)	T-S	Recorded in the Guianas: A&S. Not in N S.Am.: Peters, SFP&M.						?	?	?
1047	**Azara's Spinetail** *Synallaxis azarae*	7	*elegantior* (Co: E Andes, W Ve) *media* (N Ec, Co: W&C Andes) *ochracea* (Ec)	S-Te									
1048	**Pale-breasted Spinetail** *Synallaxis albescens*	14	*hypoleuca* (NW Co, Ve) *inequalis* (FG) *insignis* (Co, Ve: S Apure) *josephinae* (S&SE Ve, Gu, Su) *littoralis* (N Co) *nesiotis* (Ve: Marg Is) *occipitalis* (N Co, N&NW Ve) *perpallida* (NE Co, NW Ve) *trinitatis* (NC,NE&S Ve, Tr)	T									
1049	**Slaty Spinetail** *Synallaxis brachyura*	5	*brachyura* (Co: W Andes) *chapmani* (W Ec, W Co) *caucae* (C Co)	T-S									
1050	**Dark-breasted Spinetail** *Synallaxis albigularis*	M	(E Ec, S Co)	LT									
1051	**Dusky Spinetail** *Synallaxis moesta*	3	*brunneicaudalis* (E Ec) *moesta* (Co: E Andes) *obscura* (SE Co)	T									
1052	**McConnell's Spinetail** *Synallaxis macconnelli*	4	*griseipectus* (SE Ve) *macconnelli* (S Ve, Gu?) *obscurior* (Su, FG) *yavii* (S Ve)	T	Formerly *S. cabanisi macconnelli* Uncertain in Gu: Peters.						?		
1053	**Silvery-throated Spinetail** *Synallaxis subpudica*	M	(Ec, Co: E Andes)	UT-S	**Endemic**								
1054	**Blackish-headed Spinetail** *Synallaxis tithys*	M	(SW Ec)	LT	**Vulnerable**								
1055	**White-bellied Spinetail** *Synallaxis propinqua*	M	(E Ec Co, FG)	LT	Sight records in Co: SFP&M.								
1056	**Plain-crowned Spinetail** *Synallaxis gujanensis*	9?	*columbiana* (Co: E Andes) *gujanensis* (Ve, Gu, Su, FG) *maranonica* (Ec)	T-LS	*maranonica* may be a sep. sp. (Marañon Spinetail): Vaurie 1980.								
1057	**Ruddy Spinetail** *Synallaxis rutilans*	7	*caquetensis* (E Ec, SE Co) *dissors* (Co & Ve: Orinoco basin, Gu, FG) *rutilans* (Su)*	LT	Occurrence of *rutilans* in Su is doubtful.								

No.	Species	Ssp. Total	Subspecies in Northern South America	Altitude Range	References and Comments	Ec	Co	Ve	Ar Cu Bo	Tr To	Gu	Su	FC
1058	**Chestnut-throated Spinetail** *Synallaxis cherriei*	2	*napoensis* (E Ec, SE Co)	T									
1059	**Rufous Spinetail** *Synallaxis unirufa*	3	*meridana* (Co, Ve) *unirufa* (Ec, Co)	US-Te									
1060	**Black-throated Spinetail** *Synallaxis castanea*	M	(N Ve)	S-Te	Formerly *S. unirufa castanea*: Vaurie & Schwartz 1972. **Endemic**								
1061	**Rusty-headed Spinetail** *Synallaxis fuscorufa*	M	(Co: Sta Marta)	UT-Te	**Endemic**								
1062	**Stripe-breasted Spinetail** *Synallaxis cinnamomea*	7	*aveledoi* (W Ve) *bolivari* (NC Ve) *carri* (Tr) *cinnamomea* (Co: E Andes, Ve: Perija) *pariae* (Ve) *striatipectus* (E Ve) *terrestris* (To)	UT-S									
1063	**Necklaced Spinetail** *Synallaxis stictothorax*	3	*stictothorax* (Ec)	LT									
1064	**White-whiskered Spinetail** *Synallaxis candei*	3	*atrigularis* (N Co) *candei* (N Co) *venezuelensis* (NE Co, NW Ve)	T	Formerly *Poecilurus*								
1065	**Hoary-throated Spinetail** *Synallaxis kollari*	M	(S Gu)	LT	**Vulnerable** Recorded in Gu: Collar *et al.* 1994.								
1066	**White-browed Spinetail** *Hellmayrea gularis*	3	*cinereiventris* (W Ve) *gularis* (Ec, Co, W Ve)	Te-P	Formerly *Synallaxis*								
1067	**Red-faced Spinetail** *Cranioleuca erythrops*	3	*erythrops* (W Ec) *griseigularis** (Co: W&C Andes)	UT-US	* Ssp. nov.: Phelps & Phelps 1955.								
1068	**Line-cheeked Spinetail** *Cranioleuca antisiensis*	2	*antisiensis* (S Ec)	S									
1069	**Ash-browed Spinetail** *Cranioleuca curtata*	3	*cisandina* (E Ec, S Co) *curtata* (Co: E Andes)	UT-Te									
1070	**Tepui Spinetail** *Cranioleuca demissa*	M	(S Ve, S Gu)	UT-Te									
1071	**Streak-capped Spinetail** *Cranioleuca hellmayri*	M	(Co: Sta Marta, NW Ve)	LT-Te									
1072	**Crested Spinetail** *Cranioleuca subcristata*	M	*subcristata* (NW Co, NW Ve) *fuscivertex** (W Ve)	T-S	*Ssp. nov.: Phelps & Phelps 1955.								
1073	**Rusty-backed Spinetail** *Cranioleuca vulpina*	5	*alopecias* (E&SE Co) *apurensis* (SW Ve)	LT	Zimmer 1997								
1074	**Parker's Spinetail** *Cranioleuca vulpecula*	M	(E Ec)	T	Formerly *C. vulpina vulpecula*: Zimmer 1997.								
1075	**Speckled Spinetail** *Cranioleuca gutturata*	M	*gutturata* (E Ec, E Co) *hyposticta* (S Ve, Su, FG)	LT	Formerly *Certhiaxis*								
1076	**Yellow-chinned Spinetail** *Certhiaxis cinnamomea*	8	*cinnamomea* (E Ve, Tri, Gu, Su, FG) *fuscifrons* (N Co) *marabina* (NW Ve) *orenocensis* (EC Ve) *valenciana* (C Ve)	LT									
1077	**Red-and-white Spinetail** *Certhiaxis mustelina*	M	(SE Co)	LT									

No.	Species	Ssp. Total	Subspecies in Northern South America	Altitude Range	References and Comments	Ec	Co	Ve	Ar Cu Bo	Tr To	Gu	Su	FG
1078	**Streak-backed Canastero** *Asthenes wyatti*	9	*aequatorialis* (C Ec) *azuay* (S Ec) *mucuchiesi* (Ve: Merida) *sanctaemartae* (Co: Sta Marta) *wyatti* (C Co) *perijanus** (W Ve: Perijá)	P	* Ssp. nov.: Phelps 1977.								
1079	**Many-striped Canastero** *Asthenes flammulata*	5	*flammulata* (Ec, S Co) *multostriata* (Co: E Andes) *quindiana* (Co: C Andes)	P									
1080	**Orinoco Softtail** *Thripophaga cherriei*	M	(S Ve)	LT	**Vulnerable Endemic**								
1081	**Plain Softtail** *Thripophaga fusciceps*	3	*dimorpha* (Ec)	LT									
1082	**Common Thornbird** *Phacellodomus rufifrons*	6	*castilloi** (Ve: Llanos) *inornatus* (N&C Ve) *peruvianus* (NE Ec)	T-LS	* Ssp. nov.: Phelps & Aveledo 1987.								
1083	**Spectacled Prickletail** *Siptornis striaticollis*	M	(E Ec, C Co)	S									
1084	**Orange-fronted Plushcrown** *Metopothrix aurantiacus*	M	(E Ec, SE Co)	LT									
1085	**Double-banded Greytail** *Xenerpestes minlosi*	M	(NW Co)	LT									
1086	**Equatorial Greytail** *Xenerpestes singularis*	M		UT-LS									
1087	**Roraiman Barbtail** *Roraimia adusta*	3	*adusta* (E Ve, W Gu) *duidae* (S Ve) *mayri* * (S Ve) *obscurodorsalis* (SE Ve)	S	Formerly *Premnoplex*. * Phelps 1977								
1088	**Rusty-winged Barbtail** *Premnornis guttuligera*	2	*guttuligera* (Andes: Ec & Co) *venezuelana** (W Ve)	S	*Ssp. nov.: Phelps & Phelps 1956.								
1089	**Spotted Barbtail** *Premnoplex brunnescens*	7 ?	*brunnescens* (Andes: Ec, Co & Ve) *coloratus* (Co: Sta Marta) *rostratus* (NC Ve)	UT-S									
1090	**White-throated Barbtail** *Premnoplex tatei*	2	*pariae* (NE Ve: Paria) *tatei* (NE Ve: Turimiquire)	UT-S	Formerly *P. brunnescens tatei*: R&T 1994. *pariae* may be a sep. sp. (Paria Barbtail): S&M 1993. **Vulnerable Endemic**								
1091	**Fulvous-dotted Treerunner** *Margarornis stellatus*	M	(NW Ec, Co: W Andes)	UT-LS									
1092	**Pearled Treerunner** *Margarornis squamiger*	3	*perlatus* (Andes: Ec, Co & Ve)	S-P									
1093	**Pacific Tuftedcheek** *Pseudocolaptes johnsoni*	M ?	(W Ec, Co: W Andes)	T-S	Formerly *P. lawrencii johnsoni*: R&T 1994.								
1094	**Streaked Tuftedcheek** *Pseudocolaptes boissonneautii*	9	*boissoneautii* (W Ec, C Co) *meridae* (W Ve) *orientalis* (E Ec) *striaticeps* (N Ve)	S-P									
1095	**Point-tailed Palmcreeper** *Berlepschia rikeri*	M	(Ec, Co, S Ve, Gu, Su, FG)	LT									?
1096	**Chestnut-winged Hookbill** *Ancistrops strigilatus*	2	*strigilatus* (E Ec, SE Co)	LT									

No.	Species	Ssp. Total	Subspecies in Northern South America	Altitude Range	References and Comments	Ec	Co	Ve	Ar Cu Bo	Tr To	Gu	Su	FG
1097	Striped Woodhaunter *Hyloctistes subulatus*	4	*assimilis* (W Ec, SW Co) *cordobae** (NW Co) *subulatus* (E Ec, SE Co, S Ve)	T	*H.s. subulatus* differs vocally and morphologically from other forms, and is probably a sep. sp.: K. Zimmer, in prep. * Ssp. nov.: Meyer de Schauensee 1960.								
1098	Guttulated Foliage-gleaner *Syndactyla guttulata*	2	*guttulatta* (NC Ve) *pallida* (NE Ve)	UT-S	**Endemic**								
1099	Buff-browed Foliage-gleaner *Syndactyla rufosuperciliata*	5	Subspecies uncertain: *similis* ?	T-S	Recorded in Ec: SFP&M, RG&G.								
1100	Lineated Foliage-gleaner *Syndactyla subalaris*	7	*mentalis* (E Ec) *olivacea** (Ve: Tachira) *striolata* (Co: E Andes, W Ve) *subalaris* (W Ec, Co: W&C Andes)	UT-S	* Ssp. nov.: Phelps & Phelps 1956.								
1101	Rufous-necked Foliage-gleaner *Syndactyla ruficollis*	2	*celicae* (SW Ec)	T-Te	Formerly *Automolus* **Vulnerable**								
1102	Spectacled Foliage-gleaner *Anabacerthia variegaticeps*	2	*variegaticeps* (Ec, Co)	UT-S	Formerly *A. striaticollis variegaticeps*								
1103	Montane Foliage-gleaner *Anabacerthia striaticollis*	5	*anxia* (Co: Sta Marta) *montana* (E Ec) *perijana** (W Ve) *striaticollis* (Andes: Co, Ve) *venezuelana* (NC Ve)	UT-S	* Ssp. nov.: Phelps & Phelps 1952.								
1104	Rufous-tailed Foliage-gleaner *Philydor ruficaudatus*	2	*flavipectus* (S Ve) *ruficaudatus* (E Ec, SE Co, S Ve, Gu, Su, FG)	T									
1105	Cinnamon-rumped Foliage-gleaner *Philydor pyrrhodes*	M	(SE Co, S Ve, Gu, Su, FG)	LT									
1106	Slaty-winged Foliage-gleaner *Philydor fuscipennis*	2	*erythronotus* (NW Ec, Co: Andes)	T	Both ssp. formerly conspecific with *P. erythrocercus*: Vaurie 1980.								
1107	Rufous-rumped Foliage-gleaner *Philydor erythrocercus*	5	*erythrocercus* (S Gu, S Su, FG) *subflavus* (E Ec, SE Co)	LT									
1108	Chestnut-winged Foliage-gleaner *Philydor erythropterus*	2	*erythropterus* (E Ec, SE Co, S Ve)	LT									
1109	Buff-fronted Foliage-gleaner *Philydor rufus*	7	*columbianus* (N Ve) *cuchiverus* (S Ve) *panerythrus* (N Co) *riveti* (NW Ec, Co: W Andes)	T-S									
1110	Uniform Treehunter *Thripadectes ignobilis*	M	(NW Ec, Co: W Andes)	UT-Te									
1111	Streak-capped Treehunter *Thripadectes virgaticeps*	5	*klagesi* (N Ve) *magdalenae* (C Co) *sclateri* (Co: W Andes) *sumaco* (E Ec) *tachirensis** (W Ve) *virgaticeps* (NW Ec)	UT-Te	* Ssp. nov.: Phelps & Phelps 1958.								

No.	Species	Ssp. Total	Subspecies in Northern South America	Altitude Range	References and Comments	Ec	Co	Ve	Ar Cu Bo	Tr To	Gu	Su	FG
1112	**Black-billed Treehunter** *Thripadectes melanorhynchus*	2	*melanorhynchus* (E Ec) *striaticeps* (Co: E Andes)	UT-LS		■	■						
1113	**Striped Treehunter** *Thripadectes holostictus*	3	*holostictus* (E Ec, Co, Ve) *striatidorsus* (W Ec, SW Co)	S-Te		■	■	■					
1114	**Flammulated Treehunter** *Thripadectes flammulatus*	2	*bricenoi* (Ve: Merida) *flammulatus* (Ec, Co: Andes & Sta Marta, Ve)	UT-P		■	■	■					
1115	**Buff-throated Foliage-gleaner** *Automolus ochrolaemus*	8	*pallidigularis* (NW Ec, W Co) *turdinus* (E Ec, E Co, S Ve, Gu, Su, FG)	T		■	■	■			■	■	■
1116	**Rufous-necked Foliage-gleaner** *Automolus ruficollis*	2	*celicae* (SW Ec)	UT-Te		■							
1117	**Crested Foliage-gleaner** *Automolus dorsalis*	M	(E Ec, SE Co)	T		■	■						
1118	**Olive-backed Foliage-gleaner** *Automolus infuscatus*	5	*badius* (E Co, S Ve) *cervicalis* (SE Ve, Gu, Su, FG) *infuscatus* (E Ec, SE Co)	LT		■	■	■			■	■	■
1119	**White-throated Foliage-gleaner** *Automolus roraimae*	3	*duidae* (S Ve: Amazonas) *paraquensis* (S Ve: C Bolivar) *roraimae* (S Ve: E Bolivar)	S-Te	*A. albigularis* synonymous with *A. roraimae*. *Philydor hylobius* (Neblina Foliage-gleaner) now diagnosed as a juv. of *A. roraimae*: Dickerman *et al.* 1986.			■					
1120	**Brown-rumped Foliage-gleaner** *Automolus melanopezus*	M	(E Ec, SE Co)	LT		■	■						
1121	**Ruddy Foliage-gleaner** *Automolus rubiginosus*	16	*brunnescens* (E Ec) *caquetae* (SE Co) *cinnamomeigula* (E Co) *nigricauda* (W Ec, W Co) *obscurus* (Gu, Su, FG) *rufipectus* (Co: Sta Marta) *sasaimae* (C Co) *saturatus* (NW Co) *venezuelanus* (S Ve)	T-Te		■	■	■			■	■	■
1122	**Chestnut-crowned Foliage-gleaner** *Automolus rufipileatus*	2	*consobrinus* (E Ec, E Co, Ve, Gu, Su, FG)	LT		■	■	■			■	■	■
1123	**Henna-hooded Foliage-gleaner** *Hylocryptus erythrocephalus*	2	*erythrocephalus* (SW Ec)	UT-LS	**Vulnerable**	■							
1124	**Tawny-throated Leafscraper** *Sclerurus mexicanus*	7	*andinus* (N Co, S Ve, Gu) *macconnelli* (Gu, Fg) *obscurior* (W Ec, W Co) *peruvianus* (E Ec)	T		■	■	■			■		■
1125	**Short-billed Leafscraper** *Sclerurus rufigularis*	4	*fulvigularis* (Ec, Co, S&SE Ve, Gu, Su, FG)	LT		■	■	■			■	■	■
1126	**Grey-throated Leafscraper** *Sclerurus albigularis*	5	*albigularis* (E Co, N Ve, Tr) *kunanensis** (Ve: Porija) *propinquus* (Co: Sta Marta) *zamorae* (SE Ec)	T-S	*Ssp. nov.: Aveledo & Gines 1950.	■	■	■		■			
1127	**Black-tailed Leafscraper** *Sclerurus caudacutus*	6	*brunneus* (E Ec, SE Co, SW Ve) *caudacutus* (Gu, FG) *insignis* (S Ve)	T		■	■	■			■		■

No.	Species	Ssp. Total	Subspecies in Northern South America	Altitude Range	References and Comments	Ec	Co	Ve	Ar Cu Bo	Tr To	Gu	Su	F
1128	**Scaly-throated Leafscraper** *Sclerurus guatemalensis*	2	*salvini* (W Ec, W Co)	T									
1129	**Sharp-tailed Streamcreeper** *Lochmias nematura*	7	*castanonota* (SE Ve) *chimantae* (SE Ve) *sororia* (Co: C&E Andes)	T-Te	* Undescribed ssp. from Co listed in Peters.								
1130	**Rufous-tailed Xenops** *Xenops milleri*	M	(E Co, S Ve, FG)	LT									
1131	**Slender-billed Xenops** *Xenops tenuirostris*	3	*acutirostris* (E Ec, SE Co, S Ve) *hellmayri* (Su, FG) *tenuirostris* (S Ve)	LT									
1132	**Plain Xenops** *Xenops minutus*	9	*littoralis* (W Ec, W Co) *neglectus* (NE Co, NW Ve) *obsoletus* (E Ec) *olivaceus** (W Ve) *remoratus* (E Co, W Ve) *ruficaudus* (E Co, S&E Ve, Gu, Su, FG)	T	*Ssp. nov.: Aveledo & Pons 1952.								
1133	**Streaked Xenops** *Xenops rutilans*	8	*guayae* (W Ec) *heterurus* (NE Ec, Co, Ve, Tr) *perijanus** (W Ve) *peruvianus* (E Ec)	T-S	*Ssp. nov.: Phelps & Phelps 1954.								
1134	**Fasciated Antshrike** *Cymbilaimus lineatus*	4	*brangeri** (W Ve) *fasciatus* (NW Ec, Co) *intermedius* (Ec, Co, Ve) *lineatus* (S Ve, Gu, Su, FG)	T	*Ssp. nov.: Aveledo & Perez 1991; invalid ssp.: M. Isler, pers. comm.								
1135	**Black-throated Antshrike** *Frederickena viridis*	M	(SE Ve, Gu, Su, FG)	LT									
1136	**Undulated Antshrike** *Frederickena unduligera*	4	*fulva* (Ec, Co) *unduligera* (E Ec, S Co)	T									
1137	**Great Antshrike** *Taraba major*	10	*duidae* (Ve) *granadensis* (NE Co, N Ve) *melanurus* (SE Co, E Ec) *oscurus* (W Co) *semifasciata* (E Co, S&NE Ve, Tr, Gu, Su, FG) *transandeanus* (SW Co, W Ec)	T									
1138	**Black-crested Antshrike** *Sakesphorus canadensis*	7	*canadensis* (Su, FG) *fumosus* (S Ve) *intermedius* (C&S Ve) *loretoyacuensis* (S Co.) *paraguanae* (NW Ve) *phainoleucus* (NE Co, NW Ve) *pulchellus* (N Co, NW Ve) *trinitatis* (NE Ve, Tr, Gu)	LT									
1139	**Collared Antshrike** *Sakesphorus bernardi*	4	*bernardi* (W Ec) *piurae* (SW Ec)	LT									
1140	**Black-backed Antshrike** *Sakesphorus melanonotus*	M	(W&N Ve, NE Co)	LT									
1141	**Band-tailed Antshrike** *Sakesphorus melanothorax*	M		LT									

No.	Species	Ssp. Total	Subspecies in Northern South America	Altitude Range	References and Comments	Ec	Co	Ve	Ar Cu Bo	Tr To	Gu	Su	FG
1142	**Barred Antshrike** *Thamnophilus doliatus*	16	*albicans* (C Co) *doliatus* (SE Ve, Gu, Su, FG) *fraterculus* (E Co, Ve, Tr) *nigrescens* (NE Co, NW Ve) *nigricristatus* (N Co) *tobagensis* (To)	T-LS	Sight records in Ec: SFP&M.	?							
1143	**Chapman's Antshrike** *Thamnophilus zarumae*	M	(SW Ec)	T									
1144	**Bar-crested Antshrike** *Thamnophilus multistriatus*	4	*brachyurus* (C Co) *multistriatus* (Co: E slope W Andes, C Andes, W slope E Andes) *oecotonophilus* (Co, Ve) *selvae* (Co & Ve: Perija; Co: W slope W Andes)	UT-S									
1145	**Lined Antshrike** *Thamnophilus tenuepunctatus*	3	*berlepschi* (Ec) *tenuepunctatus* (Co) *tenuifasciatus* (Co, Ec)	UT-S									
1146	**Black Antshrike** *Thamnophilus nigriceps*	2	*magdalenae* (C Co) *nigriceps* (NE Co)	LT									
1147	**Cocha Antshrike** *Thamnophilus praecox*	M	(NE Ec)	LT	Endemic								
1148	**Blackish-grey Antshrike** *Thamnophilus nigrocinereus*	5	*cinereoniger* (Co & Ve: Orinoco basin) *kulczynskii* (FG)	LT									
1149	**Castelnau's Antshrike** *Thamnophilus cryptoleucus*	M	(SE Co)	LT									
1150	**White-shouldered Antshrike** *Thamnophilus aethiops*	9	*aethiops* (Ec) *polionotus* (Ve) *wetmorei* (Co)	T									
1151	**Uniform Antshrike** *Thamnophilus unicolor*	3	*grandior* (Co, Ec) *unicolor* (Ec)	UT-S									
1152	**Black-capped Antshrike** *Thamnophilus schistaceus*	5	*capitalis* (Co, Ec) *dubius* (Ec)	T									
1153	**Mouse-colored Antshrike** *Thamnophilus murinus*	3	*canipennis* (Ec, Co) *cayennensis* (FG) *murinus* (Ec, Co, Ve, Gu, Su)	T									
1154	**Eastern Slaty-Antshrike** *Thamnophilus punctatus*	9 *	*interpositus* (Co, W Ve) *leucogaster* (S Ec) *punctatus* (S&E Ve, Gu, Su, FG)	T	*leucogaster* may be a sep. sp.: Isler *et al.* 1997.								
1155	**Western Slaty-Antshrike** *Thamnophilus atrinucha*	3	*atrinucha* (W Ec, W Co, SW Ve) *gorgonae* (W coast Co: Gorgona Is.) *subcinereus* (N Co, NW Ve)	T	Formerly *T. punctatus atrinucha*: Isler *et al.* 1997.								
1156	**Streak-backed Antshrike** *Thamnophilus insignis*	2	*insignis* (S Ve.) *nigrofrotalis* (S Ve: Pantepuy)	UT									
1157	**Amazonian Antshrike** *Thamnophilus amazonicus*	5	*amazonicus* (S Co) *cinereiceps* (Co & Ve: upper Orinoco) *divaricatus* (Gu, Su, FG) *paraensis* (E Ve)	LT									
1158	**Spot-winged Antshrike** *Pygiptila stellaris*	4	*maculipennis* (SE Co, E Ec) *occipitalis* (S Co, S Ve, Su, FG)	LT									
1159	**Pearly Antshrike** *Megastictus margaritatus*	M	(S Ve, SE Co)	LT									

59

No.	Species	Ssp. Total	Subspecies in Northern South America	Altitude Range	References and Comments	Ec	Co	Ve	Ar Cu Bo	Tr To	Gu	Su	F
1160	**Black Bushbird** *Neoctantes niger*	M	(SE Co, E Ec)	LT									
1161	**Recurve-billed Bushbird** *Clytoctantes alixii*	M	(NW Ve; N, W & NC Co)	T	**Endangered**								
1162	**Spiny-faced Antshrike** *Xenornis setifrons*	M	(NW Co)	LT	**Vulnerable**								
1163	**Russet Antshrike** *Thamnistes anabatinus*	7 ?	aequatorialis (SE Co, E Ec) gularis * (Ve) intermedius (W Co, W Ec)	T	* Ssp nov.: Phelps & Phelps 1956.								
1164	**Plain Antvireo** *Dysithamnus mentalis*	18	aequatorialis (W Ec) andrei (E Ve, Tr) cumbreanus (Ve: Andes & N Range) extremus (Co: W & C Andes & mid Cauca Valley) napensis (E Ec) oberi (To) ptaritepui (Ve: Tepuis) semicinereus (NE Co, W Ve) spodionotus (Ve: Tepuis) suffusus (Co: lower Cauca Valley) viridis (Ve)	UT-S									
1165	**Spot-crowned Antvireo** *Dysithamnus puncticeps*	3	flemmingi (SW Co, W Ec) intensus (WC Co) punticeps (N Co)	T									
1166	**White-streaked Antvireo** *Dysithamnus leucostictus*	2	leucostictus (E Co, E Ec) tocuyensis (NW Ve)	UT-LS	Formerly *Thamnomanes plumbeus leucostictus*. *tocuyensis* may be a sep. sp. (Venezuelan or Tocuyo Antvireo): B.Whitney, fide R&T 1994.								
1167	**Bicolored Antvireo** *Dysithamnus occidentalis*	2	occidentalis (SW Co) punctitectus (E Ec)	UT-S	Formerly *Thamnomanes*: Whitney 1992. **Vulnerable**								
1168	**Dusky-throated Antshrike** *Thamnomanes ardesiacus*	2	ardesiacus (SE Co, E Ec) obidensis (S Ve, Gu, Su, FG)	T									
1169	**Cinereous Antshrike** *Thamnomanes caesius*	6	glaucus (E Co, E Ec, S Ve, Gu, Su, FG)	LT									
1170	**Pygmy Antwren** *Myrmotherula brachyura*	2	brachyura (E Co, E Ec, S Ve, Gu, Su, FG) ignota (W Co: Pacific slope)	T									
1171	**Short-billed Antwren** *Myrmotherula obscura*	M	(SE Co, E Ec.)	LT									
1172	**Yellow-throated Antwren** *Myrmotherula ambigua*	M	(Co & Ve: Amazonas)	LT									
1173	**Guianian Streaked Antwren** *Myrmotherula surinamensis*	M	(S&E Ve, Gu, Su, FG)	LT									
1174	**Amazonian Streaked Antwren** *Myrmotherula multostriata*	M	(E Ec, CE Co, S Ve)	LT	Formerly *M. surinamensis multostriata*: Isler et al. 1999								
1175	**Pacific Antwren** *Myrmotherula pacifica*	M	(W Ec, W Co)		Formerly *M. surinamensis pacifica*: Isler et al. 1999								

No.	Species	Ssp. Total	Subspecies in Northern South America	Altitude Range	References and Comments	Ec	Co	Ve	Ar Cu Bo	Tr To	Gu	Su	FG
1176	Cherrie's Antwren *Myrmotherula cherriei*	M	(Co & Ve: Amazonas)	LT	See Isler *et al.* 1999								
1177	Stripe-chested Antwren *Myrmotherula longicauda*	4	*pseudoaustralis* (E Ec: Zamora, Cutuco) *soderstromi* (E Ec: Rio Napo)	UT-LS									
1178	Plain-throated Antwren *Myrmotherula hauxwelli*	4	*suffusa* (SE Co)	LT									
1179	Rufous-bellied Antwren *Myrmotherula guttata*	M	(S Ve, Gu, Su, FG)	LT									
1180	Brown-bellied Antwren *Myrmotherula gutturalis*	M	(SE Vo, Gu, Su, FG)	T									
1181	Checker-throated Antwren *Myrmotherula fulviventris*	3	*fulviventris* (W Co, W Ec) *salmoni* (C Co)	T									
1182	Brown-backed Antwren *Myrmotherula fjeldsaai*	M	(E Ec)	LT	Sp. nov.: Krabbe *et al.* 1999								
1183	Stipple-throated Antwren *Myrmotherula haematonota*	4	*pyrrhonota* (SE Co, S Ve)	LT									
1184	Foothill Antwren *Myrmotherula spodionota*	2	*spodionota* (E Ec)	UT	Parker & Remsen 1987								
1185	Ornate Antwren *Myrmotherula ornata*	5	*ornata* (E Co) *saturata* (SE Co, E Ec)	T									
1186	Rufous-tailed Antwren *Myrmotherula erythrura*	2	*erythrura* (E Co, E Ec)	LT									
1187	White-flanked Antwren *Myrmotherula axillaris*	6	*albigula* (W Co, W Ec) *axillaris* (SE Ve, Tr, Gu, Su, FG) *melaena* (Co, Ve, Ec)	T									
1188	Slaty Antwren *Myrmotherula schisticolor*	3	*interior* (Andes: E Co & E Ec) *sanctaemartae* (NE Co, Ve) *schisticolor* (W Co, W Ec)	UT-S									
1189	Rio Suno Antwren *Myrmotherula sunensis*	2	*sunensis* (E Ec)	T									
1190	Plain-winged Antwren *Myrmotherula behni*	3	*behni* (Co: Sierra Macarena) *camanii* (S Ve) *inornata* (SE Ve, Gu) *yavii* (Ve: Amazonas)	UT-LS	Sight records in FG: SFP&M.								?
1191	Long-winged Antwren *Myrmotherula longipennis*	6	*longipennis* (SE Co, S&E Ve, Gu, FG) *zimmeri* (E Ec)	LT									
1192	Grey Antwren *Myrmotherula menetriesii*	5	*cinereiventris* (E Ve, Gu, FG) *pallida* (E Co, S Ve, E Ec)	T									
1193	Leaden Antwren *Myrmotherula assimilis*	M	(Extreme SE Co)	LT	Sight records in Co: SFP&M.		?						
1194	Banded Antbird *Dichrozona cincta*	3	*cincta* (E Co, S Ve) *stellata* (E Ec)	LT									
1195	Spot-tailed Antwren *Herpsilochmus sticturus*	2	*sticturus* (SE Ve, Gu, Su, FG) *dugandi* (S Co, NE Ec)	LT	*dugandi* is sometimes treated as a sep. sp. (Dugand's Antwren): R&T 1994 and RG&G.								
1196	Todd's Antwren *Herpsilochmus stictocephalus*	M	(E Ve, Gu, FG)	LT									
1197	Ancient Antwren *Herpsilochmus gentryi*	M	(SW Ec)	T	Sp. nov.: Whitney & Alonso 1998.								
1198	Spot-backed Antwren *Herpsilochmus dorsimaculatus*	M	(S Ve)	LT									

No.	Species	Ssp. Total	Subspecies in Northern South America	Altitude Range	References and Comments	Ec	Co	Ve	Ar Cu Bo	Tr To	Gu	Su	FG
1199	Roraiman Antwren *Herpsilochmus roraimae*	2	kathleenae * (S Ve) roraimae (SE Ve, S Gu)	UT-LS	*Ssp. nov.: Phelps & Dickerman 1980.								
1200	Yellow-breasted Antwren *Herpsilochmus axillaris*	4	aequatorialis (E Ec) senex (SW Co: W slopes of Andes);	UT-LS									
1201	Rufous-winged Antwren *Herpsilochmus rufimarginatus*	4	exiguus (N Co) frater (Co, Ve, E Ec: E slope of Andes)	T	Sight records in Su: SFP&M.							?	
1202	Dot-winged Antwren *Microrhopias quixensis*	10	boucardi (W Co, W Ec) consobrina (Co, ?) microsticta (FG) quixensis (E Ec, SE Co, Su, FG)	T									
1203	White-fringed Antwren *Formicivora grisea*	9	fumosa (E Co, W Ve) grisea (Gu, Su, FG) hondae (C Co) intermedia (Co: Sta Marta, N Ve, Tr) orenocensis (S Ve: Bolivar) rufiventris (E Co, S Ve: Amazonas) tobagensis (To)	T									
1204	Rusty-backed Antwren *Formicivora rufa*	3	chapmani (Su)	T									
1205	Striated Antbird *Drymophila devillei*	2	devillei (Co, Ec)	T									
1206	Long-tailed Antbird *Drymophila caudata*	3	aristiguetana * (W Ve) caudata (Co & Ec: Andes) hellmayri (N Co) klagesi (N Ve)	UT-S	* Ssp nov.: Aveledo & Perez 1994								
1207	Rufous-rumped Antwren *Terenura callinota*	4	callinota (Co & Ec: Andes) guianensis (Gu) venezuelana (Ve: Perija)	UT-S									
1208	Chestnut-shouldered Antwren *Terenura humeralis*	2	humeralis (E Ec)	LT									
1209	Ash-winged Antwren *Terenura spodioptila*	4	elaopteryx (FG) signata (SE Co) spodioptila (S Ve, Gu)	T	Sight records in Ec: RG&G.	?							
1210	Grey Antbird *Cercomacra cinerascens*	4	cinerascens (E Ec, Co: E Andes) immaculata (SE Ve, Gu, FG)	T									
1211	Dusky Antbird *Cercomacra tyrannina*	7	rufiventris (W Ec, Co: W Andes) saturatior (E Ve, Gu, Su, FG) tyrannina (Co, S Ve) vicina (Co & Ec: Andes)	LT	Bierregard et al. 1997								
1212	Parker's Antbird *Cercomacra parkeri*	M	(Co: C & W Andes)	UT-LS	Sp. nov.: Graves 1997								
1213	Blackish Antbird *Cercomacra nigrescens*	6	aequatorialis (E Ec) nigrescens (Su, FG)	T-LS									
1214	Black Antbird *Cercomacra serva*	2	serva (E Ec)	T									
1215	Jet Antbird *Cercomacra nigricans*	M ?	(Co, W Ec, SW Ve)	T									
1216	Rio Branco Antbird *Cercomacra carbonaria*	M		LT	Sight records in Gu: SFP&M. **Vulnerable**							?	

No.	Species	Ssp. Total	Subspecies in Northern South America	Altitude Range	References and Comments	Ec	Co	Ve	Ar Cu Bo	Tr To	Gu	Su	FG
1217	**White-backed Fire-eye** *Pyriglena leoconota*	10	*castanoptera* (Co, E Ec) *pacifica* (E Ec)	T-LS		▪	▪						
1218	**White-browed Antbird** *Myrmoborus leucophrys*	5	*angustirostris* (S&SE Ve, Gu, Su, FG) *erythrophrys* (W Ve, Co: E Andes) *leucophrys* (E Ec, W Ve?)	T	O'Neill & Parker 1997	▪	▪	▪			▪	▪	▪
1219	**Ash-breasted Antbird** *Myrmoborus lugubris*	4	*berlepschi* (Ve, SW Co, W Ec)	LT		▪	▪	▪					
1220	**Black-faced Antbird** *Myrmoborus myotherinus*	8	*elegans* (Co: E Andes, S Ve) *naponsis* (E Ec)	T		▪	▪	▪					
1221	**Warbling Antbird** *Hypocnemis cantator*	11	*cantator* (Su, FG) *flavescens* (Ve, E Co) *notea* (SE Ve, Gu) *saturata* (SE Co, E Ec)	T		▪	▪	▪			▪	▪	▪
1222	**Yellow-browed Antbird** *Hypocnemis hypoxantha*	2	*hypoxantha* (SE Co, E Ec)	LT		▪	▪						
1223	**Black-chinned Antbird** *Hypocnemoides melanopogon*	3	*melanopogon* (Gu, Su, FG) *occidentalis* (S Ve, SE Co, NE Ec)	LT		▪	▪	▪			▪	▪	▪
1224	**Black-and-white Antbird** *Myrmochanes hemileucus*	M	(E Ec)	LT		▪							
1225	**Bare-crowned Antbird** *Gymnocichla nudiceps*	4	*nudiceps* (NW Co) *sanctaemartae* (N Co)	LT			▪						
1226	**Silvered Antbird** *Sclateria naevia*	4	*argentata* (S Ve) *diaphora* (S Ve) *naevia* (E Ve, Tr, Gu, Su, FG)	LT				▪		▪	▪	▪	▪
1227	**Black-headed Antbird** *Percnostola rufifrons*	2	*rufifrons* (Gu, Su, FG)	LT	Capparella *et al.* 1997						▪	▪	▪
1228	**Amazonas Antbird** *Percnostola minor*	2	*minor* (SE Co, S Ve)		Formerly *P. rufifrons minor:* Capparella *et al.* 1997.		▪	▪					
1229	**Slate-colored Antbird** *Percnostola schistacea*	M	(SE Co)	LT			▪						
1230	**Spot-winged Antbird** *Percnostola leucostigma*	9	*infuscata* (Ve: S Amazonas, E Co) *leucostigma* (S Ve, Gu, Su, FG) *obscura* (SE Ve) *saturata* (SE Ve: Roraima) *subplumbea* (E Co, E Ec)	T		▪	▪	▪			▪	▪	▪
1231	**Caura Antbird** *Percnostola caurensis*	2	*australis* (Ve: S Amazonas) *caurensis* (Ve: N Bolívar & Amazonas)	T	Possibly monotypic.			▪					
1232	**Stub-tailed Antbird** *Myrmeciza berlepschi*	M	(SW Co, NW Ec)	LT	Formerly *Sipia:* Robbins & Ridgely 1991.	▪	▪						
1233	**Esmeralda's Antbird** *Myrmeciza nigricauda*	M	(SW Co, NW Ec)	T	Formerly *Sipia:* Robbins & Ridgely 1991.	▪	▪						
1234	**White-bellied Antbird** *Myrmeciza longipes*	4	*boucardi* (C Co) *griseipectus* (SE Co, S Ve, Gu) *longipes* (E Co, N Ve, Tr) *panamensis* (N Co, N Ve)	T-LS	Sight records in FG: SFP&M.		▪	▪		▪	▪		?

No.	Species	Ssp. Total	Subspecies in Northern South America	Altitude Range	References and Comments	Ec	Co	Ve	Ar Cu Bo	Tr To	Gu	Su	FG
1235	Chestnut-backed Antbird *Myrmeciza exsul*	5	cassini (N Co) · maculifer (W Co, W Ec) niglarus (extreme NW Co)	T									
1236	Ferruginous-backed Antbird *Myrmeciza ferruginea*	2	ferruginea (Ve, Gu, Su, FG)	LT									
1237	Dull-mantled Antbird *Myrmeciza laemosticta*	2	palliata (Co, W Ve)	T	Ssp. *bolivari* & *venezuelae* synonymous with *palliata*: Robbins & Ridgely 1991.								
1238	Yapacana Antbird *Myrmeciza disjuncta*	M	(Co, Ve: Cerro Yapacana)	LT									
1239	Grey-bellied Antbird *Myrmeciza pelzelni*	M	(Co & Ve: Amazonas)	LT									
1240	Chestnut-tailed Antbird *Myrmeciza hemimelaena*	2	hemimelaena (SE Co, E Ec)	T									
1241	Plumbeous Antbird *Myrmeciza hyperythra*	M	(SE Co)	LT									
1242	White-shouldered Antbird *Myrmeciza melanoceps*	M	(SE Co, E Ec)	LT									
1243	Sooty Antbird *Myrmeciza fortis*	2	fortis (SE Co)	T									
1244	Immaculate Antbird *Myrmeciza immaculata*	4	macrorhyncha (W Co, W Ec) brunnea (Perija) immaculata (C&E Co, W Ve);	T-LS	*macrorhyncha* is the new name for *berlepschi*, which is no longer valid: Robbins & Ridgely 1993.								
1245	Grey-headed Antbird *Myrmeciza griseiceps*	M	(SW Ec)	UT-Te	**Endangered**								
1246	Black-throated Antbird *Myrmeciza atrothorax*	4 ?	atrothorax (SE Co, S Ve, Gu, FG, Su) metae (E Co) tenebrosa (NE Ec)	LT									
1247	White-plumed Antbird *Pithys albifrons*	3	albifrons (S Ve, Gu, FG, Su) brevibarba (E Co, E Ec) peruviana (Co, Ve, Ec)	T									
1248	Rufous-throated Antbird *Gymnopithys rufigula*	3	pallida (S Ve) pallidigula (S Ve) rufigula (E Ve, Gu, FG, Su)	T									
1249	Bicolored Antbird *Gymnopithys leucaspis*	8	aequatorialis (SW Co, W Ec) bicolor (NW Co) castanea (E Ec) daguae (W Co) leucaspis (E Co) ruficeps (C Co)	T	AOU 1998.								
1250	Lunulated Antbird *Gymnopithys lunulata*	M	(SE Ec)	LT	Recorded in Ec: RG&G.								
1251	Wing-banded Antbird *Myrmornis torquata*	2	stictoptera (N&NW Co) torquata (SE Co, E Ec, S Ve, Gu, FG)	T									
1252	Hairy-crested Antbird *Rhegmatorhina melanosticta*	4	melanosticta (E Ec)	T									
1253	Chestnut-crested Antbird *Rhegmatorhina cristata*	M	(E Co: Vaupes)	LT									
1254	Spotted Antbird *Hylophylax naevioides*	2	naeviodes (W&N Co, W Ec)	T									

No.	Species	Ssp. Total	Subspecies in Northern South America	Altitude Range	References and Comments	Ec	Co	Ve	Ar Cu Bo	Tr To	Gu	Su	FG
1255	Spot-backed Antbird *Hylophylax naevia*	7	*consobrina* (S Ve) *naevia* (S Ve, Gu, FG + Su?) *theresae* (SE Co, E Ec)	T									
1256	Dot-backed Antbird *Hylophylax punctulata*	2	*punctulata* (Co, E&S Ve) *subochracea* (E Ec)	LT	Sight records in FG: SFP&M.								?
1257	Scale-backed Antbird *Hylophylax poecilonota*	7	*duidae* (E Co, S Ve) *lepidonota* (SE Co, E Ec) *poecilonota* (S Ve, Gu, Su, FG)	T									
1258	Black-spotted Bare-eye *Phlegopsis nigromaculata*	4	*nigromaculata* (E Ec)	LT									
1259	Argus Bare-eye *Phlegopsis barringeri*	M	(S Co: Nariño)		Diagnosed as a hybrid: (Graves 1992) but recently confirmed P. Salaman pers. Comm.								
1260	Reddish-winged Bare-eye *Phlegopsis erythroptera*	2	*erythroptera* (SE Co, E Ec, S Ve)	LT									
1261	Ocellated Antbird *Phaenostictus mcleannani*	4	*chocoanus* (W Co) *pacificus* (SW Co, NW Ec)	T									
1262	Rufous-capped Antthrush *Formicarius colma*	4	*colma* (E Co, S Ve, Gu, Su, FG) *nigrifrons* (E Ec)	LT									
1263	Black-faced Antthrush *Formicarius analis*	10	*connectens* (E Co) *crissalis* (S Ve, Gu, Su, FG) *griseioventris* (W Ve) *panamensis* (NW Co) *saturatus* (C Co, N&W Ve, Tr) *virescens* (Co: Sta Marta) *zamorae* (E Ec)	T	*saturatus, virescens & panamensis* may be part of a sep. sp.: Howell 1994.								
1264	Black-headed Antthrush *Formicarius nigricapillus*	2	*destructus* (W Ec, W Co)	T-LS									
1265	Rufous-breasted Antthrush *Formicarius rufipectus*	3	*carrikeri* (W Ec, Co: W & C Andes) *lasallei* (W Ve) *thoraccicus* (E Ec)	UT-S									
1266	Short-tailed Antthrush *Chamaeza campanisona*	11 ?	*columbiana* (Co: E Andes) *fulvescens* (SE Ve, W Gu) *obscura* (E Ve) *punctigula* (E Ec) *venezuelana* (N Ve) *yavii* (Ve: N Amazonas)	T-LS									
1267	Striated Antthrush *Chamaeza nobilis*	3	*rubida* (E Ec, SE Co)	LT									
1268	Schwartz's Antthrush *Chamaeza turdina*	2	*chinogaster* (N Ve) *turdina* (Co: C & E Andes)	S-Te	Formerly *C. ruficauda turdina*: Willis 1992.								
1269	Barred Antthrush *Chamaeza mollissima*	2	*mollissima* (Ec, C Co)	US-Te									
1270	Black-crowned Antpitta *Pittasoma michleri*	2	*michleri* (NW Co)	T									
1271	Rufous-crowned Antpitta *Pittasoma rufopileatum*	3	*harterti* (SW Co) *rosenbergi* (W Co) *rufopileatum* (NW Ec)	T									
1272	Undulated Antpitta *Grallaria squamigera*	2	*squamigera* (Andes: Ec, Co, Ve)	US-P									
1273	Giant Antpitta *Grallaria gigantea*	3	*gigantea* (E Ec) *hylodroma* (W Ec) *lehmanni* (Co: C Andes)	S-Te	Vulnerable								
1274	Great Antpitta *Grallaria excelsa*	2	*excelsa* (W Ve) *phelpsi* (N Ve)	S	Endemic								

No.	Species	Ssp. Total	Subspecies in Northern South America	Altitude Range	References and Comments	Ec	Co	Ve	Ar Cu Bo	Tr To	Gu	Su	F(
1275	Variegated Antpitta *Grallaria varia*	5	cinereiceps (S Ve) varia (Gu, Su, FG)	T-LS									
1276	Scaled Antpitta *Grallaria guatimalensis*	8	aripoensis (Tr) carmelitae (NE Co, W Ve) chocoensis (NW Co) regulus (Ec) roraimae (S Ve)	T-Te									
1277	Moustached Antpitta *Grallaria alleni*	2	alleni (Co: C Andes, W slope) andaquiensis (Co: E Andes)	US	**Endemic** **Endangered**								
1278	Tachira Antpitta *Grallaria chthonia*	M	(W Ve: Tachira)	S	Sp. nov.: Wetmore & Phelps 1956 **Endemic** **Vulnerable**								
1279	Plain-backed Antpitta *Grallaria haplonota*	3	haplonota (NC Ve) parambae (NW Ec, Co) pariae (NE Ve)	UT-S	*parambae* may be a sep. sp.: Stiles 1995.								
1280	Ochre-striped Antpitta *Grallaria dignissima*	M	(E Ec, S Co)	LT	Formerly *Thamnocharis*: Lowery & O'Neill 1969								
1281	Santa Marta Antpitta *Grallaria bangsi*	M	(Co: Sta Marta)	S	**Endemic**								
1282	Cundinamarca Antpitta *Grallaria kaestneri*	M	(Co: E Andes)	US	Sp. nov.: Stiles 1992 **Endemic** **Vulnerable**								
1283	Chestnut-crowned Antpitta *Grallaria ruficapilla*	7?	albiloris (S Ec) avilae (N Ve) connectens (SW Ec) nigrolineata (Ve: Andes) perijana (NW Ve) ruficapilla (Ec, Co: Andes)	UT-Te									
1284	Watkins's Antpitta *Grallaria watkinsi*	M ?	(SW Ec)	T	Formerly *G. ruficapilla watkinsi*: R&T 1994								
1285	Bicolored Antpitta *Grallaria rufocinerea*	2	romeroana (Co: NC Andes) rufocinerea (Co: SC Andes)	Te	**Endemic** **Endangered**								
1286	Chestnut-naped Antpitta *Grallaria nuchalis*	3	nuchalis (E Ec) obsoleta (NW Ec) ruficeps (Co: E&C Andes)	Te	Schulenberg & Williams 1982								
1287	Yellow-breasted Antpitta *Grallaria flavotincta*	M	(Co: W&C Andes)	UT-LS									
1288	Bay-backed Antpitta *Grallaria hypoleuca*	2	castanea (E Ec, SW Co) hypoleuca (Co: E Andes)	UT-LS									
1289	Grey-naped Antpitta *Grallaria griseonucha*	2	griseonucha (Ve: Merida) tachirae (Ve: Tachira)	Te	**Endemic**								
1290	Rufous Antpitta *Grallaria rufula*	7	rufula (Andes: Ec, Co & Ve) saltuensis (NE Co: Perija) spaltior (Co: Sta Marta)	Te-P									
1291	Tawny Antpitta *Grallaria quitensis*	3	alticola (Co: E Andes) quitensis (Ec, Co: C Andes)	Te									
1292	Jocotoco Antpitta *Grallaria ridgelyi*	M	(S Ec)	US	Sp. nov.: Krabbe *et al.* 1999								
1293	Brown-banded Antpitta *Grallaria milleri*	M	(Co: C Andes)	Te	**Endemic** **Endangered**								
1294	Spectacled Antpitta *Hylopezus perspicillatus*	5	pallidior (C Co) periophthalmicus (W Ec, W Co) perspicillatus (NW Co)	T	Formerly *Grallaria*: Lowery & O'Neill 1969								

No.	Species	Ssp. Total	Subspecies in Northern South America	Altitude Range	References and Comments	Ec	Co	Ve	Ar Cu Bo	Tr To	Gu	Su	FG
1295	**Spotted Antpitta** *Hylopezus macularius*	4	*diversus* (SE Co, S Ve: Amazonas) *macularius* (SE Ve, Gu, FG)	LT	Formerly *Grallaria*: Lowery & O'Neill 1969								
1296	**Thicket Antpitta** *Hylopezus dives*	3	*barbacoae* (W Co)	T	Formerly *Grallaria fulviventris dives*: AOU 1998								
1297	**White-lored Antpitta** *Hylopezus fulviventris*	2	*caquetae* (Co) *fulviventris* (E Ec)	LT	Formerly *Grallaria*: Lowery & O'Neill 1969								
1298	**Thrush-like Antpitta** *Myrmothera campanisona*	6	*campanisona* (SE Ve, Gu, Su, FG) *dissors* (SE Co, S Ve) *modesta* (Co: E Andes) *signata* (E Ec)	LT									
1299	**Tepui Antpitta** *Myrmothera simplex*	4	*duidae* (S Ve) *guaiquinimae* (S Ve) *pacaraimae** (SE Ve) *simplex* (SE Ve)	UT-Te	*Ssp. nov.: Phelps & Dickerman 1980.								
1300	**Ochre-breasted Antpitta** *Grallaricula flavirostris*	8	*flavirostris* (E Ec, Co: E Andes) *mindoensis* (N Ec) *ochraceiventris* (Co: W Andes) *zarumae* (SW Ec)	UT-S									
1301	**Rusty-breasted Antpitta** *Grallaricula ferrugineipectus*	3	*ferrugineipectus* (Co: Sta Marta, W&N Ve) *rara* (Co: E)	UT-Te									
1302	**Slate-crowned Antpitta** *Grallaricula nana*	6	*cumanensis* (NE Ve) *kukenamensis* (SE Ve) *nana* (Co: E Andes, W Ve) *occidentalis* (Co: W & C Andes) *olivascens* (NC Ve: Turimiquire) *pariae* (NE Ve: Paria)	S-Te									
1303	**Scallop-breasted Antpitta** *Grallaricula loricata*	M	(NC Ve)	S	Endemic								
1304	**Peruvian Antpitta** *Grallaricula peruviana*	M	(SW Ec)	S									
1305	**Crescent-faced Antpitta** *Grallaricula lineifrons*	M	(NE Ec)	P									
1306	**Hooded Antpitta** *Grallaricula cucullata*	2	*cucullata* (Co: Andes) *venezuelana* (SW Ve)	S-Te	Vulnerable								
1307	**Chestnut-belted Gnateater** *Conopophaga aurita*	6	*aurita* (Gu, Su, FG) *inexpectata* (SE Co) *occidentalis* (E Ec)	LT									
1308	**Ash-throated Gnateater** *Conopophaga peruviana*	M	(E Ec)	LT									
1309	**Chestnut-crowned Gnateater** *Conopophaga castaneiceps*	4	*castaneiceps* (NE Ec, Co: C&E Andes) *chapmani* (SE Ec) *chocoensis* (W Co)	S									
1310	**Rusty-belted Tapaculo** *Lioscelos thoracicus*	3	*dugandi* (SE Co) *orithacus* (E Ec)	T									
1311	**Elegant Crescentchest** *Melanopareia elegans*	2	*elegans* (W Ec)	T									
1312	**Marañon Crescentchest** *Melanopareia maranonica*	M	(SE Ec)	T	Sight records in Ec: RG&G.	?							
1313	**Ash-colored Tapaculo** *Myornis senilis*	M	(Ec, Co: C&E Andes)	Te	Formerly *Scytalopus*: H&B.								

No.	Species	Ssp. Total	Subspecies in Northern South America	Altitude Range	References and Comments	Ec	Co	Ve	Ar Cu Bo	Tr To	Gu	Su	FC
1314	**Unicolored Tapaculo** *Scytalopus unicolor*	4	*latrans* (E Ec, Co: Andes, W Ve) *subcinereus* (SW Ec)	S-P	*latrans* may be a sep. sp. (Blackish Tapaculo): S&M. *subcinereus* may be a sep. sp.: Krabbe & Schulenberg 1997.	X	X	X					
1315	**Santa Marta Tapaculo** *Scytalopus sanctaemartae*	M	(Co: Sta Marta)	S	Formerly *S. femoralis sanctaemartae*: Krabbe & Schulenberg 1997		X						
1316	**Northern White-crowned Tapaculo** *Scytalopus atratus*	3	*atratus* (Co: E Andes) *confusus* (Co: Andes) *nigricans* * (Ve)		All ssp. formerly conspecific with *S. femoralis*: Krabbe & Schulenberg 1997. * Ssp nov.: Phelps & Phelps 1963.		X	X					
1317	**Equatorial Rufous-vented Tapaculo** *Scytalopus micropterus*	M	(E Ec)	UT-Te	Formerly *S. femoralis micropterus*: Krabbe & Schulenberg 1997	X							
1318	**Pale-throated Tapaculo** *Scytalopus panamensis*	M	(Co: Panama-Co border)	UT	Krabbe & Schulenberg 1997. Pearman 1993.		X						
1319	**Choco Tapaculo** *Scytalopus chocoensis*	M	(NW Ec)	T	Sp. nov.: Krabbe & Schulenberg 1997 **Endemic**	X							
1320	**El Oro Tapaculo** *Scytalopus robbinsi*	M	(SW Ec)	UT	Sp. nov.: Krabbe & Schulenberg 1997	X							
1321	**Nariño Tapaculo** *Scytalopus vicinior*	M	(N Ec, W Co)	S-P	Formerly *S. panamensis vicinior*: Krabbe & Schulenberg 1997 **Endemic**	X	X						
1322	**Brown-rumped Tapaculo** *Scytalopus latebricola*	M	(Co: Sta Marta)	S-P	**Endemic**		X						
1323	**Merida Tapaculo** *Scytalopus meridanus*	M	(Ve: Andes)	P	Formerly *S. latebricola meridanus* (in part): Krabbe & Schulenberg 1997 **Endemic**			X					
1324	**Colombian Tapaculo** *Scytalopus infasciatus*	M	(Co: C & E Andes)	Te	Formerly *S. latebricola meridanus* (in part): Krabbe & Schulenberg 1997 (although taxonomic status remains uncertain, T. Schulenberg, pers. comm. 1999) **Endemic**		X						
1325	**Caracas Tapaculo** *Scytalopus caracae*	M	(Ve: Coastal Range)	S	Formerly *S. latebricola caracae*: Krabbe & Schulenberg 1997 **Endemic**			X					
1326	**Chusquea Tapaculo** *Scytalopus parkeri*	M	(SE Ec)	Te	Sp. nov.: Krabbe & Schulenberg 1997 **Endemic**	X							
1327	**Spillmann's Tapaculo** *Scytalopus spillmanni*	M	(Ec, Co: Andes)	US-Te	Formerly *S. latebricola spillmanni*: Krabbe & Schulenberg 1997	X	X						

No.	Species	Ssp. Total	Subspecies in Northern South America	Altitude Range	References and Comments	Ec	Co	Ve	Ar Cu Bo	Tr To	Gu	Su	FG
1328	**Rufous-rumped Tapaculo** *Scytalopus griseicollis*	2	*fuscicauda* (Ve: Andes) *griseicollis* (C Co: E Andes)	Te	Both ssp. formerly conspecific with *S. magellanica*: Krabbe & Schulenberg 1997. *fuscicauda* may be a sep. sp.: C. Sharpe pers comm.		▓						
1329	**Paramo Tapaculo** *Scytalopus canus*	2	*canus* (Co: W Andes) *opacus* (E Ec: Tambillo)	Te-P	Both ssp. formerly conspecific with *S. magellanica*: Krabbe & Schulenberg 1997.	▓	▓						
1330	**Ocellated Tapaculo** *Acropternis orthonyx*	2	*infuscata* (Ec) *orthonix* (Co: E Andes, Ve: Andes)	S-Te		▓	▓	▓					
1331	**Streak-necked Flycatcher** *Mionectes striaticollis*	6	*columbianus* (E Ec, E&C Co) *selvae* (Co: W Andes) *viridiceps* (W Ec, SW Co)	S-P		▓	▓						
1332	**Olive-striped Flycatcher** *Mionectes olivaceus*	7	*galbinus* (Co: Sta Marta) *hederaceus* (W Co, NW Ec) *meridae* (NE Co, NW Ve) *pallidus* (Co: E Andes) *venezuelensis* (Ve: N ranges, Tr)	T-LS		▓	▓	▓		▓			
1333	**Ochre-bellied Flycatcher** *Mionectes oleaginus*	15	*abdominalis* (NC Ve) *chloronotus* (E Co, W&S Ve) *dorsalis* (SE Ve: Roraima & Chimanta) *hauxwelli* (E Ec) *intensus* (SE Ve, W Gu) *pacificus* (SW Co, W Ec) *pallidiventris* (NE Ve, Tr, To) *parcus* (N Co, NW Ve) *wallacei* (Gu, Su, FG)	T	Formerly *Pipromorpha*	▓	▓	▓		▓	▓	▓	▓
1334	**McConnell's Flycatcher** *Mionectes macconnelli*	4	*macconnelli* (E Ve, Gu, FG) *roraimae* (S Ve, W Gu)	T-LS	Formerly *Pipromorpha*			▓			▓		▓
1335	**Rufous-breasted Flycatcher** *Leptopogon rufipectus*	2	*rufipectus* (NE Ec, S Co: C & E Andes) *venezuelanus* (W Ve: Táchira)	S-Te		▓	▓	▓					
1336	**Sepia-capped Flycatcher** *Leptopogon amaurocephalus*	8	*diversus* (NC&NE Co, NW Ve) *faustus* (NW Co) *obscuritergum* (S Ve, Gu, Su, FG) *orinocensis* (C&WC Ve) *peruvianus* (SE Co, E Ec?)	T		▓	▓	▓			▓	▓	▓
1337	**Slaty-capped Flycatcher** *Leptopogon superciliaris*	7	*pariae* (NE Ve, Tr) *poliocephalus* (C&CE Co) *superciliaris* (E Ec, SE Co) *transandinus* (W Ec, Co: W Andes) *venezueliensis* (N Ve)	UT-S		▓	▓	▓		▓			
1338	**Bronze-olive Pygmy-Tyrant** *Pseudotriccus pelzelni*	4	*annectens* (NW Ec, SW Co) *berlepschi* (NW Co) *pelzelni* (E Ec, E Co)	UT-S		▓	▓						
1339	**Rufous-headed Pygmy-Tyrant** *Pseudotriccus ruficeps*	M	(Ec, S Co)	S-Te		▓	▓						

No.	Species	Ssp. Total	Subspecies in Northern South America	Altitude Range	References and Comments	Ec	Co	Ve	Ar Cu Bo	Tr To	Gu	Su	F(
1340	**Rufous-crowned Tody-Tyrant** *Poecilotriccus ruficeps*	4	*melanomystax* (NC Co: C Andes) *ruficeps* (NE Ec, Co: E Andes, Ve: Táchira) *rufigenis* (W Ec, SW Co)	S-Te									
1341	**Black-and-white Tody-Tyrant** *Poecilotriccus capitalis*	M	(E Ec, SE Co)	T									
1342	**Black-chested Tyrant** *Taeniotriccus andrei*	2?	*andrei* (SE Ve)	LT	Formerly *Poecilotriccus*								
1343	**Snethlage's Tody-Tyrant** *Hemitriccus minor*	3	*pallens* (S Ve)	T	Formerly *Idioptilon*								
1344	**Boat-billed Tody-Tyrant** *Hemitriccus josephinae*	M	(Gu, W Su)	LT	Formerly *Idioptilon*								?
1345	**White-eyed Tody-Tyrant** *Hemitriccus zosterops*	4	*zosterops* (E Ec, S Co, S Ve, Su, FG)	LT	Formerly *Idioptilon*								
1346	**Johannes's Tody-Tyrant** *Hemitriccus iohannis*	M	(S Co)	LT	Formerly *Idioptilon*								
1347	**Stripe-necked Tody-Tyrant** *Hemitriccus striaticollis*	2	*striaticollis* (E Co: Meta)	LT	Formerly *Idioptilon*								
1348	**Pearly-vented Tody-Tyrant** *Hemitriccus margaritaceiventer*	8	*auyantepui* (SE Ve) *broweri* * (S Ve: Sarisariñama) *duidae* (S Ve) *impiger* (NE Co,Ve: N & Marg) *septentrionalis* (S Co)	T-S	Formerly *Idioptilon* * Phelps 1977								
1349	**Black-throated Tody-Tyrant** *Hemitriccus granadensis*	7	*andinus* (N Co: E Andes, Ve: Táchira) *federalis* (NC Ve) *granadensis* (NE Ec, Co) *intensus* (W Ve) *lehmani* (Co: Sta Marta)	T-S	Formerly *Idioptilon*								
1350	**Buff-throated Tody-Tyrant** *Hemitriccus rufigularis*	M	(C&SE Ec)	UT-S	Formerly *Idioptilon*								
1351	**Cinnamon-breasted Tody-Tyrant** *Hemitriccus cinnamomeipectus*		(Extreme S Ec)	S	Formerly *Idioptilon*								
1352	**Ruddy Tody-Flycatcher** *Todirostrum russatum*	M	(S Ve)	S									
1353	**Rusty-fronted Tody-Flycatcher** *Todirostrum latirostre*	7	*caniceps* (E Ec, SE Co) *mituensis* (S Co)	T									
1354	**Smoky-fronted Tody-Flycatcher** *Todirostrum fumifrons*	2	*penardi* (Su, FG)	LT									
1355	**Slate-headed Tody-Flycatcher** *Todirostrum sylvia*	5	*griseolum* (SE Co, Ve) *superciliare* (Co) *sylvia* (Gu, Su)	T									
1356	**Spotted Tody-Flycatcher** *Todirostrum maculatum*	5	*amacurense* (Ve) *maculatum* (Tr?, Su, FG) *signatum* (SE Co)	LT									
1357	**Common Tody-Flycatcher** *Todirostrum cinereum*	8	*cinereum* (N&E Co, C&E Ve, Gu, Su, FG) *peruanum* (E Ec) *sclateri* (W Ec, SW Co)	T									
1358	**Short-tailed Tody-Flycatcher** *Todirostrum viridanum*	M	(NW Ve)	LT	**Endemic**								

No.	Species	Ssp. Total	Subspecies in Northern South America	Altitude Range	References and Comments	Ec	Co	Ve	Ar Cu Bo	Tr To	Gu	Su	FG
1359	**Black-headed Tody-Flycatcher** *Todirostrum nigriceps*	M	(W Ec, N&W Co, W Ve)	T		■	■	■					
1360	**Painted Tody-Flycatcher** *Todirostrum pictum*	M	(S Ve, Gu, Su, FG)	LT				■			■	■	■
1361	**Yellow-browed Tody-Flycatcher** *Todirostrum chrysocrotaphum*	5	guttatum (E Ec, E Co)	T		■	■						
1362	**Golden-winged Tody-Flycatcher** *Todirostrum calopterum*	2	calopterum (E Ec, SE Co)	T		■	■						
1363	**Ringed Antpipit** *Corythopis torquata*	4	sarayacuensis (E Ec, SE Co) anthoides (S&SE Ve, Gu, Su, FG)	T	Removed from Gnateaters, Conopophagidae: Ames *et al.* 1968.	■	■	■			■	■	■
1364	**White-fronted Tyrannulet** *Phyllomyias zeledoni*	5	bunites (SE Ve) leucogonys (Ec, E Co) viridiceps (CN Ve) wetmorei (NW Ve)	UT-S	Formerly *P. burmeisteri zeledoni*: SFP&M, R&T.	■	■	■					
1365	**Greenish Tyrannulet** *Phyllomyias virescens*	2	urichi (NE Ve)	T	*urichi* may be a sep. sp.: R&T 1994.			■					
1366	**Sooty-capped Tyrannulet** *Phyllomyias griseiceps*	4	caucae (CW Co) cristatus (N Co, N Ve) griseiceps (Ec) pallidiceps (SE Ve, Gu)	T		■	■	■			■		
1367	**Plumbeous-crowned Tyrannulet** *Phyllomyias plumbeiceps*	M	(E Ec, S Co)	S		■	■						
1368	**Black-capped Tyrannulet** *Phyllomyias nigrocapillus*	3	aureus (W Ve) flavimentum (N Co) nigrocapillus (Ec, Co: Andes, W Ve)	Te		■	■	■					
1369	**Ashy-headed Tyrannulet** *Phyllomyias cinereiceps*	M	(N Ec, Co)	UT-Te		■	■						
1370	**Tawny-rumped Tyrannulet** *Phyllomyias uropygialis*	M	(W Ec, EC&SW Co, W Ve)	S-P		■	■	■					
1371	**Paltry Tyrannulet** *Zimmerius vilissimus*	2	parvus (NW Co: Chocó)	T-Te	*parvus* may be a sep. sp. (Mistletoe Tyrannulet): S&M.		■						
1372	**Venezuelan Tyrannulet** *Zimmerius improbus*	3	improbus (N Co, NW Ve) petersi (Co: Sta Marta, Ve: Perijá & Tamá) tamae (N Ve)	T-Te	R&T 1994		■	■					
1373	**Red-billed Tyrannulet** *Zimmerius cinereicapillus*	M	(NE Ec)	T		■							
1374	**Slender-footed Tyrannulet** *Zimmerius gracilipes*	3	acer (Ve, Gu, Su, FG) gracilipes (SE Co, S&SE Ve)	T	*acer* may be a sep. sp. (Guianian Tyrannulet): S&M.		■	■			■	■	■
1375	**Golden-faced Tyrannulet** *Zimmerius chrysops*	5	albigularis (SW Co, NW Ec) chrysops (E Ec, Co: Andes, NW Ve) cumanensis (NE Ve) flavidifrons (SW Ec) minimus (Co: Sta Marta)	UT-Te		■	■	■					
1376	**White-lored Tyrannulet** *Ornithion inerme*	M	(E Ec, E&SE Co, S Ve, Gu, Su, FG)	T		■	■	■			■	■	■
1377	**Brown-capped Tyrannulet** *Ornithion brunneicapillum*	2	brunneicapillum (W&C CO, NW Ec) dilutum (NE Co, NW Ve)	T		■	■	■					

No.	Species	Ssp. Total	Subspecies in Northern South America	Altitude Range	References and Comments	Ec	Co	Ve	Ar Cu Bo	Tr To	Gu	Su	F
1378	Southern Beardless Tyrannulet *Camptostoma obsoletum*	15	*bogotensis* (E Co) *caucae* (C Co: W Andes) *napaeum* (SC Ve, Gu, Su, FG) *olivaceum* (E Ec, SE Co) *pusillum* (N Co, & NW Ve) *sclateri* (W Ec) *venezuelae* (NC,NE&C Ve, Tr)	T									
1379	Mouse-colored Tyrannulet *Phaeomyias murina*	8	*incomta* (N&W Co, Ve, Tr) *tumbezana* (SW Ec)	T-LS	*tumbezana,* together with NW Peru ssp., may be a sep. sp. (Tumbes Tyrannulet): R&T 1994.								
1380	Yellow Tyrannulet *Capsiempis flaveolus*	6	*amazonus* (Gu, Su, FG) *cerulus* (NE Ec, E Co, E&S Ve) *leucophrys* (CN Co, NW Ve) *magnirostris* (SW Ec)	T	Formerly *Phylloscartes*								
1381	Northern Scrub-Flycatcher *Sublegatus arenarum*	6 ?	*atrirostris* (N Co) *glaber* (Ve: N coast & Marg, Tr, Su, FG) *orinocensis* (E Co, C Ve) *pallens* (Ve: Los Roques, Ar, Bo, Cu) *tortuguensis* (Ve: La Tortuga Is.)	T	Formerly *S. modestus* (in Peters), but now S S.Am ssp. considered to be a sep. sp.: S&M, SFP&M.								
1382	Amazonian Scrub-Flycatcher *Sublegatus obscurior*	M	(E Ec, E Co, C&NE Ve, Gu, Su, FG)	T									
1383	Suiriri Flycatcher *Suiriri suiriri*	3	*affinis* (Su)	T									
1384	Yellow-crowned Tyrannulet *Tyrannulus elatus*	M		T									
1385	Forest Elaenia *Myiopagis gaimardii*	6	*bogotensis* (NE Co, N Ve) *gaimardii* (S Ec) *guianensis* (E Co, SE Ve, Gu, Su, FG) *macilvainii* (N Co) *trinitatis* (Tr)	T									
1386	Grey Elaenia *Myiopagis caniceps*	4	*cinerea* (E Ec, E Co, NW&S Ve) *parambae* (NW Ec, W Co)	T									
1387	Pacific Elaenia *Myiopagis subplacens*	M	(W Ec)	T-S									
1388	Yellow-crowned Elaenia *Myiopagis flavivertex*	M	(S&SE Ve, Su, FG)	T									
1389	Greenish Elaenia *Myiopagis viridicata*	10	*accola* (Co, Ve: Táchira) *implacens* (W Ec, SW Co) *pallens* (NE Co) *restricta* (Ve) *zuliae* (Ve: Perijá)	T-S									
1390	Grey-and-white Tyrannulet *Pseudoelaenia leucospodia*	2	*cinereifrons* (SW Ec)	T	Formerly *Phaeomyias* or *Myiopagis*: Lanyon 1988.								
1391	Caribbean Elaenia *Elaenia martinica*	7	*riisii* (Cu, Bo, Ar)	T									
1392	Yellow-bellied Elaenia *Elaenia flavogaster*	4	*flavogaster* (Co, Ve, Marg, Tr, To, Gu, Su, FG) *semipagana* (W Ec)	T-S									

No.	Species	Ssp. Total	Subspecies in Northern South America	Altitude Range	References and Comments	Ec	Co	Ve	Ar Cu Bo	Tr To	Gu	Su	FG
393	Large Elaenia *Elaenia spectabilis*	2	*spectabilis* (extreme SE Co)	T									
394	White-crested Elaenia *Elaenia albiceps*	6	*griseigularis* (SW Co, W&NE Ec)	T-P									
395	Small-billed Elaenia *Elaenia parvirostris*	M	(Austral migrant: winters to Caribbean coasts of N. S.Am.)	T									
396	Slaty Elaenia *Elaenia strepera*	M	(Austral migrant: winters to E Co, Ve)	S- Te	Marantz & Remsen 1991								
397	Mottle-backed Elaenia *Elaenia gigas*	M	(Ec, E Co)	T									
398	Brownish Elaenia *Elaenia pelzelni*	M		T	Sight records in Co: SFP&M.		?						
399	Plain-crested Elaenia *Elaenia cristata*	2	*alticola* (SE Ve: Tepuis) *cristata* (SE Co, C&E Ve, Gu, Su, FG)	T	Recorded in Co: Rojas *et al.* 1997.								
400	Rufous-crowned Elaenia *Elaenia ruficeps*	M	(E Co, S Ve, Gu, Su, FG)	T									
401	Lesser Elaenia *Elaenia chiriquensis*	3	*albivertex* (Co, Ve, Gu, Su, FG) *brachyptera* (SW Co, NW Ec)	T-P									
402	Mountain Elaenia *Elaenia frantzii*	4	*browni* (NE Co, NW Ve) *pudica* (Co, N Ve)	UT-P									
403	Highland Elaenia *Elaenia obscura*	2	*obscura* (extreme S Ec)	UT-Te	Recorded in Ec: R&T 1994.								
404	Great Elaenia *Elaenia dayi*	3	*auyantepui* (Ve: Auyantepui) *dayi* (Ve: eastern tepuis) *tyleri* (Ve: Amazonas tepuis)	UT-Te	**Endemic**								
405	Sierran Elaenia *Elaenia pallatangae*	4	*olivina* (S Ve, Gu) *pallatangae* (Ec, S Co)	S-P									
406	White-throated Tyrannulet *Mecocerculus leucophrys*	12	*gularis* (NW Ve) *montensis* (Co: Sta Marta) *nigriceps* (NE Ve) *notatus* (Co: W & C Andes) *palliditergum* (CN Ve) *parui* (S Ve) *roraimae* (SC Ve) *rufomarginatus* (SW Co, Ec) *setophagoides* (Co: E Andes)	S-P									
407	White-tailed Tyrannulet *Mecocerculus poecilocercus*	M	(Ec, Co)	S-Te									
408	Rufous-winged Tyrannulet *Mecocerculus calopterus*	M		UT-S									
409	Sulphur-bellied Tyrannulet *Mecocerculus minor*	M	(E Co, Ve: Táchira)	S-Te									
410	White-banded Tyrannulet *Mecocerculus stictopterus*	3	*albocaudatus* (Ve: Andes) *stictopterus* (Ec, Co)	Te-P									
411	Torrent Tyrannulet *Serpophaga cinerea*	2	*cinerea* (Ec, Co, NW Ve)	UT-Te									
412	River Tyrannulet *Serpophaga hypoleuca*	3	*hypoleuca* (SE Co) *venezuelana* (C&E Ve, CE Co)	T	Recorded in Co: Rojas *et al.* 1997.								
413	Slender-billed Inezia *Inezia tenuirostris*	M	(NE Co, NW Ve)	T	Formerly Slender-billed Tyrannulet: Zimmer & Whittaker, in prep.								
414	Pale-tipped Inezia *Inezia caudata*	2	*caudata* (C Ve, Gu, Su) *intermedia* (NE Co, C Ve)	T	Formerly Pale-tipped Tyrannulet: Zimmer & Whittaker, in prep.								

No.	Species	Ssp. Total	Subspecies in Northern South America	Altitude Range	References and Comments	Ec	Co	Ve	Ar Cu Bo	Tr To	Gu	Su	F
1415	**Amazonian Inezia** *Inezia subflava*	2	*obscura* (S Ve, extreme E Co)	T	Formerly Pale-tipped Tyrannulet: Zimmer & Whittaker, in prep.		■	■					
1416	**Lesser Wagtail-Tyrant** *Stigmatura napensis*	2	*napensis* (Ec, SE Co, Ve)	T		■	?	■					
1417	**Agile Tit-Tyrant** *Anairetes agilis*	M	(N Ec, S Co)	Te-P		■	■						
1418	**Black-crested Tit-Tyrant** *Anairetes nigrocristatus*	M ?	(Extreme S Ec)	Te-P	Formerly *A. reguloides nigrocristatus*: F&K. Sight records in Ec.: SFP&M	?							
1419	**Tufted Tit-Tyrant** *Anairetes parulus*	3	*aequatorialis* (S Co, Ec)	T-P		■	■						
1420	**Bearded Tachuri** *Polystictus pectoralis*	3	*bogotensis* (C Co) *brevipennis* (S Ve, Gu, Su)	T	Sight records in FG: SFP&M.		■	■			■	■	
1421	**Crested Doradito** *Pseudocolopteryx sclateri*	M		T									
1422	**Subtropical Doradito** *Pseudocolopteryx acutipennis*	M	(Ec, Co: C Andes)	UT-S		■	■						
1423	**Tawny-crowned Pygmy-Tyrant** *Euscarthmus meloryphus*	3	*fulviceps* (SW Ec) *paulus* (NE Co, N,C&SE Ve)	T-S		■	■	■					
1424	**Rufous-sided Pygmy-Tyrant** *Euscarthmus rufomarginatus*	2	*savannophilus* (Su)	T								■	
1425	**Marbled-faced Bristle-Tyrant** *Phylloscartes ophthalmicus*	3	*ophthalmicus* (NW&E Ec, Co: W & C Andes) *purus* (N Ve)	UT-S		■	■	■					
1426	**Venezuelan Bristle-Tyrant** *Phylloscartes venezuelanus*	M	(N Ve)	UT	Endemic			■					
1427	**Spectacled Bristle-Tyrant** *Phylloscartes orbitalis*	M	(S Co, E Ec)	T		■	■						
1428	**Variegated Bristle-Tyrant** *Phylloscartes poecilotis*	2	*pifanoi* (Perijá: Co & Ve) *poecilotis* (Andes: Ve, Co & Ec)	UT-S		■	■	■					
1429	**Black-fronted Tyrannulet** *Phylloscartes nigrifrons*	M	(S Ve)	UT-S	Endemic			■					
1430	**Chapman's Tyrannulet** *Phylloscartes chapmani*	2	*chapmani* (SE Ve) *duidae* (S Ve)	UT-S				■					
1431	**Ecuadorean Tyrannulet** *Phylloscartes gualaquizae*	M	(E Ec, Co)	T-LS		■	■						
1432	**Yellow-bellied Bristle-Tyrant** *Phylloscartes flaviventris*	M	(N Ve)	T	Endemic			■					
1433	**Olive-green Tyrannulet** *Phylloscartes virescens*	M		T									
1434	**Rufous-browed Tyrannulet** *Phylloscartes superciliaris*	3	*griseocapillus* (Ve: Perijá) *palloris* (S Ec, N Co)	UT-LS	Recorded in Ec & Co: R&T.	■	■	■					
1435	**Antioquia Bristle-Tyrant** *Phylloscartes lanyoni*	M	(Co: C Andes)	T	Sp. nov.: Graves 1988; known from a single specimen. **Endemic**		■						
1436	**Black-capped Pygmy-Tyrant** *Myiornis atricapillus*	M ?	(NW Ec, W Co)	LT	Formerly *M. ecaudatus atricapillus*: AOU 1998	■	■						
1437	**Short-tailed Pygmy-Tyrant** *Myiornis ecaudatus*	2 ?	*miserabilis* (E Co, N&C Ve, Tr, Gu, Su)	T			■	■		■	■	■	

No.	Species	Ssp. Total	Subspecies in Northern South America	Altitude Range	References and Comments	Ec	Co	Ve	Ar Cu Bo	Tr To	Gu	Su	FG
1438	**Scale-crested Pygmy-Tyrant** *Lophotriccus pileatus*	5	*pileatus* (E Ec) *sanctaeluciae* (NE Co, NW Ve) *squamaecrista* (Andes: Co & Ec)	LT-LS									
1439	**Double-banded Pygmy-Tyrant** *Lophotriccus vitiosus*	4	*affinis* (E Ec, SE Co) *guianensis* (Gu, Su, FG)	T-LT									
1440	**Helmeted Pygmy-Tyrant** *Lophotriccus galeatus*	M	(E Co, E&S Ve, Gu, Su, FG)	T									
1441	**Pale-eyed Pygmy-Tyrant** *Atalotriccus pilaris*	4	*griseiceps* (E Co, C&E Ve, W Gu) *pilaris* (N&C Co) *venezuelensis* (N&C Ve)	T									
1442	**Northern Bentbill** *Oncostoma cinereigulare*	M		T	Romero & Rodriguez 1980		?						
1443	**Southern Bentbill** *Oncostoma olivaceum*	M	(N Co)	T									
1444	**Brownish Flycatcher** *Cnipodectes subbrunneus*	3	*minor* (SE Co) *panamensis* (NW Co) *subbrunneus* (W Co, W Ec)	LT									
1445	**Large-headed Flatbill** *Ramphotrigon megacephala*	4	*pectoralis* (SE Co, S Ve) *venezuelensis* (WC Ve)	T-LS									
1446	**Dusky-tailed Flatbill** *Ramphotrigon fuscicauda*	M	(S Co, NE Ec)	T									
1447	**Rufous-tailed Flatbill** *Ramphotrigon ruficauda*	M	(E Co, S Ve, Gu, Su, FG)	LT									
1448	**Eye-ringed Flatbill** *Rhynchocyclus brevirostris*	3 ?	*hellmayri* (NW Co)	T-Te									
1449	**Pacific Flatbill** *Rhynchocyclus pacificus*	M	(NW Ec, W Co)	T	Formerly *R. brevirostris pacificus*: Zimmer 1939, R&T 1994.								
1450	**Olivaceous Flatbill** *Rhynchocyclus olivaceus*	9	*aequinoctialis* (SE Co, E Ec) *bardus* (NW Co) *flavus* (NE&E Co, W Ve: W Zulia) *guianensis* (S&SE Ve, Gu, Su, FG) *jelambianus* * (W Ve: E&S Zulia) *mirus* (NW Co) *tamborensis* (Co: Santander)	T	* Ssp nov.: Aveledo & Perez 1994								
1451	**Fulvous-breasted Flatbill** *Rhynchocyclus fulvipectus*	M	(W Ve, C&W Co, NW&E Ec)	UT-S									
1452	**Yellow-olive Flycatcher** *Tolmomyias sulphurescens*	16	*aequatorialis* (W Ec) *asemus* (W Co) *berlepschi* (Tr) *cherriei* (S Ve, Gu, Su, FG) *confusus* (NE Ec, Co: E Andes, W Ve) *duidae* (S Ve) *exortivus* (NE Co, N Ve) *flavoolivaceus* (NW Co) *peruvianus* (SE Ec)	T-LS									
1453	**Yellow-margined Flycatcher** *Tolmomyias assimilis*	8	*examinatus* (SE Ve, Gu, Su, FG) *flavotectus* (NW Ec, W Co) *neglectus* (E Co, SW Ve) *obscuriceps* (NE Ec, SE Co)	T									

No.	Species	Ssp. Total	Subspecies in Northern South America	Altitude Range	References and Comments	Ec	Co	Ve	Ar Cu Bo	Tr To	Gu	Su	F(
1454	**Grey-crowned Flycatcher** *Tolmomyias poliocephalus*	3	*klagesi* (CE Ve) *poliocephalus* (E Ec, SE Co, SW Ve) *sclateri* (Gu, Su, FG)	LT									
1455	**Yellow-breasted Flycatcher** *Tolmomyias flaviventris*	7	*aurulentus* (N Co, NW Ve) *collingwoodi* (E Co, C,N&E Ve, Tr, To, Gu, Su, FG) *dissors* (SW Ve) *flaviventris* (S Ve?) *viridiceps* (E Ec, SE Co)	LT	Ssp. divided into 3 groups: '*aurulentus* ': N Co to E Brazil '*flaviventris* ': extreme S Ve & S Amazonia '*viridiceps* ': W Amazonia. Perhaps best considered 3 sep. sp.: R&T 1994, SFP&M.								
1456	**Orange-eyed Flycatcher** *Tolmomyias traylori*	M	(E Ec, SE Co)		Sp. nov.: Schulenberg & Parker 1997								
1457	**Cinnamon-crested Spadebill** *Platyrinchus saturatus*	2	*saturatus* (E Co, S Ve, Gu, Su, FG)	T									
1458	**White-throated Spadebill** *Platyrinchus mystaceus*	14	*albogularis* (W Ec, Co: W Andes) *duidae* (S Ve, Gu) *imatacae* (E Ve) *insularis* (N Ve, Tr, To) *neglectus* (Co, Ve: Táchira) *perijanus* (W Ve) *ptaritepui* (SE Ve) *ventralis* (Ve: Neblina) *zamorae* (E Ec)	T-S	Ssp. *mystaceus* of Brazil may be a sep. sp. (Yellow-crested Spadebill); all ssp. here then become *P. albogularis*: S&M. Recorded in FG (but no data for ssp): SFP&M.								
1459	**Golden-crowned Spadebill** *Platyrinchus coronatus*	3	*coronatus* (SE Co, SW Ve) *gumia* (SE Ve, Gu, Su, FG) *superciliaris* (W Co, NW Ec)	LT									
1460	**Yellow-throated Spadebill** *Platyrinchus flavigularis*	2	*flavigularis* (NE Ec, Co: E Andes) *vividus* (W Ve)	LS-TeT									
1461	**White-crested Spadebill** *Platyrinchus platyrhynchos*	4	*platyrhynchos* (E Co, S Ve, Gu, Su) *senex* (E Ec)	T									
1462	**Amazonian Royal-Flycatcher** *Onychorhynchus coronatus*	3	*coronatus* (S&E Ve, Gu, Su, FG) *castelnaui* (S Ve?, SE Co, E Ec) *fraterculus* (NE Co, W Ve)	T-LS	*Onychorhynchus* formerly considered a monotypic genus; now often treated as 4 sep. spp.: AOU 1998.								
1463	**Western Royal-Flycatcher** *Onychorhynchus occidentalis*	M	(W Ec)	T	Formerly *O. coronatus occidentalis*								
1464	**Northern Royal-Flycatcher** *Onychorhynchus mexicanus*	M		T	Formerly *O. coronatus mexicanus*. Recorded in Co & Ve: SFP&M.								
1465	**Ornate Flycatcher** *Myiotriccus ornatus*	4	*ornatus* (N Co: C & E Andes) *phoenicurus* (S Co: E Andes, E Ec) *stellatus* (W Ec, W Co)	UT-LS									
1466	**Flavescent Flycatcher** *Myiophobus flavicans*	5	*caripensis* (E Ve: Turimiquire Range) *flavicans* (Co, Ec) *perijanus* (Ve: Perijá & Tamá) *venezuelanus* (N Ve)	LS-Te									

76

No.	Species	Ssp. Total	Subspecies in Northern South America	Altitude Range	References and Comments	Ec	Co	Ve	Ar Cu Bo	Tr To	Gu	Su	FG
1467	**Orange-crested Flycatcher** *Myiophobus phoenicomitra*	2	litae (W Ec, Co: W Andes) phoenicomitra (E Ec)	UT		X	X						
1468	**Unadorned Flycatcher** *Myiophobus inornatus*	M	(S Ec)	S		X							
1469	**Roraiman Flycatcher** *Myiophobus roraimae*	2	roraimae (SE Co, S Ve, W Gu) rufipennis (E Ec)	UT-LS		X	X	X			X		
1470	**Handsome Flycatcher** *Myiophobus pulcher*	3	bellus (NE Ec, Co: C & E Andes) pulcher (NW Ec, SW Co: W Andes)	S		X	X						
1471	**Orange-banded Flycatcher** *Myiophobus lintoni*	M	(SE Ec)	US-Te		X							
1472	**Bran-colored Flycatcher** *Myiophobus fasciatus*	7	crypterythrus (Ec, SW Co) fasciatus (Co, N&SE Ve, Tr, Gu, Su, FG)	T-S		X	X	X		X	X	X	X
1473	**Olive-crested Flycatcher** *Myiophobus cryptoxanthus*	M	(E Ec)	UT		X							
1474	**Ruddy-tailed Flycatcher** *Myiobius erythrurus*	7	erythrurus (SE Ve, Gu, Su, FG) fulvigularis (N&W Co, NW Ec) signatus (E Ec, E Co) venezuelensis (extreme E Co, S Ve)	T	Formerly *Terenotriccus*	X	X	X			X	X	X
1475	**Tawny-breasted Flycatcher** *Myiobius villosus*	4	clarus (E Ec) schaeferi (N Co: E Andes, W Ve) villosus (W Co, W Ec)	UT-S		X	X	X					
1476	**Sulphur-rumped Flycatcher** *Myiobius sulphureipygius*	3	aureatus (W Co, W Ec) semiflavus (Co: Antioquía)	T	AOU 1983	X	X						
1477	**Whiskered Flycatcher** *Myiobius barbatus*	3	barbatus (SE Co, S ve, Gu, Su, FG)	LT	Hellmayr 1927.		X	X			X	X	X
1478	**Black-tailed Flycatcher** *Myiobius atricaudus*	7	adjacens (E Ec, S Co) atricaudus (W Co) modestus (SE Ve) portovelae (W Ec)	T		X	X	X					
1479	**Cinnamon Tyrant** *Neopipo cinnamomea*	2	cinnamomea (E Ec, extreme E Co, S Ve) helenae (Gu, Su, FG)	LT	Formerly Cinnamon Tyrant-Manakin: Mobley & Prum 1995.	X	X	X			X	X	X
1480	**Cinnamon Flycatcher** *Pyrrhomyias cinnamomea*	6	assimilis (Co: Sta Marta) pariae (NE Ve: Paria) pyrrhoptera (Ec, Co, W Ve) spadix (NE Ve) vieillotioides (CNW Ve)	UT-Te		X	X	X					
1481	**Cliff Flycatcher** *Hirundinea ferruginea*	4	ferruginea (Co: E Andes, Ve: Perijá) sclateri (extreme E Co, SE Ve, SW Gu, FG)	UT-LS			X	X			X		X
1482	**Fuscous Flycatcher** *Cnemotriccus fuscatus*	7	cabanisi (N&E Co, N&C Ve, Tr, To) duidae (S Ve) fumosus (Gu, Su, FG)	T			X	X		X	X	X	X
1483	**Euler's Flycatcher** *Lathrotriccus euleri*	5	bolivianus (E Ec, S Ve, migrant to N Co) flaviventris (E Co, N&C Ve, Tr, Su, FG)	T	Formerly *Empidonax*. *lawrencei* = *flaviventris*: S&M 1993, AOU 1998.	X	X	X		X		X	X

No.	Species	Ssp. Total	Subspecies in Northern South America	Altitude Range	References and Comments	Ec	Co	Ve	Ar Cu Bo	Tr To	Gu	Su	FG
1484	**Grey-breasted Flycatcher** *Lathrotriccus griseipectus*	M	(SW Ec)	T	Formerly *Empidonax*								
1485	**Black-billed Flycatcher** *Aphanotriccus audax*	M	(NW Co)	LT									
1486	**Tufted Flycatcher** *Mitrephanes phaeocercus*	8	*berlepschi* (W Co, NW Ec) *eminulus* (Co: Chocó)	UT-P									
1487	**Olive-tufted Flycatcher** *Mitrephanes olivaceus*	M	(Extreme SE Ec)	S	Recorded in Ec?: R&T 1994.	?							
1488	**Olive-sided Flycatcher** *Contopus borealis*	M	(Boreal migrant: winters to mountains in Ec, Co, Ve)	S-Te									
1489	**Greater Pewee** *Contopus fumigatus*	10	*ardosiacus* (E Ec, Co, NW Ve) *cineraceus* (N Ve) *duidae* (S Ve, S Gu) *zarumae* (W Ec, SW Co)	UT-S									
1490	**Western Wood Pewee** *Contopus sordidus*	7	Boreal migrants: *sordidulus* (winters to Co, Ec) *griscomi, peninsulae, veliei* (winter to N S.Am.?)	UT-Te									
1491	**Eastern Wood Pewee** *Contopus virens*	M	(Boreal migrant: winters to Ec, Co, Ve)	T									
1492	**Tropical Pewee** *Contopus cinereus*	8	*bogotensis* (N&E Co, N&C Ve, Tr) *punensis* (W Ec) *surinamemnsis* (SE Ve, Gu, Su, FG)	T-S									
1493	**Blackish Pewee** *Contopus nigrescens*	2	*canescens* (S Gu) *nigrescens* (E Ec)	UT									
1494	**White-throated Pewee** *Contopus albogularis*	M		LT									
1495	**Acadian Flycatcher** *Empidonax virescens*	M	(Boreal migrant: winters to W Ec, Co, NW Ve)	T-S									
1496	**Alder Flycatcher** *Empidonax alnorum*	M	(Boreal migrant: winters to N S.Am.)	T									
1497	**Willow Flycatcher** *Empidonax traillii*	M	(Boreal migrant: winters to N S.Am.)	T	Uncertain in Ec: SFP&M.	?							
1498	**Black Phoebe** *Sayornis nigricans*	6	*angustirostris* (Ec, Co, W&N Ve)	T-S									
1499	**Vermilion Flycatcher** *Pyrocephalus rubinus*	13	*piurae* (W Ec, C&W Co) *rubinus* (austral migrant: winters to E Ec, SE Co) *saturatus* (NE Co, N&SE Ve, Gu)	T-S									
1500	**Crowned Chat-Tyrant** *Silvicultrix frontalis*	4	*albidiadema* (Co: E Andes) *frontalis* (NW Ec, Co: C Andes) *orientalis* (NE Ec)	Te-P	Formerly *Ochthoeca*: Lanyon 1986 *orientalis* treated as synonymous with *frontalis* byTraylor 1985.								
1501	**Jelski's Chat-Tyrant** *Silvicultrix jelskii*	M	(SW Ec)	S-Te	Formerly *Ochthoeca frontalis jelskii*: Traylor 1985. Lanyon 1986.								
1502	**Yellow-bellied Chat-Tyrant** *Silvicultrix diadema*	7	*gratiosa* (N Ec, Co: Andes) *jesupi* (Co: Sta Marta) *meridana* (Ve: Andes) *rubella* (Perijá: Co & Ve) *tovarensis* (NC Ve)	S-P	Formerly *Ochthoeca*: Lanyon 1986								

No.	Species	Ssp. Total	Subspecies in Northern South America	Altitude Range	References and Comments	Ec	Co	Ve	Ar Cu Bo	Tr To	Gu	Su	FG
503	**Slaty-backed Chat-Tyrant** *Ochthoeca cinnamomeiventris*	4	*cinnamomeiventris* (Andes: N Ec, Co, Ve) *nigrita* (Ve: Andes)	S-P		▓	▓	▓					
504	**Rufous-breasted Chat-Tyrant** *Ochthoeca rufipectoralis*	7	*obfuscata* (Ec, Co: C & W Andes) *poliogastra* (Co: Sta Marta) *rubicunda* (Perijá: Co & Ve) *rufopectus* (N Co: E Andes)	Te-P		▓	▓	▓					
505	**Brown-backed Chat-Tyrant** *Ochthoeca fumicolor*	5	*brunneifrons* (Ec, S Co: C & W Andes) *ferruginea* (N Co: C & W Andes) *fumicolor* (N Co: E Andes, Ve: Táchira) *superciliosa* (Ve: Andes)	Te-P		▓	▓	▓					
506	**White-browed Chat-Tyrant** *Ochthoeca leucophrys*	6	*dissors* (extreme S Ec?)	UT-P	Sight records in Ec: RG&G.	?							
507	**Drab Water-Tyrant** *Ochthornis littoralis*	M	(Ec, S Co, S Ve, Gu, FG)			▓	▓	▓			▓		▓
508	**Red-rumped Bush-Tyrant** *Cnemarchus erythropygius*	2	*erythropygius* (Ec, S Co) *orimonus* (N Co)	Te-P	Formerly *Myotheretes*	▓	▓						
509	**Streak-throated Bush-Tyrant** *Myiotheretes striaticollis*	2	*striaticollis* (Ec, Co, W Ve)	S-P		▓	▓	▓					
510	**Santa Marta Bush-Tyrant** *Myiotheretes pernix*	M	(Co: Sta Marta)	Te	**Endemic**		▓						
511	**Smoky Bush-Tyrant** *Myiotheretes fumigatus*	4	*cajamarcae* (S Ec) *fumigatus* (N Ec, Co) *lugubris* (W Ve: Andes) *olivaceus* (Perijá: Co & Ve)	S-P		▓	▓	▓					
512	**Grey Monjita** *Xolmis cinerea*	2	*cinerea* (Su)	T								▓	
513	**Black-billed Shrike-Tyrant** *Agriornis montana*	6	*solitaria* (Ec, S Co)	S-P		▓	▓						
514	**White-tailed Shrike-Tyrant** *Agriornis andicola*	2	*andicola* (Ec)	P	*A. albicauda* synonymous with *A. andicola*.	▓							
515	**Spot-billed Ground-Tyrant** *Muscisaxicola maculirostris*	3	*niceforoi* (N Co: E Andes) *rufescens* (Ec)	Te		▓	▓						
516	**Dark-faced Ground-Tyrant** *Muscisaxicola macloviana*	2	*mentalis* (austral migrant: vagrant to Ec)	T	Sight records in Ec: SFP&M, RG&G.	?							
517	**Little Ground-Tyrant** *Muscisaxicola fluviatilis*	M	(Extreme SE Co, E Ec)	T	Sight records in Ec & Co: SFP&M.	?	?						
518	**White-browed Ground-Tyrant** *Muscisaxicola albilora*	M	(Austral migrant: winters to S Ec)	P	Recorded in Co: Ortiz-Von Halle 1990.	▓	▓						
519	**Plain-capped Ground-Tyrant** *Muscisaxicola alpina*	4	*alpina* (N Ec) *columbiana* (N Co: C Andes) *quesadae* (C Co: C Andes)	P		▓	▓						
520	**Short-tailed Field-Tyrant** *Muscigralla brevicauda*	M	(S Ec, Co)	T	Recorded in Co: Ortiz-Von Halle 1990.	▓	▓						
521	**Amazonian Black-Tyrant** *Knipolegus poecilocercus*	M	(Ec, Co, S Ve, Gu)	T		▓	▓	▓			▓		
522	**Rufous-tailed Tyrant** *Knipolegus poecilurus*	5	*paraquensis* (S Ve: Paraque) *peruanus* (SE Ec) *poecilurus* (Co) *salvini* (S Ve) *venezuelanus* (W&N Ve)	T-Te		▓	▓	▓					

No.	Species	Ssp. Total	Subspecies in Northern South America	Altitude Range	References and Comments	Ec	Co	Ve	Ar Cu Bo	Tr To	Gu	Su	F
1523	**Riverside Tyrant** *Knipolegus orenocensis*	3	orenocensis (Co: Meta, C Ve) sclateri (E Ec)	T									
1524	**Pied Water-Tyrant** *Fluvicola pica*	2	pica (Co, Ve, Tr, Gu, Su, FG)	T	Sight records in Ec: RG&G.								
1525	**Masked Water-Tyrant** *Fluvicola nengeta*	2	atripennis (SW Ec)	T									
1526	**White-headed Marsh-Tyrant** *Arundinicola leucocephala*	M	(N&E Co, N&C Ve, Tr, Gu, Su, FG)	T	Formerly *Fluvicola*. Sight records in Ec: RG&G.								
1527	**Yellow-browed Tyrant** *Satrapa icterophrys*	M	(Austral migrant: winters to Co, Ve)	T-S									
1528	**Long-tailed Tyrant** *Colonia colonus*	5	fuscicapillus (N Ec, Co: E Andes) leuconotus (NW Ec, W Co) poecilonotus S Ve, Gu, Su, FG)	T-S									
1529	**Cattle Tyrant** *Machetornis rixosus*	3	flavigularis (N Co, N&C Ve) obscurodorsalis (E Co, SW Ve)	T									
1530	**Rufous-tailed Attila** *Attila phoenicurus*	M	(S Ve)	T-S									
1531	**Cinnamon Attila** *Attila cinnamomeus*	M	(E Ec, SE Co, E Ve, Gu, Su, FG)	T									
1532	**Ochraceous Attila** *Attila torridus*	M	(W Ec, SW Co)	T									
1533	**Citron-bellied Attila** *Attila citriniventris*	M	(E Ec, SE Co, S Ve)	T									
1534	**Dull-capped Attila** *Attila bolivianus*	2	nattereri (extreme SE Co)	T	Sight records in Ec: RG&G.								
1535	**Bright-rumped Attila** *Attila spadiceus*	12	caniceps (N Co) parambae (NW Ec, W Co) parvirostris (NE Co, NW Ve) sclateri (NW Co) spadiceus (S Co, C&E Ve, Gu, Su, FG)	L-T									
1536	**Rufous Mourner** *Rhytipterna holerythra*	2	rosenbergi (NW Ec, W Co)	T									
1537	**Greyish Mourner** *Rhytipterna simplex*	2	frederici (E Co, Gu, Su, FG)	T									
1538	**Pale-bellied Mourner** *Rhytipterna immunda*	M	(E Co, Su, FG)	T									
1539	**Speckled Mourner** *Laniocera rufescens*	3	griseigula (N Co) rufescens (NW Co: Chocó) tertia (NW Ec, SW Co)	T									
1540	**Cinereous Mourner** *Laniocera hypopyrra*	M	(E Ec, E Co, S Ve, Gu, Su, FG)	T									
1541	**Sirystes** *Sirystes sibilator*	5	albocinereus (E Ec, E Co) albogriseus (NW Co: Chocó)	T									
1542	**Rufous Flycatcher** *Myiarchus semirufus*	M	(S Ec?)	T	Lanyon 1978 Recorded in Ec: A&S.	?							
1543	**Dusky-capped Flycatcher** *Myiarchus tuberculifer*	12	atriceps (S Ec) brunneiceps (W Co) nigriceps (W Ec, SW Co) pallidus (N Co, N&WC Ve) tuberculifer (E Ec, E Co, S Ve, Gu, Su, FG)	T-P									

80

No.	Species	Ssp. Total	Subspecies in Northern South America	Altitude Range	References and Comments	Ec	Co	Ve	Ar Cu Bo	Tr To	Gu	Su	FG
1544	**Swainson's Flycatcher** *Myiarchus swainsoni*	4	*amazonus* (Su, FG) *fumosus* (SE Ve) *pelzelni* & *ferocior* (austral migrants to SE Co) *phaeonotus* (E&S Ve, S Gu) *swainsoni* (austral migrant to E Co, N Ve, Tr)	T-S	*amazonus, fumosus* and *phaeonotus* may be a sep. sp. (Whitely's Flycatcher, *M. phaeonotus*); *pelzelni* and *ferocior* may be a sep. sp. (Pelzeln's Flycatcher): S&M.								
1545	**Venezuelan Flycatcher** *Myiarchus venezuelensis*	M	(NE Co, NW Ve, To)	T									
1546	**Panama Flycatcher** *Myiarchus panamensis*	2	*panamensis* (W,C&N Co, NW Ve)	T									
1547	**Short-crested Flycatcher** *Myiarchus ferox*	3	*brunnescens* (Llanos: Ve & Co) *ferox* (E Ec, E Co, S Ve, Gu, Su, FG)	T	Lanyon 1978								
1548	**Pale-edged Flycatcher** *Myiarchus cephalotes*	2	*caribbaeus* (N Ve) *cephalotes* (C&S Co, E Ec)	T-P									
1549	**Sooty-crowned Flycatcher** *Myiarchus phaeocephalus*	2	*phaeocephalus* (W Ec)	T-S									
1550	**Apical Flycatcher** *Myiarchus apicalis*	M	(C&W Co)	T-Te	Endemic								
1551	**Great Crested Flycatcher** *Myiarchus crinitus*	M	(Boreal migrant: winters to Co & Ve)	T	Sight records in Ec: RG&G.	?							
1552	**Brown-crested Flycatcher** *Myiarchus tyrannulus*	6	*tyrannulus* (N&E Co, N Ve, Tr, To, Gu, Su, FG)	T-S	In Peters, ssp. *blanquillae* (Ve: Blanquilla), *tobagensis* (To) & *brevipennis* (Ar, Cu, Bo) are all synonyms of *tyrannulus*.								
1553	**Snowy-throated Kingbird** *Tyrannus niveigularis*	M	(SW Co, W Ec)	T									
1554	**White-throated Kingbird** *Tyrannus albogularis*	M	(NE Ve, Gu, Su, FG)	T	Sight records in Ec: RG&G.	?							
1555	**Tropical Kingbird** *Tyrannus melancholicus*	3	*melancholicus* (Ec, Co, Ve, Gu, Su, FG) *satrapa* (N Co, Ve, Tr, To)	T-S									
1556	**Scissor-tailed Flycatcher** *Tyrannus forficatus*	M	(Boreal migrant: winter vagrant to N S. Am.?)	T-S	Sight records in Ec: RG&G.	?							
1557	**Fork-tailed Flycatcher** *Tyrannus savanna*	4	*monachus* (N&C Co, Ve, Su) *sanctaemartae* (NE Co, NW Ve) *savana* (austral migrant: winters to E Co, Ve, Tr, To, Gu, Su, FG)	T-S									
1558	**Eastern Kingbird** *Tyrannus tyrannus*	M	(Boreal migrant: winters to Andes of Ec, Co & occasionally Ve)	T									
1559	**Grey Kingbird** *Tyrannus dominicensis*	2	*dominicensis* (boreal migrant: winters to N&W Co, Cu, Bo, N Ve, Marg, Tr, To) *vorax* (trans-Caribbean migrant: Tr, Gu, Su, FG in winter)	T	Sight records in Ec: RG&G.	?							
1560	**Variegated Flycatcher** *Empidonomus varius*	2	*rufinus* (WC,S&E Ve, Gu, Su, FG) *varius* (austral migrant: winters to E Co, N Ve, Gu, Su, FG)	T									

81

No.	Species	Ssp. Total	Subspecies in Northern South America	Altitude Range	References and Comments	Ec	Co	Ve	Ar Cu Bo	Tr To	Gu	Su	FG
1561	**Crowned Slaty Flycatcher** *Griseo-tyrannus aurantioatrocristatus*	2	*pallidiventris* (austral migrant: winters to E Ec, SE Co, S Ve)	T-S									
1562	**Sulphury Flycatcher** *Tyrannopsis sulphurea*	M	(E Ec, SE Co, S&E Ve, Gu, Su, FG)	T									
1563	**Boat-billed Flycatcher** *Megarhynchus pitangua*	6	*chrysogaster* (W Ec) *mexicanus* (NW Co) *pitangua* (E Ec, C&E Co, Ve, Gu, Su, FG)	T-S									
1564	**White-ringed Flycatcher** *Conopias albovittata*	M ?	(NW Ec, W Co)	T	Formerly *C. parva albovittata*: S&M.								
1565	**Yellow-throated Flycatcher** *Conopias parva*	2	*parva* (S Ve, Gu, Su, FG)	T									
1566	**Three-striped Flycatcher** *Conopias trivirgata*	2	*berlepschi* (S Ve)	T									
1567	**Lemon-browed Flycatcher** *Conopias cinchoneti*	2	*cinchoneti* (E Ec) *icterophrys* (Co: Andes, Ve: Perijá)	T-S									
1568	**Golden-crowned Flycatcher** *Myiodynastes chrysocephalus*	3	*cinerascens* (Co: Sta Marta, W Ve) *minor* (Ec, Co)	T-Te									
1569	**Baird's Flycatcher** *Myiodynastes bairdii*	M	(CW Ec)	T									
1570	**Streaked Flycatcher** *Myiodynastes maculatus*	7	*chapmani* (W Ec, W Co) *difficilis* (NW Co, W Ve) *insolens* (boreal migrant: winters to N S.Am.: NW Co?) *maculatus* (Su, FG) *nobilis* (NE Co) *solitarius* (austral migrant: winters to Co, Ve , Gu, Su, FG) *tobagensis* (C&E Ve, Tr, To, Gu)	T-S	*solitarius* may be a sep. sp. (Solitary Flycatcher): S&M.								
1571	**Sulphur-bellied Flycatcher** *Myiodynastes luteiventris*	M	(Boreal migrant: winters to Ec, Co)	T-S									
1572	**Rusty-margined Flycatcher** *Myiozetetes cayanensis*	4	*cayanensis* (S Ve, Gu, Su, FG) *hellmayri* (W Ec, W&C Co, W Ve) *rufipennis* (E Ec, E Co, N&C Ve)	T-S									
1573	**Social Flycatcher** *Myiozetetes similis*	7	*columbianus* (N Co, N&C Ve) *grandis* (W Ec) *similis* (E Ec, E Co, S&SW Ve)	T									
1574	**Grey-capped Flycatcher** *Myiozetetes granadensis*	3	*obscurior* (E Ec, E Co, CS Ve) *occidentalis* (W Ec, W Co)	T									
1575	**Dusky-chested Flycatcher** *Myiozetetes luteiventris*	2	*luteiventris* (SE Co, S Ve) *septentrionalis* (Su)	T									
1576	**Piratic Flycatcher** *Legatus leucophaius*	2	*leucophaius* (NW&E Ec, Co, Ve, Gu, Su, FG)	T									
1577	**Lesser Kiskadee** *Pitangus lictor*	2	*lictor* (Ve, Gu, Su, FG) *panamensis* (N Co)	T									

No.	Species	Ssp. Total	Subspecies in Northern South America	Altitude Range	References and Comments	Ec	Co	Ve	Ar Cu Bo	Tr To	Gu	Su	FG
578	Great Kiskadee *Pitangus sulphuratus*	10	*caucensis* (W&S Co) *rufipennis* (N Co, N&C Ve) *sulphuratus* (SE Co, Gu, Su, FG) *trinitatis* (E Co: Meta, E Ve, Tr)	T-S									
579	White-bearded Flycatcher *Phelpsia inornata*	M	(C Ve, CE Co)	LT	Formerly *Myiozetetes* or *Conopius*: Lanyon 1984								
580	Xenopsaris *Xenopsaris albinucha*	2	*minor* (C Ve)	T									
581	Green-backed Becard *Pachyramphus viridis*	2	*griseigularis* (SE Ve, W Gu)	T-S									
582	Yellow-cheeked Becard *Pachyramphus xanthogenys*	2	*xanthogenys* (E Ec)	T-S	Formerly *P. viridis xanthogenys*: R&T 1994.								
583	Barred Becard *Pachyramphus versicolor*	3	*meridionalis* (S Ec) *versicolor* (N&C Ec, Co: E & C Andes, W Ve)	S-P									
584	Cinnamon Becard *Pachyramphus cinnamomeus*	4	*badius* (Ve: Tachira) *cinnamomeus* (W Ec, W&NW Co) *magdalenae* (N Co, W Ve)	T									
585	Chestnut-crowned Becard *Pachyramphus castaneus*	5	*intermedius* (N Ve) *parui* (S Ve) *saturatus* (E Ec, SE Co)	T-S									
586	White-winged Becard *Pachyramphus polychopterus*	8	*cinereiventris* (N Co) *dorsalis* (NW Ec, C&SW Co) *nigriventris* (CE Co, S Ve) *similis* (NW Co) *tenebrosus* (E Ec, SE Co) *tristis* (NE Co, Ve, Tr, To, Gu, Su, FG)	T									
587	Black-and-white Becard *Pachyramphus albogriseus*	5	*albogriseus* (Co: E Andes, W&N Ve) *coronatus* (N Co, NW Ve) *guayaquilensis* (W Ec) *salvini* (E Ec)	T-S									
588	Black-capped Becard *Pachyramphus marginatus*	2	*nanus* (E Ec, E Co, Ve, Gu, Su, FG)	T									
589	Glossy-backed Becard *Pachyramphus surinamus*	M	(Su, FG)	T									
590	Cinereous Becard *Pachyramphus rufus*	2	*rufus* (N Co, Ve, Gu, Su, FG)	T									
591	Slaty Becard *Pachyramphus spodiurus*	M	(W Ec, SW Co)	T									
592	One-colored Becard *Pachyramphus homochrous*	3	*canescens* (NE Co, NW Ve) *homochrous* (W Ec, W Co) *quimarinus* (NW Co)	T									
593	Pink-throated Becard *Pachyramphus minor*	M	(E Ec, SE Co, CS Ve, Gu, Su, FG)	T									
594	Black-tailed Tityra *Tityra cayana*	2	*cayana* (E Ec, E Co, Ve, Tr, Gu, Su, FG)	LT									
595	Masked Tityra *Tityra semifasciata*	8	*columbiana* (N Co, NW&N Ve) *fortis* (E Ec, SE Co) *nigriceps* (NW Ec, SW Co)	T									

No.	Species	Ssp. Total	Subspecies in Northern South America	Altitude Range	References and Comments	Ec	Co	Ve	Ar Cu Bo	Tr To	Gu	Su	F
1596	**Black-crowned Tityra** *Tityra inquisitor*	6	*albitorques* (W Ec, N&W Co) *buckleyi* (NE Ec, SE Co) *erythogenys* (E Co, N&C Ve, Gu, Su, FG)	T									
1597	**Greater Schiffornis** *Schiffornis major*	2	*duidae* (S Ve) *major* (SE Co)	T	Formerly Greater Manakin								
1598	**Thrush-like Schiffornis** *Schiffornis turdinus*	13 ?	*acrolophites* (NW Co) *aeneus* (E Ec) *amazonus* (E Ec, SE Co, S Ve) *olivaceus* (SE Ve, Gu) *panamensis* (NW Co) *rosenbergi* (W Ec, W Co) *stenorhynchus* (NE Co, W&NC Ve) *wallacii* (Su, FG)	T	Formerly Thrush-like Manakin								
1599	**Crimson-hooded Manakin** *Pipra aureola*	4	*aureola* (E&SE Ve, Gu, Su, FG)	T									
1600	**Wire-tailed Manakin** *Pipra filicauda*	2	*filicauda* (E Ec, SE Co, S Ve) *subpallida* (Co: E Andes, W&NC Ve)	T									
1601	**Red-capped Manakin** *Pipra mentalis*	3	*minor* (NW Ec, W Co)	T									
1602	**Golden-headed Manakin** *Pipra erythrocephala*	3	*berlepschi* (E Ec, SE Co) *erythrocephala* (N Co, Ve, Tr, Gu, Su, FG) *flammiceps* (E Co)	T									
1603	**Scarlet-horned Manakin** *Pipra cornuta*	M	(S Ve, S Gu)	UT-S									
1604	**White-crowned Manakin** *Pipra pipra*	13	*bolivari* (NW Co) *coracina* (E Ec, Co: E Andes, NW Ve) *minimus* (S Co: W Andes) *pipra* (E Co, S&E Ve, Gu, Su, FG) *unica* (NC&S Co)	T-S									
1605	**Blue-crowned Manakin** *Pipra coronata*	8	*caquetae* (SE Co) *carbonata* (C&SE Co, S Ve) *coronata* (E Ec) *minuscula* (W&NC Co, NW Ec)	T	Formerly sometimes *Lepidothrix*								
1606	**Blue-rumped Manakin** *Pipra isidorei*	2	*isidorei* (E Ec, Co: E Andes)	UT-LS									
1607	**White-fronted Manakin** *Lepidothrix serena*	M	(Su, FG)	LT									
1608	**Tepui Manakin** *Lepidothrix suavissima*	M	(E &SE Ve, Gu)	UT-LS	Formerly *L. serena suavissima:* Prum 1994								
1609	**Lance-tailed Manakin** *Chiroxiphia lanceolata*	M	(N&NE Co, N Ve)	T									
1610	**Blue-backed Manakin** *Chiroxiphia pareola*	5	*atlantica* (To) *napensis* (E Ec, SE Co) *pareola* (E Ve, Gu, Su, FG)	LT									
1611	**Golden-winged Manakin** *Masius chrysopterus*	5	*bellus* (WC Co: C Andes) *chrysopterus* (C&E Co, W Ve) *coronatus* (W Ec, SW Co) *pax* (E Ec, SE Co)	ST	Prum 1992								
1612	**White-throated Manakin** *Corapipo gutturalis*	M	(S Ve, Gu, Su, FG)	T	Prum 1992								

No.	Species	Ssp. Total	Subspecies in Northern South America	Altitude Range	References and Comments	Ec	Co	Ve	Ar Cu Bo	Tr To	Gu	Su	FG
1613	White-ruffed Manakin *Corapipo altera*	M	(NW Co)	T	Formerly *C. leucorrhoa altera*: Wetmore 1972.		▓						
1614	White-bibbed Manakin *Corapipo leucorrhoa*	2	leucorrhoa (C&E Co, W&NW Ve)	T	Prum 1992		▓	▓					
1615	Orange-collared Manakin *Manacus aurantiacus*	3	viridiventris (NW Co) milleri (N Co)	T	Formerly *M. manacus aurantiacus*: AOU 1998. viridiventris (and milleri) may be a sep. sp. (Greenish-bellied Manakin), or perhaps conspecific with *M. vitellinus*.		▓						
1616	Golden-collared Manakin *Manacus vitellinus*	2	vitellinus (NW Co)	T	Formerly *M. manacus vitellinus*: AOU 1998		▓						
1617	White-bearded Manakin *Manacus manacus*	15	abditivua (CN Co) bangsi (NW Ec, SW Co) flaveolus (CE Co) interior (E Ec, E Co, NW&SC Ve) leucochlamys (NW&W Ec) manacus (S Ve, Gu, Su, FG) maximus (SW Ec) trinitatis (Tr) umbrosus (Ve: C Amazonas)	T		▓	▓	▓		▓	▓	▓	▓
1618	Club-winged Manakin *Machaeropterus deliciosus*	M	(W Ec, SW Co)	T-LS		▓	▓						
1619	Striped Manakin *Machaeropterus regulus*	6	antioquiae (C&W Co) auropectus * (SE&SC Ve, Gu) obscurostriatus (W Ve: Marida) striolatus (E Ec, Co: E Andes) zulianus (NW Ve)	T-LS	*Recorded in Gu: Agro & Ridgely 1998	▓	▓	▓			▓		
1620	Fiery-capped Manakin *Machaeropterus pyrocephalus*	2	pallidiceps (SC Ve)	T				▓					
1621	Black Manakin *Xenopipo atronitens*	M	(SE Co, SC&SE Ve, Gu, Su, FG)	T			▓	▓			▓	▓	▓
1622	Jet Manakin *Chloropipo unicolor*	M	(S Ec)	UT-S		▓							
1623	Olive Manakin *Chloropipo uniformis*	2	duidae (S Ve) uniformis (SE Ve, W Gu)	UT-S				▓			▓		
1624	Green Manakin *Chloropipo holochlora*	4	holochlora (E Ec, SE Co) litae (NW Ec, W Co) suffusa (NW Co)	T	Merged into *Xenopipo* by Prum 1992.	▓	▓						
1625	Yellow-headed Manakin *Chloropipo flavicapilla*	M	(NE Ec, S Co: Andes)	S		▓	▓						
1626	Yellow-crowned Manakin *Heterocercus flavivertex*	M	(E Co, S Ve)	T			▓	▓					
1627	Orange-crowned Manakin *Heterocercus aurantiivertex*	M	(E Ec)	T		▓							
1628	Saffron-crested Tyrant-Manakin *Neopelma chrysocephalum*	M	(S Ve, Gu, Su, FG)	T				▓			▓	▓	▓
1629	Dwarf Tyrant-Manakin *Tyranneutes stolzmanni*	M	(E Co, S Ve)	T			▓	▓					
1630	Tiny Tyrant-Manakin *Tyranneutes virescens*	M	(E Ve, Gu)	T				▓			▓		▓

No.	Species	Ssp. Total	Subspecies in Northern South America	Altitude Range	References and Comments	Ec	Co	Ve	Ar Cu Bo	Tr To	Gu	Su	F
1631	**Wing-barred Manakin** *Piprites chloris*	7	*antioquiae* (NW Ec, Co: C Andes) *chlorion* (S&N Ve, Gu, Su, FG) *perijanus* (W Ve: Perija & Tachira) *tschudii* (E Ec, S Ve, SE Co)	T									
1632	**Broad-billed Manakin** *Sapayoa aenigma*	M	(NW Ec, W&N Co)	T									
1633	**Black-necked Red-Cotinga** *Phoenicircus nigricollis*	M	(E Ec, SE Co, S Ve)	LT									
1634	**Guianan Red-Cotinga** *Phoenicircus carnifex*	M	(E Ve, Gu, Su, FG)	LT									
1635	**Shrike-like Cotinga** *Laniisoma elegans*	4	*buckleyi* (E Ec, SE Co) *venezuelensis* (SW Ve, E Co)	T	Snow 1975								
1636	**Red-crested Cotinga** *Ampelion rubrocristatus*	M	(Ec, Co: Andes & Sta Marta, Ve)	S-Te									
1637	**Chestnut-crested Cotinga** *Ampelion rufaxilla*	2	*antioquiae* (Se Ec, C&SW Co)	S									
1638	**Chestnut-bellied Cotinga** *Doliornis remseni*	M	(E Ec, Co: S of C Andes)	P	Sp. nov.: Robbins *et al.* 1994. Formerly *Ampelion*. Sight records in Co: SFP&M **Vulnerable**								
1639	**Green-and-black Fruiteater** *Pipreola riefferii*	5	*confusa* (E Ec) *melanolaema* (N&NW Ve) *occidentalis* (SW Co: W & C Andes, W Ec) *riefferii* (C Co: E Andes, W Ve)	UT-Te									
1640	**Barred Fruiteater** *Pipreola arcuata*	2	*arcuata* (NW & E Ec, Co, NW Ve)	S-Te									
1641	**Golden-breasted Fruiteater** *Pipreola aureopectus*	4 ?	*aureopectus* (Co: E & C Andes, Ve: Perija & Andes) *decora* (Co: Sta Marta) *festiva* (Ve: N Range)	S									
1642	**Orange-breasted Fruiteater** *Pipreola jucunda*	M ?	(NW Ec, SW Co)	S	Formerly *P. aureopectus jucunda*								
1643	**Black-chested Fruiteater** *Pipreola lubomirskii*	M ?	(E Ec, SE Co)	S	Formerly *P. aureopectus lubomirskii*								
1644	**Fiery-throated Fruiteater** *Pipreola chlorolepidota*	M	(E Ec, Co)	UT									
1645	**Scarlet-breasted Fruiteater** *Pipreola frontalis*	2	*squamipectus* (SE Ec)	S									
1646	**Handsome Fruiteater** *Pipreola formosa*	3	*formosa* (CN Ve) *pariae* (NE Ve: Paria) *rubidior* (NE Ve: Turimiquire)	S	**Endemic**								
1647	**Red-banded Fruiteater** *Pipreola whitleyi*	2	*kathleenae* (SE Ve: Ptaritepui) *whitelyi* (SE Ve: Roraima, W Gu)	S									
1648	**Scaled Fruiteater** *Ampelioides tschudii*	M	(Ec, Co, NW Ve)	UT-S									
1649	**Buff-throated Purpletuft** *Iodopleura pipra*	2	*leucopygia* (Gu)	T	Uncertain in Gu: SFP&M						?		

No.	Species	Ssp. Total	Subspecies in Northern South America	Altitude Range	References and Comments	Ec	Co	Ve	Ar Cu Bo	Tr To	Gu	Su	FG
1650	White-browed Purpletuft *Iodopleura isabellae*	2	*isabellae* (E Ec, SE Co, S Ve)	T									
1651	Dusky Purpletuft *Iodopleura fusca*	M	(SE Ve, Gu, Su, FG)	T									
1652	Grey-tailed Piha *Lipaugus subalaris*	M	(NE Ec, Co)	T									
1653	Olivaceous Piha *Lipaugus cryptolophus*	2	*cryptolophus* (E Ec, S Co) *mindoensis* (SW Co)	UT-S									
1654	Dusky Piha *Lipaugus fuscocinereus*	M	(E Ec, Co: C & E Andes)	S-Te									
1655	Screaming Piha *Lipaugus vociferans*	M	(E Ec, SE Co, S&E Ve, Gu, Su, FG)	T									
1656	Rufous Piha *Lipaugus unirufus*	2	*castaneotinctus* (NW Ec, SW Co) *unirufus* (N&C Co)	T									
1657	Rose-collared Piha *Lipaugus streptophorus*	M	(SE Ve, Gu)	S									
1658	Purple-throated Cotinga *Porphyrolaema porphyrolaema*	M	(E Ec, S Co)	T									
1659	Blue Cotinga *Cotinga nattererii*	M	(NW Ec, W&NC Co, W Ve)	T									
1660	Plum-throated Cotinga *Cotinga maynana*	M	(E Ec, S Co)	T									
1661	Purple-breasted Cotinga *Cotinga cotinga*	M	(SE Co, S Ve, Gu, Su, FG)	T									
1662	Spangled Cotinga *Cotinga cayanna*	M	(E Ec, E Co, S Ve, Gu, Su, FG)	T									
1663	Pompadour Cotinga *Xipholena punicea*	M	(E Ec, E Co, S Ve, Gu, Su, FG)	T-LS									
1664	Black-tipped Cotinga *Carpodectes hopkei*	M	(NW Ec, W Co)	T									
1665	Bare-necked Fruitcrow *Gymnoderus foetidus*	M	(E Ec, E Co, S Ve, Gu, Su, FG)	T									
1666	Crimson Fruitcrow *Haematoderus militaris*	M		T				?					
1667	Purple-throated Fruitcrow *Querula purpurata*	M	(NW&E Ec, Co, Ve: Bolivar, Gu, Su, FG)	T									
1668	Red-ruffed Fruitcrow *Pyroderus scutatus*	5	*granadensis* (Co: E&C Andes, W&N Ve) *occidentalis* (Co: W Andes) *orenocensis* (E Ve, N Gu)	UT-LS									
1669	Long-wattled Umbrellabird *Cephalopterus penduliger*	M	(W Ec, Co: W Andes)	UT-S	Vulnerable								
1670	Amazonian Umbrellabird *Cephalopterus ornatus*	M	(E Ec, Co: E Andes, SC Ve, S Gu)	T									
1671	Capuchinbird *Perissocephalus tricolor*	M	(S&SE Ve, Gu, Su, FG)	T-LS	Sight records in Co: SFP&M.		?						
1672	White Bellbird *Procnias alba*	M	(SE Ve, Gu, Su, FG)	T									
1673	Bearded Bellbird *Procnias averano*	2	*carbonara* (NE Co: Perija, Ve: all mountain ranges)	UT-S									
1674	Guianan Cock-of-the-Rock *Rupicola rupicola*	M	(E Co, S Ve, Gu, Su, FG)	T-S									
1675	Andean Cock-of-the-Rock *Rupicola peruviana*	4	*aequatorialis* (E Ec, Co: C & E Andes, Ve: Andes) *sanguinolenta* (NW Ec, Co)	UT-S									
1676	Sharpbill *Oxyruncus cristatus*	7?	*hypoglaucus* (Ve, Gu) *phelpsi* (Ve: Bolivar & N Amazonas, Gu: Acary)	UT-S	Sight records in Ec: RG&G.	?							

87

No.	Species	Ssp. Total	Subspecies in Northern South America	Altitude Range	References and Comments	Ec	Co	Ve	Ar Cu Bo	Tr To	Gu	Su	FG
1677	**Horned Lark** *Eremophila alpestris*	40	*peregrina* (Co: savanna of Bogota)	T-P									
1678	**Tree Swallow** *Tachycineta bicolor*	M	(Boreal migrant; winters occasionally Co, Ve, Tr, Gu)	T-P							?		?
1679	**Mangrove Swallow** *Tachycineta albilinea*	2	*albilinea* (Co) *stolzmanni* (S Ec)	LT	Sight records in Co & Su: Gochfeld *et al.* 1980. *stolzmanni* maybe a sep. sp.: RG&G.		?					?	
1680	**White-winged Swallow** *Tachycineta albiventer*	M	(E Ec, N Co, Ve, Tr, Gu, Su, FG)	LT				?					
1681	**Chilean Swallow** *Tachycineta meyeni*	M	(Austral migrant: occasional record Tr, To, Ar, Cu, Bo?)	T-LS	Formerly *T. leucopyga*: Turner & Rose 1989				?	?			
1682	**Violet-green Swallow** *Tachycineta thalassina*	3	Subspecies uncertain: *thalassina*, *lepida* or *brachyptera*?	T-Te	Sight records in Co: H&B, SFP&M.		?						
1683	**Brown-chested Martin** *Progne tapera*	2	*tapera* (resident: S Ec, N&E Co, Ve, Gu, Su, FG) *fusca* (austral migrant: winters to N&E Co, Ve, Gu, Su, FG)	T-LS									
1684	**Purple Martin** *Progne subis*	3	*subis* (boreal migrant: winters to Co, Ve) *hesperia* & *arboricola* (boreal migrants: in transit through N S.Am.?)	T-P	Sight records in Ec: RG&G.	?							
1685	**Caribbean Martin** *Progne dominicensis*	M	(Resident in To & also boreal winter migrant: in transit through N S.Am.?)	T	Sight records in Gu: SFP&M.		?	?			?		
1686	**Sinaloa Martin** *Progne sinaloae*	M	(Boreal migrant: winter range unknown. N S.Am.?)		Sometimes considered conspecific with *subis* and *dominicensis*: AOU 1998.	?	?	?					
1687	**Cuban Martin** *Progne cryptoleuca*	M	(Boreal winter range unknown; apparently transient in N S.Am.)	T	Variously treated as a sep. sp. or a ssp of *P. dominicensis* or *P. subis*: AOU 1998.								
1688	**Grey-breasted Martin** *Progne chalybea*	2	*chalybea* (resident: Ec, Co, Ve, Tr, Gu, Su, FG) *macrorhamphus* (austral migrant: winters to Ve, Cu, Su)	T-LS	*domestica* synonymous with *macrorhamphus*: Brooke 1974								
1689	**Southern Martin** *Progne modesta*	3	*elegans* (austral migrant: winters to Co, Su)	T-LS	Sight records in Ec: RG&G.								
1690	**Brown-bellied Swallow** *Notiochelidon murina*	3	*murina* (Co, Ec), *meridensis* (W Ve)	Te-P									
1691	**Blue-and-white Swallow** *Notiochelidon cyanoleuca*	3	*cyanoleuca* (resident: Ec, Co, Ve, Tr, Gu) *patagonica* (austral migrant: winters to Ec, E Co, N Ve)	T-P									
1692	**Pale-footed Swallow** *Notiochelidon flavipes*	M	(E Ec, Co: C Andes, W Ve)	US-P		?							
1693	**White-banded Swallow** *Atticora fasciata*	M	(E Ec, SE Co, S Ve, Gu, Su, FG)	T	Zimmer 1955.								
1694	**Black-collared Swallow** *Atticora melanoleuca*	M	(SE Co, S Ve, Gu, Su, FG)	LT									
1695	**White-thighed Swallow** *Neochelidon tibialis*	3	*minima* (W&C Co, W Ec) *griseiventris* (E Ec, S Co, SE Ve, Su, FG)	T									
1696	**Tawny-headed Swallow** *Stelgidopteryx fucata*	M	(N&SE Ve, E Co)	T-LS	Formerly *Alopochelidon*								

No.	Species	Ssp. Total	Subspecies in Northern South America	Altitude Range	References and Comments	Ec	Co	Ve	Ar Cu Bo	Tr To	Gu	Su	FG
1697	**Northern Rough-winged Swallow** *Stelgidopteryx serripennis*	4	*ridgwayi* & *stuarti* (boreal migrants: winter regularly in West Indies, vagrant to Ar/Cu/Bo) *psammochrous* (boreal migrant: possibly to Co)	T-Te	Formerly *S. ruficollis serripennis*: Stiles 1981. Turner & Rose 1989		?						
1698	**Southern Rough-winged Swallow** *Stelgidopteryx ruficollis*	4	*ruficollis* * (SE Co, E Ec, SE Ve, Gu, Su, FG) *uropygialis* (W&C Co, W Ec) *aequalis* (N Co, Ve, Tr)	T-S	* Austral migrant *ruficollis* collected in Su, Co: Turner & Rose 1989.								
1699	**Sand Martin** *Riparia riparia*	4	*riparia* (boreal migrant: in transit through N S.Am.)	LT									
1700	**Barn Swallow** *Hirundo rustica*	6	*erythrogaster* (boreal migrant: winters to all N S.Am.)	T-Te	Winter range of austral populations uncertain.								
1701	**Cliff Swallow** *Petrochelidon pyrrhonota*	4	*pyrrhonota* & *melanogaster* (boreal migrants: in transit through N S.Am.) *tachina* & *hypopolia* (boreal migrants: winter range not known)	T-Te	AOU 1998. Formerly *Hirundo*: Turner & Rose 1989.								
1702	**Cave Swallow** *Petrochelidon fulva*	8?	*aequatorialis* (resident: SW Ec) *cavicola*? (vagrant to Ar, Cu, Bo)	T-S	Garrido *et al.* 1999 separate the ssp. of *P. fulva* into 3 spp.: *pelodoma* (= *pallida*, Mex.) [Cave Swallow], *fulva* (with 5 ssp.) [Fulvous Swallow], and *rufocollaris* (including *aequatorialis*) [Chestnut-collared Swallow].								
1703	**White Wagtail** *Motacilla alba*		(Boreal migrant: winter vagrant to Tr)		Recorded in Trinidad: SFP&M								
1704	**Paramo Pipit** *Anthus bogotensis*	4	*bogotensis* (Ec, Co: E & C Andes, Nariño) *meridae* (Ve: Andes)	Te-P									
1705	**Yellowish Pipit** *Anthus lutescens*	3	*lutescens* (E Co, C,E&SE Ve, Gu, Su, FG)	T									
1706	**Cedar Waxwing** *Bombycilla cedrorum*	M	(Boreal migrant: winters irregularly to Co, Ve)	T-S									
1707	**Grey Catbird** *Dumetella carolinensis*	M	(Boreal migrant: winters irregularly to Co)	T-S									
1708	**Tropical Mockingbird** *Mimus gilvus*	10	*gilvus* (Su, FG) *melanopterus* (NE&E Co, Ve, Gu) *rostratus* (Ar, Cu, Ve: Marg, Orchila, Tortuga, Blanquilla, Hermanos, Testigos) *tobagensis* (Tr, To) *tolimensis* (W&C Co)	T-Te									
1709	**Chalk-browed Mockingbird** *Mimus saturninus*	4	*saturninus* (S Su)	T-Te									
1710	**Long-tailed Mockingbird** *Mimus longicaudatus*	4	*albogriseus* (SW Ec) *platensis* (Ec: Plata Is.)	T-S									
1711	**Brown Thrasher** *Toxostoma rufum*	2	Ssp. uncertain: *rufum* or *longicauda*? (boreal migrants: may winter occasionally to Cu)	T	Accidental in Cu: AOU 1998.								
1712	**Pearly-eyed Thrasher** *Margarops fuscatus*	4	*bonairensis* (Bo, Ve: Los Hermanos Arch.)	T	Garrido & Remsen 1996								

No.	Species	Ssp. Total	Subspecies in Northern South America	Altitude Range	References and Comments	Ec	Co	Ve	Ar Cu Bo	Tr To	Gu	Su	FG
1713	White-capped Dipper *Cinclus leucocephalus*	4	*leuconotus* (Andes of Ec, Co & Ve) *rivularis* (Co: Sta Marta)	T-P		■	■	■					
1714	Varied Solitaire *Myadestes coloratus*	M	(NW Co)	UT-S			■						
1715	Andean Solitaire *Myadestes ralloides*	5	*candelae* (C Co) *plumbeiceps* (Co: W&C Andes, W Ec) *venezuelensis* (Co: E Andes, N Ve, E Ec)	UT-Te		■	■	■					
1716	Rufous-brown Solitaire *Cichlopsis leucogenys*	4	*chubbi* (W Ec, Co) *gularis* (SE Ve, Gu)	T	Formerly *Myadestes*. Sight records in Su: SFP&M.	■	■	■			■	?	
1717	Black Solitaire *Entomodestes coracinus*	M	(W Co, W Ec)	T-LS		■	■						
1718	Orange-billed Nightingale-Thrush *Catharus aurantiirostris*	13	*aurantiirostris* (E Co, N&SW Ve) *barbaritoi* (Ve: Perija) *birchalli* (NE Ve, Tri) *inornatus* (Co: E Andes) *insignis* (C Co) *phaeopleurus* (W Co)	T-S			■	■		■			
1719	Spotted Nightingale-Thrush *Catharus dryas*	4	*dryas* (W Ec) *ecuadoreanus* (W Ec: Andes) *maculatus* (E Co, E Ec)	T-S		■	■						
1720	Slaty-backed Nightingale-Thrush *Catharus fuscater*	7	*fuscater* (Co: E Andes, Ve: Andes, Ec) *opertaneus* (Co: W Andes) *sanctamartae* (N Co)	UT-Te		■	■	■					
1721	Veery *Catharus fuscescens*	4	*fuscescens* (winters Co, Ve, Gu) *subpallidus* (winters ?) *fuliginosa* (winters S.Am.?) *salicicola* (winters Co, Ve)	T	Sight records in FG: SFP&M.		■	■			■		?
1722	Grey-cheeked Thrush *Catharus minimus*	M*	(Boreal migrant: winters Ec, Co, Ve, Gu)	T	* Bicknell's Thrush *C. bicknelli*, formerly ssp. of *C. minimus* (Ouellet 1993), not recorded in N. S.Am. Sight records in Su: SFP&M.	■	■	■			■	?	
1723	Swainson's Thrush *Catharus ustulatus*	5	*swainsoni* (winters in Ec, Co, Ve)	T-Te		■	■	■					
1724	Wood Thrush *Hylocichla mustelina*	M	(Migrant: winters Co)	T	Formerly *Catharus*		■						
1725	Yellow-legged Thrush *Platycichla flavipes*	5	*venezuelensis* (Co, Ve) *xanthoscelus* (To) *melanopleura* (NE Ve, Tr) *polionota* (S Ve, Gu)	T-Te			■	■		■	■		
1726	Pale-eyed Thrush *Platycichla leucops*	M		UT-S		■	■	■					
1727	Chiguanco Thrush *Turdus chiguanco*	3	*conradi* (S Ec)	UT-P		■							
1728	Great Thrush *Turdus fuscater*	7	*cacozelus* (N Co) *clarus* (Perija) *gigas* (Ve: Andes, Co: E Andes) *quindio* (Co: C & W Andes, Ec) *gigantoides* (S Ec)	S-P		■	■	■					

No.	Species	Ssp. Total	Subspecies in Northern South America	Altitude Range	References and Comments	Ec	Co	Ve	Ar Cu Bo	Tr To	Gu	Su	FG
1729	Glossy-black Thrush *Turdus serranus*	5	atrocericeus (N Ve, NE Co) cumanensis (NE Ve) fuscobrunneus (Co, Ec)	UT-Te									
1730	Andean Slaty-Thrush *Turdus nigriceps*	2	nigriceps (austral migrant: winters to SE Ec)	T-S	Uncertain in Ec: SFP&M.	?							
1731	Plumbeous-backed Thrush *Turdus reevei*	M	(W Ec)	T									
1732	Black-hooded Thrush *Turdus olivater*	7	caucae (Co: C Andes) duidae (Ve) kemptoni (Ve: Neblina) olivator (N Vo, N Co) paraquensis (S Ve) roraimae (Ve, Gu) sanctaemartae (Co)	UT-Te	Sight records in Su: SFP&M.							?	
1733	Marañón Thrush *Turdus maranonicus*	M	(SE Ec)	UT-S									
1734	Chestnut-bellied Thrush *Turdus fulviventris*	M	(Ve: Andes, Co: E Andes, Ec)	S-Te									
1735	Pale-breasted Thrush *Turdus leucomelas*	3	albiventer (Co, Ve, Gu, Su, FG) cantor (Co: Guajira)	T-LS									
1736	Black-billed Thrush *Turdus ignobilis*	5	arthuri (S Ve, Gu, FG) debilis (E Co, W Ve, E Ec) goodfellowi (W Co) ignobilis (E Co) murinus (S Ve, W Gu)	T-S									
1737	Lawrence's Thrush *Turdus lawrencei*	M	(S Ve, E Ec, SE Co)	LT									
1738	Pale-vented Thrush *Turdus obsoletus*	3	colombianus (Co: E slope of W Andes) obsoletus (NW Co) parambanus (W Co, W Ec)	T-LS	Formerly T. hauxwelli colombianus, T. fumigatus obsoletus & T. f. parambanus: Snow 1985.								
1739	Cocoa Thrush *Turdus fumigatus*	5	aquilonalis (Tr, N Ve, NE Co) fumigatus (Gu, Su, FG) orinocensis (S Ve, SE Co),	T-LS									
1740	Hauxwell's Thrush *Turdus hauxwelli*	M	(SE Co, S Ve)	LT									
1741	Clay colored Thrush *Turdus grayi*	6	casius (NW Co) incoptus (N Co)	T-Te									
1742	Bare-eyed Thrush *Turdus nudigenis*	2	nudigenis (Tr, To, Ve, Marg, Gu, Su, FG, E Co)	T-LS									
1743	Ecuadorean Thrush *Turdus maculirostris*	M	(W Ec)	T-LS	Formerly T. nudigenis maculirostris								
1744	Dagua Thrush *Turdus dague*	M	(SE Co, S Ve)	T-Te	Formerly T. assimilis dague								
1745	White-necked Thrush *Turdus albicollis*	5 ?	phaeopygoides (NE Co, N Ve, Tr, To) phaeopygus (E Co, S Ve, Gu, Su, FG) spodiolaemus (E Ec)	T-LS									
1746	Northern Wheatear *Oenanthe oenanthe*	6 ?	(Boreal migrant: winters to Ar, Cu, Bo)	T	Two or more ssp. possible, but no data on subspecific identity. AOU 1998								
1747	Black-capped Donacobius *Donacobius atricapillus*	4	atricapillus (Ve, Gu, Su, FG) brachypterus (N Co) nigrodorsalis (E Ec, SE Co)	T	Formerly considered a member of the family Mimidae.								

No.	Species	Ssp. Total	Subspecies in Northern South America	Altitude Range	References and Comments	Ec	Co	Ve	Ar Cu Bo	Tr To	Gu	Su	FG
1748	**Bicolored Wren** *Campylorhynchus griseus*	6	*albicilius* (N Co, NW Ve) *bicolor* (C Co) *griseus* (S&SE Ve, Gu) *minor* (CE Co, N Ve) *pallidus* (Ve: NE Amazonas)	T-S			▓	▓			▓		
1749	**Thrush-like Wren** *Campylorhynchus turdinus*	3 *	*hypostictus* (E Ec, E Co)	T	* Ssp. E of Andes (*hypostictus, turdinus & unicolor*) considered to be a sep. sp. from ssp. W of Andes (*C. albobrunneus*): Haffer 1975.	▓	▓						
1750	**White-headed Wren** *Campylorhynchus albobrunneus*	3	*aenigmaticus* * (SW Co) *harterti* (W Co)	T	Formerly *C. turdinus harterti* & *C. t. aenigmaticus.* * Possibly a hybrid population: *C. zonatus* x *C. a. albobrunneus*: Haffer 1975.		▓						
1751	**Black-backed Wren** *Campylorhynchus zonatus*	6	*brevirostris* (NW Ec, N Co) *curvirostris* (Co: Sta Marta)	T-S		▓	▓						
1752	**Stripe-backed Wren** *Campylorhynchus nuchalis*	3	*brevipennis* (N Ve) *nuchalis* (W,C&S Ve) *pardus* (N&C Co)	T			▓	▓					
1753	**Fasciated Wren** *Campylorhynchus fasciatus*	2	*pallescens* (SW Ec)	T-Te		▓							
1754	**Grey-mantled Wren** *Odontorchilus branickii*	2	*branickii* (S Co, E Ec) *minor* (N Ec)	UT-S		▓	▓						
1755	**Rufous Wren** *Cinnycerthia unirufa*	3	*chakei* (Perijá: Co, Ve) *unibrunnea* (Ec, Co) *unirufa* (C&N Co, Ve)	Te-P		▓	▓	▓					
1756	**Sharpe's Wren** *Cinnycerthia olivascens*	2	*bogotensis* (Co: E Andes) *olivascens* (Ec, Co: W & C Andes)	S-P	Brumfield & Remsen 1996	▓	▓						
1757	**Sedge Wren** *Cistothorus platensis*	16	*aequatorialis* (Ec, SW Co) *alticola* (Co: Sta Marta, N&SE Ve, E Gu) *tamae* (CE Co, Ve: Táchira) *tolimae* (C Co)	T-P		▓	▓	▓			▓		
1758	**Apolinar's Marsh-Wren** *Cistothorus apolinari*	M	(C Co)	US-P	**Endemic**		▓						
1759	**Paramo Wren** *Cistothorus meridae*	M	(Ve: Merida & Trujillo)	P	**Endemic**			▓					
1760	**Sooty-headed Wren** *Thryothorus spadix*	2	*spadix* (NW & C Co: W Andes)	T-LS	Formerly *T. atrogularis spadix*: Wetmore *et al.* 1984		▓						
1761	**Black-bellied Wren** *Thryothorus fasciatoventris*	3	*albigularis* (W Co: Chocó) *fasciatoventris* (N Co)	T			▓						
1762	**Plain-tailed Wren** *Thryothorus euophrys*	4	*euophrys* (W Ec, Co) *longipes* (E Ec, Co)	UT-P	Parker & O'Neill 1985	▓	▓						
1763	**Whiskered Wren** *Thryothorus mystacalis*	8	*amaurogaster* (NE&E Co) *consobrinus* (NW Ve) *macrurus* (CE Co: C & E Andes) *mystacalis* (Ec) *ruficaudatus* (NC Ve) *saltuensis* (W Co: W Andes) *tachirensis* (Ve: Táchira) *yananchae* (S Co: Nariño)	T-Te	Formerly *T. genibarbis*, now separated into 2 spp. – Andean ssp. are now *T. mystacalis*, while Amazonian ssp. remain *T. genibarbis* (Moustached Wren): R&T 1994.	▓	▓	▓					

No.	Species	Ssp. Total	Subspecies in Northern South America	Altitude Range	References and Comments	Ec	Co	Ve	Ar Cu Bo	Tr To	Gu	Su	FG
1764	**Coraya Wren** *Thryothorus coraya*	10	*barrowcloughiana* * (Ve: Roraima & Cuquenan) *caurensis* (E Co, S Ve) *coraya* (E Gu, Su, FG) *griseipectus* (E Ec, S Co) *obscurus* (SE Ve: Auyantepui) *ridgwayi* (SE Ve: Gran Sabana, W Gu)	T	* Ssp nov.: Aveledo & Perez 1994	█	█	█			█	█	█
1765	**Rufous-breasted Wren** *Thryothorus rutilus*	7	*hyspodius* (Co: E Andes) *intensus* (NW Ve) *interior* (N Co, E Andes) *laetus* (NE Co, NW Ve) *rutilus* (C, N&NE Ve, Tr) *tobagensis* (To)	T-LS	Formerly (as in Peters), *T. rutilus* included *T. sclateri*: Wetmore *et al.* 1984 and AOU 1998.		█	█		█			
1766	**Speckle-breasted Wren** *Thryothorus sclateri*	3	*columbianus* (Co: C Andes in Valle & E Andes in Bogota) *paucimaculatus* (SW Ec)	T-LS	Formerly *T. rutilus columbianus* & *T. r. paucimaculatus*: Wetmore *et al.* 1984 and AOU 1998.	█	█						
1767	**Bay Wren** *Thryothorus nigricapillus*	7	*connectens* (SW Co) *nigricapillus* (W Ec) *schottii* (NW Co)	T-LS		█	█						
1768	**Stripe-throated Wren** *Thryothorus leucopogon*	2	*grisescens* (NW Co) *leucopogon* (W Ec, W Co)	T	Formerly *T. thoracicus leucopogon* & *T. t. grisescens*: Wetmore *et al.* 1984 and AOU 1998.	█	█						
1769	**Rufous-and-white Wren** *Thryothorus rufalbus*	5	*cumanensis* (Co: N coast, N Ve) *minlosi* (NE Co, CNW Ve)	T-LS			█	█					
1770	**Niceforo's Wren** *Thryothorus nicefori*	M	(Co: E Andes in Santander)	UT	**Endemic**		█						
1771	**Buff-breasted Wren** *Thryothorus leucotis*	11	*albipectus* (NE Ve, Gu, Su, FG) *bogotensis* (E Co, C Ve) *collinus* (Co: Guajira) *galbraithii* (NW Co) *hypoleucus* (NC Ve) *leucotis* (NC Co) *venezuelanus* (NE Co, NW Ve) *zuliensis* (Co: N Santander, Ve: Maracaibo basin)	LT			█	█			█	█	█
1772	**Superciliated Wren** *Thryothorus superciliaris*	2	*baroni* (SW Ec: El Oro) *superciliaris* (SW Ec: Manabi & Guayas)	T		█							
1773	**House Wren** *Troglodytes aedon*	29	*albicans* (Ec: W & La Plata & Puná Is., S&SE Co, Ve) *atopus* (N Co) *columbae* (Co: E Andes) *striatulus* (Co: W & C Andes, Ve: Andes) *tobagensis* (To)	T-P	Howell & Webb 1995	█	█	█		█			
1774	**Santa Marta Wren** *Troglodytes monticola*	M	(Co: Sta Marta)	P	Formerly *T. solstitialis monticola*: S&M **Endemic**		█						
1775	**Mountain Wren** *Troglodytes solstitialis*	5	*solitarius* (Andes: Co & Ve) *solstitialis* (Ec, SW Co)	S-P	Andean ssp. are a sep. sp. from C.Am. ssp.: S&M.	█	█	█					

No.	Species	Ssp. Total	Subspecies in Northern South America	Altitude Range	References and Comments	Ec	Co	Ve	Ar Cu Bo	Tr To	Gu	Su	FG
1776	**Tepui Wren** *Troglodytes rufulus*	6	*duidae* (S Ve: C Amazonas) *fulvigularis* (SE Ve: CE Bolivar) *marahuacae** (SE Ve: C Amazonas) *rufulus* (SE Ve: E Bolivar) *wetmorei* (S Ve: extreme S Amazonas) *yavii* (S Ve: N Amazonas)	S-Te	* Ssp. nov.: Phelps & Aveledo 1984.			■					
1777	**White-breasted Wood-Wren** *Henicorhina leucosticta*	9	*albilateralis* (C Cu) *darienensis* (NW Co) *eucharis* (W Co: Valle) *hauxwelli* (E Ec, E Co) *inornata* (NW Ec, W Co) *leucosticta* (S Ve, Gu, Su)	T		■	■	■	■		■	■	
1778	**Grey-breasted Wood-Wren** *Henicorhina leucophrys*	16	*anachoreta* (Co: Sta Marta heights) *bangsi* (Co: Sta Marta slopes) *brunneiceps* (extreme N Ec, SW Co: W Andes) *hilaris* (SW Ec) *leucophrys* (Ec, C Co: E, C & W Andes) *manastarae* (W Ve: S Zulia) *meridana* (Ve: Andes) *tamae* (NE Co: E Andes, Ve: W Táchira) *venezuelensis* (N Ve: Coastal Range)	UT-Te		■	■	■					
1779	**Scaly-breasted Wren** *Microcerculus marginatus*	4	*corrasus* (Co: Sta Marta) *marginatus* (E Ec, SE Co, SW Ve) *squamulatus* (NE Co, NW&N Ve) *taeniatus* (W Ec, W Co)	T	Formerly Southern Nightingale Wren: AOU 1998. Stiles 1983	■	■	■					
1780	**Flutist Wren** *Microcerculus ustulatus*	4	*duidae* (S Ve) *lunatipectus* (S Ve) *obscurus* (Ve: Gran Sabana tepuis) *ustulatus* (Ve & Gu)	UT-S				■			■		
1781	**Wing-banded Wren** *Microcerculus bambla*	3	*albigularis* (E Ec) *bambla* (SE Ve, Gu, FG) *caurensis* (S&SC Ve)	T		■		■			■		■
1782	**Chestnut Wren** *Cyphorhinus thoracicus*	2	*dichrous* (Ec, Co: C & W Andes)	T-Te		■	■						
1783	**Song Wren** *Cyphorhinus phaeocephalus*	6	*chocoanus* (Co: Chocó) *lawrencii* (NW Co) *phaeocephalus* (W Ec, W Co) *propinquus* (N Co)	T	Formerly conspecific with *C. aradus*: S&M	■	■						
1784	**Musician Wren** *Cyphorhinus aradus*	8 *	*aradus* (SE Ve, Gu, Su, FG) *salvini* (E Ec, SE Co) *transfluvialis* (SE Co) *urbanoi* (SE Ve)	T	* Revision: S&M.	■	■	■			■	■	■
1785	**Collared Gnatwren** *Microbates collaris*	3	*paraguensis* (SE Ve) *collaris* (SW Ve, SE Co, FG)	T			■	■					■
1786	**Tawny-faced Gnatwren** *Microbates cinereiventris*	4	*cinereiventris* (W Co, W Ec) *magdalenae* (N Co) *peruvianus* (S Co, E Ec)	T		■	■						

No.	Species	Ssp. Total	Subspecies in Northern South America	Altitude Range	References and Comments	Ec	Co	Ve	Ar Cu Bo	Tr To	Gu	Su	FG
1787	**Long-billed Gnatwren** *Ramphocaenus melanurus*	14	*albiventris* (SE Ve, Gu, Su, FG) *duidae* (S Ve, NE Ec, SW Co) *griseodorsalis* (WC Co) *rufiventris* (N Co, E Ec) *pallidus* (NE Co, N Ve) *sanctaemartae* (N Co, NW Ve) *trinitatis* (E Co, Tr, NE&C&W Ve)	T-S									
1788	**Tropical Gnatcatcher** *Polioptila plumbea*	11	*anteocularis* (NW Co) *bilineata* (W Ec, N Co) *daguae* (W Co) *innotata* (E Co, S Ve, Gu) *plumbea* (Su, FG) *plumbeiceps* (N Co, N Ve)	T	Sight records in Co: SFP&M.								
1789	**Guianan Gnatcatcher** *Polioptila guianensis*	3	*facilis* (S Ve) *guianensis* (Gu, Su, FG)	LT	Sight records in Co: SFP&M.		?						
1790	**Slate-throated Gnatcatcher** *Polioptila schistaceigula*	M	(W Co, W Ec)	T									
1791	**Lincoln's Sparrow** *Melospiza lincolnii*	3	*lincolnii* (boreal migrant: N Ve?)	S	Single record from Portachuelo Pass, Henri Pittier N.P., Ve.								
1792	**Rufous-collared Sparrow** *Zonotrichia capensis*	26	*capensis* (FG) *costaricensis* (Ec, Co, W Ve) *inaccessibilis* (Ve: Neblina) *insularis* (Ar, Cu) *macconnelli* (Ve: Roraima) *perezchinchillae* * (Ve: Marahuaca) *roraimae* (SE Co, S&E Ve, W Gu) *venezuelae* (N Ve)	T-P	* Ssp nov.: Phelps & Aveledo 1984. *macconnelli*, with *perezchinchillae* and *inaccessibilis*, a distinctly darker and larger group occurring at higher elevations, may be a sep. sp.: Lentino & Restall in prep.								
1793	**White-throated Sparrow** *Zonotrichia albicollis*	M	(Boreal migrant: occasionally winters to S Caribbean islands)	T-LS	Uncertain in Ar, Cu, Bo: SFP&M.				?				
1794	**Grasshopper Sparrow** *Ammodramus savannarum*	11	*caribaeus* (Bo, Cu) *caucae* (N Ec, Co)	T-S									
1795	**Grassland Sparrow** *Ammodramus humeralis*	5 ?	*colombiana* (Co: Cauca & Valle, Ve: NW Llanos & Amazonas) *humeralis* (Ve, Gu, Su) *pallidulus* (Guajira: Co & Ve)	T-LS	Sometimes still listed in the genus *Myiospiza*.								
1796	**Yellow-browed Sparrow** *Ammodramus aurifrons*	4	*apurensis* (CNE Co, W Ve) *aurifrons* (E Ec, SE Co) *cherriei* (E Co) *tenebrosus* (SE Co, SW Ve)	T	Sometimes still listed in the genus *Myiospiza*.								
1797	**Tumbes Sparrow** *Aimophila stolzmanni*	M	(SW Ec)	T									
1798	**Pileated Finch** *Coryphospingus pileatus*	3	*rostratus* (C Co) *brevicaudus* (Co: Sta Marta, N Ve)	T	Sight records in FG: SFP&M.								?
1799	**Red-crested Finch** *Coryphospingus cucullatus*	3	*cucullatus* (Gu, Su, FG)	T-S									
1800	**Crimson Finch** *Rhodospingus cruentus*	M	(W Ec, Co: Gorgona Is.)	T	Recorded in Co: Ortiz-Von Halle 1990								
1801	**Plumbeous Sierra-Finch** *Phrygilus unicolor*	6	*nivarius* (Co, Ve: Andes) *geospizopsis* (Ec, S Co: C & E Andes)	Te-P									

No.	Species	Ssp. Total	Subspecies in Northern South America	Altitude Range	References and Comments	Ec	Co	Ve	Ar Cu Bo	Tr To	Gu	Su	FG
1802	**Ash-breasted Sierra Finch** *Phrygilus plebejus*	2	*ocularis* (Ec)	T-P									
1803	**Band-tailed Sierra-Finch** *Phrygilus alaudinus*	6 *	*bipartitus* (W Ec) *humboldti* (S Ec)	T-P	* Revision: O'Neill & Parker 1997								
1804	**Cinereous Finch** *Piezorhina cinerea*	M	(Extreme SW Ec)	T	Sight records in Ec: RG&G.	?							
1805	**Slaty Finch** *Haplospiza rustica*	4	*arcana* (S Ve) *rustica* (Ec, Co, N Ve)	UT-S									
1806	**Collared Warbling-Finch** *Poospiza hispaniolensis*	M	(SW Ec)	T									
1807	**Striped Yellow-Finch** *Sicalis citrina*	3	*browni* (C&NE Co, S Ve, Gu, Su)	T-Te									
1808	**Orange-fronted Yellow-Finch** *Sicalis columbiana*	3	*columbiana* (E Co, S&E Ve, Tr)	T	Uncertain in Tr: SFP&M.					?			
1809	**Saffron Yellow-Finch** *Sicalis flaveola*	4	*flaveola* (N&E Co, N Ve, Tr, Gu) *valida* (Ec)	T									
1810	**Grassland Yellow-Finch** *Sicalis luteola*	8	*bogotensis* (E Ec, Co: E Andes, W Ve) *luteola* (Co, N Ve, Gu)	T-P									
1811	**Sulphur-throated Yellow-Finch** *Sicalis taczanowskii*	M	(SW Ec)	T									
1812	**Wedge-tailed Grass-Finch** *Emberizoides herbicola*	6	*apurensis* (E Co, W Ve) *sphenurus* (N Co, Ve, Gu, Su, FG)	T-S									
1813	**Duida Grass-Finch** *Emberizoides duidae*	M	(S Ve)	T-S	Endemic								
1814	**Blue-black Grassquit** *Volatinia jacarina*	3	*peruviensis* (W Ec) *splendens* (Co, Ve, Tr, Gu, Su, FG)	T									
1815	**Slate-colored Seedeater** *Sporophila schistacea*	4	*incerta* (Ec, SW Co) *longipennis* (W Co, Ve, Gu, Su, FG) *schistacea* (N Co)	T									
1816	**Plumbeous Seedeater** *Sporophila plumbea*	3	*colombiana* (NC Co) *whiteleyana* (E Co, S&E Ve, Gu, Su, FG)	T									
1817	**Grey Seedeater** *Sporophila intermedia*	4 ?	*agustini* (Co) *anchicayae* (Co: Valle) *bogotensis* (Co: Cauca) *intermedia* (C&E Co, N Ve, Tr, Gu)	T	*agustini* = *bogotensis*; *anchicayae* = hybrid *bogotensis* x *S. americana hicksii*: Stiles 1996.								
1818	**Ring-necked Seedeater** *Sporophila insularis*	M	(N Ve, Tr)	T-LS	Formerly *S. intermedia insularis*: Restall 2000.								
1819	**Variable Seedeater** *Sporophila corvina*	4	*ophthalmica* (W Ec, SW Co) *hicksii* * (NW Co)	T	Ssp. revision: Stiles 1996 * Ssp nov.: Olson 1981.								
1820	**Caqueta Seedeater** *Sporophila murallae*	M	(Co: Caqueta)	T	Formerly *S. americana murallae*: Stiles 1996								
1821	**Wing-barred Seedeater** *Sporophila americana*	2	*americana* (NE Ve, To, Gu, Su, FG)	T	Stiles 1996								
1822	**Lesson's Seedeater,** *Sporophila bouvronides*	M	(NE Co, N Ve, Tr, Gu, Su, FG. Intertropical migrant: winters south to Amazonia.)	T	Uncertain in Ec: SFP&M.	?							
1823	**Lined Seedeater** *Sporophila lineola*	2	*lineola* (austral migrant: winters to (E Ec, Ve, Gu, Su, FG) *restricta* (austral migrant: winters to C&E Co)	T									

No.	Species	Ssp. Total	Subspecies in Northern South America	Altitude Range	References and Comments	Ec	Co	Ve	Ar Cu Bo	Tr To	Gu	Su	FG
1824	Black-and-white Seedeater *Sporophila luctuosa*	M	(Ec, Co, W Ve)	T-Te									
1825	Yellow-bellied Seedeater *Sporophila nigricollis*	3	nigricollis (Co, Ve, To, Tr, Gu, Su, FG) vivida (W Ec, SW Co)	T-S									
1826	Double-collared Seedeater *Sporophila caerulescens*	3	yungae (austral migrant: winters to extreme SE Co)	T-S									
1827	White-bellied Seedeater *Sporophila leucoptera*	4	cinerola (S Su)	T	Haverschmidt & Mees 1994								
1828	Parrot-billed Seedeater *Sporophila peruviana*	2	devronis (SE Ec)	T	Recorded in Ec: RG&G.								
1829	Drab Seedeater *Sporophila simplex*	M	(SE Ec)	T-S									
1830	Capped Seedeater *Sporophila bouvreuil*	4	bouvreuil (S Su)	T	Haverschmidt & Mees 1994								
1831	Ruddy-breasted Seedeater *Sporophila minuta*	3	minuta (NW Ec, Co, Ve, Tr, To, Gu, Su, FG)	T									
1832	Chestnut-bellied Seedeater *Sporophila castaneiventris*	M	(E Ec, SE Co, S Ve, Gu, Su, FG)	T									
1833	Rufous-rumped Seedeater *Sporophila hypochroma*	M		T	Uncertain in Gu: SFP&M.						?		
1834	Chestnut-throated Seedeater *Sporophila telasco*	M	(W Ec, SW Co)	T									
1835	Tumaco Seedeater *Sporophila insulata*	M	(Co: Tumaco Is.)	T	**Endemic Critically threatened**								
1836	Large-billed Seed-Finch *Oryzoborus crassirostris*	2	crassirostris (E Co, Ve, Gu, Su, FG) occidentalis (NW Ec, W Co)	T									
1837	Black-billed Seed-Finch *Oryzoborus atrirostris*	M	(S Ec)	T									
1838	Great-billed Seed-Finch *Oryzoborus maximilianus*	3	magnirostris (Ec, Co, E&SE Ve, Tr, Gu, FG)	T									
1839	Lesser Seed-Finch *Oryzoborus angolensis*	2	angolensis (E Ec, E Co, Ve, Tr, Gu, Su, FG) theobromae* (Co)	T	Ssp torridus is invalid. * Ssp. nov.: Olson 1981.								
1840	Thick-billed Seed-Finch *Oryzoborus funereus*	4	aethiops (W Ec, SW Co) ochrogyne (W Co)	T	= O. angolensis: Olson 1981; retained as a sep. sp. in AOU 1998.								
1841	Dusky-blue Seedeater *Amaurospiza equatorialis*	M	(Ec, SW Co)	T-S	Formerly A. concolor equatorialis: Restall in prep.								
1842	White-naped Seedeater *Dolospingus fringilloides*	M	(E Co, S Ve)	T									
1843	Band-tailed Seedeater *Catamenia analis*	8	alpica (Co: Sta Marta) schistaceifrons (C Co) soederstromi (NC Ec)	S-Te									
1844	Plain-colored Seedeater *Catamenia inornata*	3	minor (Ec, E&C Co, W Ve) mucuchiesi (Ve: Merida)	Te-P									
1845	Paramo Seedeater *Catamenia homochroa*	3	duncani (S Ve) homochroa (Ec, Co, W Vc) oreophila * (Co: Sta Marta)	Tc P	* Ssp. nov.: Romero 1977								
1846	Dull-colored Grassquit *Tiaris obscura*	5	haplochroma (NE Co, NW Ve) pauper (Ec, SW Co)	UT-S									
1847	Yellow-faced Grassquit *Tiaris olivacea*	5	pusilla (N Ec, W Co, Ve: Tachira)										

No.	Species	Ssp. Total	Subspecies in Northern South America	Altitude Range	References and Comments	Ec	Co	Ve	Ar Cu Bo	Tr To	Gu	Su	F
1848	**Black-faced Grassquit** *Tiaris bicolor*	8	*huilae* (C Co: Magdalena Val.) *johnstonei* (Ve: Blanquilla & Hermanos Is.) *omissa* (NE Co) *sharpei* (Ar, Cu, Bo) *tortugensis* (Ve: Tortuga Is.)	T-S			X	X	X				
1849	**Sooty Grassquit** *Tiaris fuliginosa*	3	*fumosa* (N Ve, Tr) *zuliae* (Ve: Perijá)	T-S	Probably monotypic: Bates 1997.			X		X			
1850	**Bananaquit** *Coereba flaveola*	41	*bolivari* (E&NE Ve) *bonarensis* (Bo) *caucae* (W Co) *columbiana* (SW Co, SC Ve) *ferryi* (Ve: Tortuga Is.) *frailensis* (Ve: Los Frailes & Los Hermanos Is.) *gorgonae* (Co: Gorgona Is.) *guianensis* (E Ve, Gu) *intermedia* (Ec, SW Co, Ve: SW Amazonas) *laurae* (Ve: Los Testigos Is.) *lowii* (Ve: Los Roques) *luteola* (N Co, N Ve, Tr, To) *melanurus* (Ve: Cayo Sal) *minima* (E Co, S Ve, Su, FG) *montana* (SW Ve) *obscura* (NE Co, W Ve) *roraimae* (S&SE Ve, S Gu) *uropygialis* (Ar, Cu)	T		X	X	X	X	X	X	X	X
1851	**Orange-billed Sparrow** *Arremon aurantiirostris*	8	*erythrorhynchus* (N Co) *spectabilis* (E Ec, SE Co) *occidentalis* (NW Ec, W Co) *sanctarosae* (SW Ec) *strictocollaris* (NW Co)	T		X	X						
1852	**Golden-winged Sparrow** *Arremon schlegeli*	3	*canidorsum* (Co: E Andes) *fratruelis* (Co: Guajira) *schlegeli* (NE Co, N Ve)	T-LS			X	X					
1853	**Pectoral Sparrow** *Arremon taciturnus*	4	*axillaris* (W Ve) *taciturnus* (E Co, SE Ve, Gu, Su, FG)	T			X	X			X	X	
1854	**Black-capped Sparrow** *Arremon abeillei*	2	*abeillei* (SW Ec)	T		X							
1855	**Tocuyo Sparrow** *Arremonops tocuyensis*	M	(NE Co, NW Ve)	T			X	X					
1856	**Black-striped Sparrow** *Arremonops conirostris*	6	*conirostris* (N&E Co, N&S Ve) *inexpectatus* (CW Co) *striaticeps* (W Ec, W Co) *umbrinus* (NC Co, NW Ve)	T-LS		X	X	X					
1857	**Chestnut-capped Brush-Finch** *Buarremon brunneinuchus*	9	*alliornatus* (NW Ve) *frontalis* (Ec, Co, N&W Ve) *innornatus* (CW Ec)	T-Te	Formerly *Atlapetes*: Hackett 1992, fide Remsen & Graves 1995.	X	X	X					
1858	**Black-headed Brush-Finch** *Buarremon atricapillus*	2	*atricapillus* (N Co: E & C Andes)	T	Formerly *Atlapetes*. Formerly included in *B. torquatus*: Hackett 1992, fide Remsen & Graves 1995.		X						

98

No.	Species	Ssp. Total	Subspecies in Northern South America	Altitude Range	References and Comments	Ec	Co	Ve	Ar Cu Bo	Tr To	Gu	Su	FG
1859	Stripe-headed Brush-Finch *Buarremon torquatus*	14	*assimilis* (C&N Ec, Co: Andes, Ve: Merida) *basilicus* (N Co) *larensis* (Ve: N Andes) *nigrifrons* (SW Ec) *perijanus* (NC Co: E Andes, NW Ve) *phaeopleurus* (Ve: Coastal Range) *phygas* (NE Ve)	S-Te	Formerly *Atlapetes*: Hackett 1992, fide Remsen & Graves 1995.								
1860	Sooty-faced Finch *Lysurus crassirostris*	M		T-S									
1861	Olive Finch *Lysurus castaneiceps*	M		T-S									
1862	Yellow-throated Brush-Finch *Atlapetes gutturalis*	M ?	(Co: Sta Marta & S)	UT-S	Formerly *A. albinucha gutturalis*: S&M.								
1863	Pale-naped Brush-Finch *Atlapetes pallidinucha*	2	*pallidinucha* (Co: C Andes, Ve: Tachira) *papallactae* (Co: C Andes, Ec)	S-P									
1864	Northern Rufous-naped Brush-Finch *Atlapetes latinuchus*	9?	*caucae* (Co: W & C Andes) *comptus* (SW Ec) *elaeoprorus* (N Co: C Andes) *latinuchus* (SE Ec) *phelpsi* (E Co, Ve: Perija) *simplex* (Co: E Andes) *spodionotus* (N Ec, SW Co)	S-Te	Garcia-Moreno & Fjeldså 1999; the taxonomic status of *phelpsi* was not re-evaluated in the above study.								
1865	White-rimmed Brush-Finch *Atlapetes leucopis*	M	(SW Co, W Ec)	Te									
1866	Santa Marta Brush-Finch *Atlapetes melanocephalus*	M	(Co: Sta Marta)	S-Te	Endemic								
1867	Yellow-headed Brush-Finch *Atlapetes flaviceps*	M	(Co: C Andes)	UT-S	Endemic								
1868	Dusky-headed Brush-Finch *Atlapetes fuscoolivaceus*	M	(C Co)	S	Endemic								
1869	Tricolored Brush-Finch *Atlapetes tricolor*	2	*crassus* (Ec, Co: W Andes)	T-LS	*crassus* is very probably a sep. sp.: Garcia-Moreno & Fjeldså 1999.								
1870	Moustached Brush-Finch *Atlapetes albofrenatus*	2	*albofrenatus* (Co: E Andes) *meridae* (W Ve)	UT-S									
1871	Slaty Brush-Finch *Atlapetes schistaceus*	5	*castaneifrons* (Ve: Andes) *fumidus* (E Co, Ve: Perija) *tamae* (CE Co, Ve: Tachira) *schistaceus* (Ec, Co: Andes)	S-Te	Garcia-Moreno & Fjeldså 1999								
1872	Bay-crowned Brush-Finch *Atlapetes seebohmi*	3	*seebohmi* (S Ec) *simonsi* (SW Ec) *celicae* (SW Ec)	T-Te	Meyer de Schauensee 1966 and 1970.								
1873	White-winged Brush-Finch *Atlapetes leucopterus*	2	*dresseri* (SW Ec) *leucopterus* (W Ec)	T-Te									
1874	White-headed Brush-Finch *Atlapetes albiceps*	M	(SE Ec)	T									
1875	Pale-headed Brush-Finch *Atlapetes pallidiceps*	M	(S Ec)	UT-LS	Endemic								

No.	Species	Ssp. Total	Subspecies in Northern South America	Altitude Range	References and Comments	Ec	Co	Ve	Ar Cu Bo	Tr To	Gu	Su	F
1876	Ochre-breasted Brush-Finch *Atlapetes semirufus*	6	albigula (Ve: NE Táchira) benedettii (NW Ve) denisei (Ve: Coastal Range) majusculus (Co: C Andes) semirufus (C Co: E Andes) zimmeri (NC Co, Ve)	S-P									
1877	Tepui Brush-Finch *Atlapetes personatus*	6	collaris (Ve: Gran Sabana) duidae (Ve: Duida) jugularis (Ve: SE Amazonas) paraquensis (Ve: NW Amazonas) parui (Ve: N Amazonas) personatus (Gu & Ve: Roraima & nearby tepuis)	T-S									
1878	Red-capped Cardinal *Paroaria gularis*	3	gularis (E Ec, E Co, Gu, Su, FG) nigrogenis (EC Co,Ve, Tr)	T									
1879	Dickcissel *Spiza americana*	M	(Boreal migrant: winters mainly to Ve W Llanos, also Tr, E Co, Gu, Su)	T	Sight records in Ec: RG&G.	?							
1880	Yellow Grosbeak *Pheucticus chrysogaster*	2?	chrysogaster (Ec, SW Co) laubmanni (N Co, N Ve)	T-S	Formerly *P. chryso-peplus chrysogaster*								
1881	Black-backed Grosbeak *Pheucticus aureoventris*	5	chrysalis (Ec, Sw Co) meridensis (Ve: Merida) uropygialis (W Co)	T-Te									
1882	Rose-breasted Grosbeak *Pheucticus ludovicianus*	2	ludovicianus (Boreal migrant: winters to E Ec, E&N Co, Ve)	T-S	Phillips 1994								
1883	Black-headed Grosbeak *Pheucticus melanocephalus*	2	maculatus (Boreal migrant: Cu)	S-Te	Sight records in Cu: A&S.				?				
1884	Vermilion Cardinal *Cardinalis phoeniceus*	M	(NE Co, N Ve)	T									
1885	Green Grosbeak *Caryothraustes canadensis*	6	canadensis (SE Co, S Ve, Gu, Su, FG)	T									
1886	Yellow-shouldered Grosbeak *Parkerthraustes humeralis*	M	(E Ec)	T	Formerly *Caryothraustes*: Remsen 1997. Uncertain in Co: SFP&M.		?						
1887	Red-and-black Grosbeak *Periporphyrus erythromelas*	M	(Ve: Roraima, Gu, Su, FG)	T									
1888	Slate-colored Grosbeak *Saltator grossus*	3	grossus (E Ec, S Ve, Gu, Su, FG) saturatus (W Ec, N&W Co)	T	Formerly *Pitylus*: Demastes & Remsen 1994.								
1889	Buff-throated Saltator *Saltator maximus*	5	iungens (NW Co) maximus (E Ec, E&NE Co, Ve, Gu, Su, FG)	T-S									
1890	Black-winged Saltator *Saltator atripennis*	2	atripennis (NW Ec, W Co) caniceps (W Ec, Co)	T-S									
1891	Greyish Saltator *Saltator coerulescens*	13	azarae (E Ec, E Co) brewsteri (NE Co, N Ve, Tr) olivascens (S Ve, Gu, Su, FG) plumbeus (Co: N coast)	T									
1892	Orinocan Saltator *Saltator orenocensis*	2	orenocensis (CN&E Ve) rufescens (NE Co, NW Ve)	T									
1893	Black-cowled Saltator *Saltator nigriceps*	M	(S Ec)	T-S	F&K								
1894	Masked Saltator *Saltator cinctus*	M	(E Ec)	S-Te									

No.	Species	Ssp. Total	Subspecies in Northern South America	Altitude Range	References and Comments	Ec	Co	Ve	Ar Cu Bo	Tr To	Gu	Su	FG
895	**Streaked Saltator** *Saltator striatipectus*	10	*flavidicollis* (W Ec, SW Co) *perstriatus* (NE Co, N Ve, Tr) *striatipectus* (W Co)	T-S	Formerly *S. albicollis* (in part): Seutin *et al.* 1993.								
896	**Blue-black Grosbeak** *Cyanocompsa cyanoides*	4	*cyanoides* (CW Ec, N Co: E Andes, NW Ve) *rothschildii* (E Ec, E Co, NE&S Ve, Tr, Gu, Su, FG)	T	AOU 1998								
897	**Ultramarine Grosbeak** *Cyanocompsa cyanea*	5	*caucae* (W Co) *minor* (N Ve)	T	In S&M and R&T = *C. brissonii* In SFP&M = *Passerina brissonii*								
898	**Blue Grosbeak** *Guiraca caerulea*	6	*caoruloa* (Boreal migrant: winters to E Ec, E Co)		R&T 1989, AOU 1998								
899	**Indigo Bunting** *Passerina cyanea*	M	(Boreal migrant: occasionally winters to Co, W Ve, Ar, Cu, Bo, Tr)	T-S	Sight records in Tr: SFP&M.					?			
900	**Black-faced Tanager** *Schistochlamys melanopis*	5	*aterrima* (E Co, Ve, W Gu) *melanopis* (E Gu, Su, FG)	T-S	Sight records in Ec: SFP&M.	?							
901	**White-rumped Tanager** *Cypsnagra hirundinacea*	2	*pallidigula* (Su)	T	Sight records in FG: SFP&M.								?
902	**Black-and-white Tanager** *Conothraupis speculigera*	M	(S Ec)	T-S									
903	**Red-billed Pied Tanager** *Lamprospiza melanoleuca*	M	(Gu, Su, FG)	T									
904	**Magpie Tanager** *Cissopis leveriana*	2	*leveriana* (E Ec, E Co, W&SE Ve, Gu, Su, FG)	T	Sight records in FG: SFP&M.								?
905	**Grass-green Tanager** *Chlorornis riefferii*	5	*riefferi* (Andes: Co & Ec)	Te-P									
906	**White-capped Tanager** *Sericossypha albocristata*	M	(E Ec, C Co, SW Ve)	S-P									
1907	**Common Bush-Tanager** *Chlorospingus ophthalmicus*	25	*eminens* (Co: E Andes) *exitelis* (Co: W & C Andes) *falconensis* (NE Ve) *flavopectus* (Co: E Andes) *hiaticolus* (Co) *jacqueti* (Co: E Andes, Ve: Coastal Range) *macarenae* (Co: Macarena Mts) *nigriceps* (Co: C Andes & upper Magdalena Valley) *phaeocephalus* (Ec) *ponsi* (Co & Ve: Perija) *trudis* (Co: E Andes) *venezuelanus* (Ve: Andes)	T-S									
1908	**Tacarcuna Bush-Tanager** *Chlorospingus tacarcunae*	M	(NW Co)	T									
1909	**Pirre Bush-Tanager** *Chlorospingus inornatus*	M	(NW Co)	T	Possible in Co: H&B.		?						
1910	**Dusky-bellied Bush-Tanager** *Chlorospingus semifuscus*	2	*livingstoni* (W Co) *semifuscus* (Ec, SW Co)	T-S									
1911	**Short-billed Bush-Tanager** *Chlorospingus parvirostris*	3	*huallagae* (Ec , C&S Co)	S									
1912	**Yellow-throated Bush-Tananger** *Chlorospingus flavigularis*	3	*flavigularis* (E Ec, C Co) *marginatus* (W Ec, SW Co)	T									
1913	**Yellow-green Bush-Tanager** *Chlorospingus flavovirens*	M	(W Ec, Co)	T									

No.	Species	Ssp. Total	Subspecies in Northern South America	Altitude Range	References and Comments	Ec	Co	Ve	Ar Cu Bo	Tr To	Gu	Su	F
1914	**Ashy-throated Bush-Tanager** *Chlorospingus canigularis*	5	*canigularis* (C Co, SW Ve) *conspicillatus* (NW Ec, W Co) *paulus* (SW Ec) *signatus* (E Ec)	T-Te									
1915	**Grey-hooded Bush-Tanager** *Cnemoscopus rubrirostris*	2	*rubrirostris* (Andes: W Ve, Co, Ec)	S-P									
1916	**Black-capped Hemispingus** *Hemispingus atropileus*	2	*atropileus* (Andes: W Ve, Co, Ec)	Te-P									
1917	**Superciliaried Hemispingus** *Hemispingus superciliaris*	7	*chrysophrys* (Ve: Andes) *maculifrons* (SW Ec) *nigrifrons* (Ec, Co) *superciliaris* (Ec, C Co)	Te-P									
1918	**Grey-capped Hemispingus** *Hemispingus reyi*	M	(Ve: Andes)	S-P	**Endemic**								
1919	**Oleaginous Hemispingus** *Hemispingus frontalis*	5	*flavidorsalis* (Ve: Perija) *frontalis* (E Ec, Co) *hanieli* (N Ve) *ignobilis* (Ve: Andes) *iteratus* (NE Ve)	S-Te									
1920	**Black-eared Hemispingus** *Hemispingus melanotis*	6	*melanotis* (E Ec, Co, SW Ve) *ochraceus* (W Ec, SW Co) *piurae* (SE Ec)	S-Te	Each ssp. to be given specific rank - *H. ochraceus* (Western Hemispingus), *H. piurae* (Piura Hemispingus): Ridgely & Greenfield, in prep.								
1921	**Slaty-backed Hemispingus** *Hemispingus goeringi*	M	(Ve: Andes)	Te	**Endemic**								
1922	**Black-headed Hemispingus** *Hemispingus verticalis*	M	(Andes: E Ec, S&C Co, Ve)	Te-P									
1923	**Fulvous-headed Tanager** *Thlypopsis fulviceps*	4	*fulviceps* (NE Co, N&W Ve) *intensa* (NE&C Co) *meridensis* (Ve: Merida) *obscuriceps* (Ve: Perijá)	T-S									
1924	**Buff-bellied Tanager** *Thlypopsis inornata*	M		T-S	Recorded in Ec: RG&G.								
1925	**Rufous-chested Tanager** *Thlypopsis ornata*	3	*media* (S Ec) *ornata* (W Ec, SW Co)	S-P									
1926	**Orange-headed Tanager** *Thlypopsis sordida*	3	*chrysopis* (E Ec, S Co) *orinocensis* (CE Ve)	T									
1927	**Guira Tanager** *Hemithraupis guira*	8	*guirina* (W Ec, W&C Co) *huambina* (E Ec, SE Co) *nigrigula* (NC Co, N Ve, Gu, Su, FG) *roraimae* (SE Ve, Gu)	T									
1928	**Yellow-backed Tanager** *Hemithraupis flavicollis*	11	*albigularis* (C Co) *aurigularis* (SE Co, S Ve) *flavicollis* (Su, FG) *hellmayri* (SE Ve, W Gu) *ornata* (NW Co) *peruana* (E Ec, SC Co)	T									
1929	**Scarlet-and-white Tanager** *Chrysothlypis salmoni*	M	(NW Ec, W Co)	T									
1930	**Hooded Tanager** *Nemosia pileata*	6	*hypoleuca* (N Co, N Ve) *pileata* (FG) *surinamensis* (Gu, Su)	T									

No.	Species	Ssp. Total	Subspecies in Northern South America	Altitude Range	References and Comments	Ec	Co	Ve	Ar Cu Bo	Tr To	Gu	Su	FG
931	**Rosy Thrush-Tanager** *Rhodinocichla rosea*	5	beebei (NE Co, NW Ve) harterti (C Co) rosea (NW Ve)	T-S									
932	**Dusky-faced Tanager** *Mitrospingus cassinii*	2	cassinii (W Ec, W Co)	T									
933	**Olive-backed Tanager** *Mitrospingus oleagineus*	2	obscuripectus (SE Ve) oleagineus (SE Ve, W Gu)	T-S									
934	**Olive Tanager** *Chlorothraupis carmioli*	3	lutescens (NW Co) frenata (SW Co)	T	frenata may be a sep. sp. (Olive Tanager); carmioli then becomes Carmiol's Tanager: S&M.								
935	**Lemon-browed Tanager** *Chlorothraupis olivacea*	M	(NW Ec, W Co)	T-S									
936	**Ochre-breasted Tanager** *Chlorothraupis stolzmanni*	2	dugandi (SW Co) stolzmanni (W Ec)	T-S									
937	**Grey-headed Tanager** *Eucometis penicillata*	7	affinis (N Ve) cristata (N&NW Co, W ve) penicillata (E Ec, SE Co, Ve, Gu, Su, FG)	T									
938	**Fulvous Shrike-Tanager** *Lanio fulvus*	2	fulvus (S Ve, Gu, Su, FG) peruvianus (E Ec, S Co, Ve: Táchira)	T									
939	**Rufous-crested Tanager** *Creurgops verticalis*	M	(E Ec, W Co, SW Ve)	T-Te									
940	**Scarlet-browed Tanager** *Heterospingus xanthopygius*	2	berliozi (NW Ec, W Co) xanthopygius (N Co)	T									
941	**Flame-crested Tanager** *Tachyphonus cristatus*	10	cristatellus (SE Co) cristatus (FG) fallax (E Ec, S Co) intercedens (E Ve, Gu, Su) orinocensis (E Co, S Ve)	T									
942	**Fulvous-crested Tanager** *Tachyphonus surinamus*	4	brevipes (E Ec, E Co, S Ve) surinamus (E&S Ve, Gu, Su, FG)	T									
943	**White-shouldered Tanager** *Tachyphonus luctuosus*	5	flaviventris (NE Ve, Tr) luctuosus (E Ec, SE Co, Ve, Gu, Su, FG) panamensis (W Ec, N&W Co, W Ve)	T									
944	**Tawny-crested Tanager** *Tachyphonus delatrii*	M	(W Ec, W Co)	T									
945	**White-lined Tanager** *Tachyphonus rufus*	M	(NW Ec, Co, Ve, Tr, Gu, Su, FG)	T									
946	**Red-shouldered Tanager** *Tachyphonus phoenicius*	M	(C Co, S Ve, Gu, Su, FG)	T-S									
1947	**Red-crowned Ant-Tanager** *Habia rubica*	17	coccinea (NC Co, W Ve) crissalis (NE Ve) mesopotamia (SE Ve) perijana (Perijá: Co & Ve) rhodinolaema (E Ec, SE Co) rubra (Tr)	T									
1948	**Red-throated Ant-Tanager** *Habia fuscicauda*	6	erythrolaema (N Co)	T									
1949	**Sooty Ant-Tanager** *Habia gutturalis*	M	(NW Co)	T	Endemic								
1950	**Crested Ant-Tanager** *Habia cristata*	M	(W Co)	T-S	Endemic								

No.	Species	Ssp. Total	Subspecies in Northern South America	Altitude Range	References and Comments	Ec	Co	Ve	Ar Cu Bo	Tr To	Gu	Su	F
1951	**Hepatic Tanager** *Piranga flava*	15	*desidiosa* (SW Co) *faceta* (N Co, N Ve, Tr) *haemalea* (S Ve, W Gu) *lutea* (W Ec, SW Co) *macconnelli* (S Gu, Su, FG) *toddi* (C Co)	T-Te									
1952	**Summer Tanager** *Piranga rubra*	2	*rubra* (winters in Ec, N Co, N&SE Ve)	T-S									
1953	**Scarlet Tanager** *Piranga olivacea*	M	(Winters in Ec, W&C Co)	T									
1954	**White-winged Tanager** *Piranga leucoptera*	4	*ardens* (Ec, SW Co) *venezuelae* (Co & Ve)	T-S									
1955	**Red-hooded Tanager** *Piranga rubriceps*	M	(W Ec, W Co)	S-Te									
1956	**Vermilion Tanager** *Calochaetes coccineus*	M	(E Ec, S Co)	T-S									
1957	**Masked Crimson Tanager** *Ramphocelus nigrogularis*	M	(E Ec, SE Co)	T									
1958	**Crimson-backed Tanager** *Ramphocelus dimidiatus*	5	*dimidiatus* (NW Co, W Ve) *mochinus* (NW Co)	T-S									
1959	**Silver-beaked Tanager** *Ramphocelus carbo*	8	*capitalis* (NE Ve) *carbo* (E Ec, SE Co, S Ve, Gu, Su, FG) *magnirostris* (NE Ve, Tr) *unicolor* (E Co) *venezuelensis* (E Co, W Ve)	T									
1960	**Flame-rumped Tanager** *Ramphocelus flammigerus*	M	(W&C Co)	T									
1961	**Blue-grey Tanager** *Thraupis episcopus*	13	*berlepschi* (To) *caerulea* (SE Ec) *cana* (Co, N Ve) *coelestis* (NE&EC Ec, SE Co) *episcopus* (Gu, Su, FG) *leucoptera* (C Co) *mediana* (SE Co, SE Ve) *nesophilus* (E Co, E Ve, Tr) *quaesita* (W Ec, SW Co)	T-S									
1962	**Glaucous Tanager** *Thraupis glaucocolpa*	M	(N Co, N Ve)	T	Formerly *T. sayaca glaucocolpa*								
1963	**Palm Tanager** *Thraupis palmarum*	4	*atripennis* (N Co, NW Ve) *melanoptera* (E Co, Ve, Tr, Gu, Su, FG) *violilavata* (W Ec, SW Co)	T									
1964	**Blue-capped Tanager** *Thraupis cyanocephala*	8	*annectes* (C Co) *auricrissa* (NC Co, W Ve) *buesingi* (NE Ve, Tr) *cyanocephala* (W Ec) *hypophaea* (NW Ve) *margaritae* (N Co) *olivicyanea* (N Ve) *subcinerea* (NE Ve)	S-Te									
1965	**Blue-and-yellow Tanager** *Thraupis bonariensis*	4	*darwinii* (W Ec)	T-Te									
1966	**Blue-backed Tanager** *Cyanicterus cyanicterus*	M	(E Ve, Gu, Su, FG)	T									
1967	**Black-and-gold Tanager** *Bangsia melanochlamys*	M	(W Co)	T-S	Formerly *Buthraupis* **Endemic**								
1968	**Golden-crested Tanager** *Bangsia rothschildi*	M	(NW Ec, SW Co)	T	Formerly *Buthraupis*								

No.	Species	Ssp. Total	Subspecies in Northern South America	Altitude Range	References and Comments	Ec	Co	Ve	Ar Cu Bo	Tr To	Gu	Su	FG
969	**Moss-backed Tanager** *Bangsia edwardsi*	M	(NW Ec, SW Co)	T-S	Formerly *Buthraupis*	■	■						
970	**Gold-ringed Tanager** *Bangsia aureocincta*	M	(W Co)	S	Formerly *Buthraupis* **Endemic**		■						
971	**Hooded Mountain-Tanager** *Buthraupis montana*	5	cucullata (W Ec, W Co) gigas (NC Co, NW&SW Ve)	S-P		■	■	■					
972	**Black-chested Mountain-Tanager** *Buthraupis eximia*	4	chloronota (NW Ec, SE Co) cyanocalyptra (SC Ec) eximia (NC Co, SW Ve) zimmeri (WC Co)	Te-P		■	■	■					
973	**Masked Mountain-Tanager** *Buthraupis wetmorei*	M	(SC Ec, SW Co)	Te-P		■	■						
974	**Orange-throated Tanager** *Wetmorethraupis sterrhopteron*	M	(SE Ec)	T	Listed in RG&G.	■							
975	**Santa Marta Mountain-Tanager** *Anisognathus melanogenys*	M	(Co: Sta Marta)	S-Te	Formerly *A. lacrymosus melanogenys* **Endemic**		■						
976	**Lacrimose Mountain-Tanager** *Anisognathus lacrymosus*	8	caerulescens (S Ec) intensus (SW Co) melanops (Ve: Andes) olivaceiceps (W Co) pallididorsalis (Perijá) palpebrosus (E Ec, SW Co) tamae (NC Co, W Ve)	S-P		■	■	■					
977	**Scarlet-bellied Mountain-Tanager** *Anisognathus igniventris*	4	erythrotus (Ec, S co) lunulatus (NC Co, W Ve)	Te-P		■	■	■					
978	**Blue-winged Mountain-Tanager** *Anisognathus somptuosus*	9	alamoris (SW Ec) antioquiae (N Co) baezae (E Ec, S Co) cyanopterus (W Ec, SW Co) somptuosus (extreme SE Ec) venezuelanus (N Ve) victorini (C Co, SW Ve) viridorsalis (N Ve)	T-S	Formerly *A. flavinucha*, but older name *somptuosus* Lesson 1831 takes priority: S&M (ssp. *flavinucha* occurs in Peru).	■	■	■					
979	**Black-chinned Mountain-Tanager** *Anisognathus notabilis*	M	(NW Ec, SW Co)	T-S		■	■						
980	**Purplish-mantled Tanager** *Iridosornis porphyrocephala*	M	(W Ec, W Co)	S		■	■						
981	**Yellow-throated Tanager** *Iridosornis analis*	M	(E Ec)	T-S	Uncertain in Co: SFP&M.	■	?						
982	**Golden-crowned Tanager** *Iridosornis rufivertex*	5	caeruleoventris (N Co) ignicapillus (SW Co) rufivertex (E Ec, C Co, W Ve) subsimilis (W Ec)	Te-P		■	■	■					
983	**Buff-breasted Mtn-Tanager** *Dubusia teniata*	3	carrikeri (N Co) teniata (Ec, Co, W Ve)	S-P		■	■	■					
984	**Fawn-breasted Tanager** *Pipraeidea melanonota*	2	venezuelensis (Ec, Co, Ve)	T-S		■	■	■					
985	**Plumbeous Euphonia** *Euphonia plumbea*	M	(S Ve, Gu, Su)	T				■			■	■	
986	**Purple-throated Euphonia** *Euphonia chlorotica*	5	chlorotica (Gu, Su, FG) cyanoptera (E Co, S Ve)	T			■	■			■	■	■
987	**Trinidad Euphonia** *Euphonia trinitatis*	M		T				■	■				
988	**Velvet-fronted Euphonia** *Euphonia concinna*	M	(C Co)	T	**Endemic**		■						

No.	Species	Ssp. Total	Subspecies in Northern South America	Altitude Range	References and Comments	Ec	Co	Ve	Ar Cu Bo	Tr To	Gu	Su	F
1989	**Orange-crowned Euphonia** *Euphonia saturata*	M	(W Ec, W Co)	T									
1990	**Finsch's Euphonia** *Euphonia finschi*	M	(E Ve, Gu, Su, FG)	T									
1991	**Violaceous Euphonia** *Euphonia violacea*	3	rodwayi (E Ve, Tr, To) violacea (Gu, Su, FG)	T									
1992	**Thick-billed Euphonia** *Euphonia laniirostris*	5	crassirostris (C Co, W Ve) hypoxantha (W Ec) melanura (E Ec, SE Co, S Ve)	T-S									
1993	**Golden-rumped Euphonia** *Euphonia cyanocephala*	9	cyanocephala (Tr) insignis (S Ec) intermedia (N&SE Ve, Gu, Su, FG) pelzelni (S Co, W Ec)	T-S									
1994	**Fulvous-vented Euphonia** *Euphonia fulvicrissa*	3	fulvicrissa (NW Co) omissa (C Co) purpurascens (NW Ec, SW Co)	T									
1995	**Golden-bellied Euphonia** *Euphonia chrysopasta*	2	chrysopasta (E Ec, SE Co) nitida (E Co, S Ve, Gu, Su, FG)	T									
1996	**Bronze-green Euphonia** *Euphonia mesochrysa*	3	mesochrysa (E Ec, C Co)	T-S									
1997	**White-vented Euphonia** *Euphonia minuta*	2	humilis (W Ec, W Co) minuta (E Co, S Ve, Gu, Su, FG)	T									
1998	**Tawny-capped Euphonia** *Euphonia anneae*	2	rufivertex (NW Co)	T									
1999	**Orange-bellied Euphonia** *Euphonia xanthogaster*	10	badissima (NW Co, W Ve) brevirostris (E Ec, E Co, S Ve, Gu) chocoensis (NW Ec, W Co) dilutior (SE Co) exsul (NE Co, N Ve) quitensis (W Ec)	T-S	lecroyana (Aveledo & Perez 1994) synonymous with badissima: Lentino in prep.								
2000	**Rufous-bellied Euphonia** *Euphonia rufiventris*	2	carnegiei* (S Ve) rufiventris (E Ec, E Co)	T	* ssp. nov.: Dickerman 1988.								
2001	**Golden-sided Euphonia** *Euphonia cayennensis*	M	(S Ve, Gu, Su, FG)	T									
2002	**Yellow-collared Chlorophonia** *Chlorophonia flavirostris*	M	(W Ec, SW Co)	T-S									
2003	**Blue-naped Chlorophonia** *Chlorophonia cyanea*	7	frontalis (N Ve) intensa (W Co) longipennis (Andes: Ec, Co & Ve) minuscula (NE Ve) psittacina (N Co) roraimae (S Ve, Gu)	T-S									
2004	**Chestnut-breasted Chlorophonia** *Chlorophonia pyrrhophrys*	M	(E Ec, Co, W Ve)	S-P									
2005	**Glistening-green Tanager** *Chlorochrysa phoenicotis*	M	(W Ec, W Co)	T-S									
2006	**Orange-eared Tanager** *Chlorochrysa calliparaea*	3	bourcieri (E Ec, C Co)	T-S	Sight records in Ve: S. Hilty pers. comm.			?					
2007	**Multicolored Tanager** *Chlorochrysa nitidissima*	M	(W Co)	T-S	**Endemic**								
2008	**Plain-colored Tanager** *Tangara inornata*	3	inornata (N Co) languens (NW Co)	T									

No.	Species	Ssp. Total	Subspecies in Northern South America	Altitude Range	References and Comments	Ec	Co	Ve	Ar Cu Bo	Tr To	Gu	Su	FG
2009	**Turquoise Tanager** *Tangara mexicana*	5	*boliviana* (E Ec, E Co) *media* (E Co, S&E Ve) *mexicana* (Gu, Su, FG) *veilloti* (Tr)	T									
2010	**Grey-and-gold Tanager** *Tangara palmeri*	M	(W Ec, W Co)	T									
2011	**Paradise Tanager** *Tangara chilensis*	4	*chilensis* (E Ec, SE Co) *coelicolor* (E Co, S Ve) *paradisea* (Su, FG)	T									
2012	**Blue-whiskered Tanager** *Tangara johannae*	M	(NW Ec, W Co)	T									
2013	**Green-and-gold Tanager** *Tangara schrankii*	3	*anchicayae* (W Co) *schrankii* (E Ec, SE Co) *venezuelana* (S Ve)	T									
2014	**Emerald Tanager** *Tangara florida*	2	*auriceps* (W Co)	T									
2015	**Golden Tanager** *Tangara arthus*	9	*aequatorialis* (E Ec) *arthus* (N&E Ve) *aurulenta* (C Co, NW Ve) *goodsoni* (W Ec) *occidentalis* (W Co) *palmitae* (C Co) *sclateri* (E Co)	T-S									
2016	**Silver-throated Tanager** *Tangara icterocephala*	3	*icterocephala* (W Ec, W Co)	T-S									
2017	**Saffron-crowned Tanager** *Tangara xanthocephala*	3	*venusta* (Ec, Co, W Ve)	T-S									
2018	**Golden-eared Tanager** *Tangara chrysotis*	M	(E Ec, S Co)	T-S									
2019	**Flame-faced Tanager** *Tangara parzudakii*	3	*lunigera* (W Ec, W Co) *parzudakii* (E Ec, C&E Co, SW Ve)	T-S									
2020	**Yellow-bellied Tanager** *Tangara xanthogastra*	2	*phelpsi* (S Ve) *xanthogastra* (E Ec, E Co, S Ve)	T									
2021	**Spotted Tanager** *Tangara punctata*	5	*punctata* (S Ve, Gu, Su, FG) *zamorae* (E Ec)	T									
2022	**Speckled Tanager** *Tangara guttata*	6	*bogotensis* (E Co, W Ve) *chrysophrys* (Ve) *guttata* (SE Ve) *tolimae* (C Co) *trinitatis* (Tr)	T-S	Sight records in Su: SFP&M.							?	
2023	**Dotted Tanager** *Tangara varia*	M	(E Co, S Ve, Gu, Su, FG)	T									
2024	**Rufous-throated Tanager** *Tangara rufigula*	M	(NW Ec, W Co)	T-S									
2025	**Bay-headed Tanager** *Tangara gyrola*	9	*catharinae* (E Ec, E Co) *delecticia* (N Co) *gyrola* (S Ve, Gu, Su, FG) *nupera* (W Ec, SW Co) *parva* (SE Co, S Ve) *toddi* (N Co, N Ve) *viridissima* (NW Ve, Tr)	T-S									
2026	**Rufous-winged Tanager** *Tangara lavinia*	3	*lavinia* (NW Ec, W Co)	T									
2027	**Burnished-buff Tanager** *Tangara cayana*	7	*cayana* (E Co, S Ve, Gu, Su, FG) *fulvescens* (C Co)	T-S									
2028	**Scrub Tanager** *Tangara vitriolina*	M	(NW Ec, W&C Co)	T-Te									
2029	**Rufous-cheeked Tanager** *Tangara rufigenis*	M	(N Ve)	T	Endemic								

No.	Species	Ssp. Total	Subspecies in Northern South America	Altitude Range	References and Comments	Ec	Co	Ve	Ar Cu Bo	Tr To	Gu	Su	FG
2030	**Golden-naped Tanager** *Tangara ruficervix*	6	leucotis (W Ec) ruficervix (Co) taylori (E Ec, SE Co)	T-S	In RG&G: erroneously called *rufivertex*.								
2031	**Metallic-green Tanager** *Tangara labradorides*	2	labradorides (W Ec, W Co)	T-Te									
2032	**Blue-browed Tanager** *Tangara cyanotis*	2	lutleyi (E Ec, S Co)	T-S									
2033	**Blue-necked Tanager** *Tangara cyanicollis*	7	caeruleocephala (E Ec, Co) cyanopygia (W Ec) granadensis (C Co) hannahiae (E Co, NW Ve)	T-S									
2034	**Golden-masked Tanager** *Tangara larvata*	4	fanny (NW Ec, W Co)	T									
2035	**Masked Tanager** *Tangara nigrocincta*	M	(E Ec, E Co, S Ve, Gu)	T									
2036	**Green-naped Tanager** *Tangara fucosa*	M	(Extreme NW Co)	S	Recorded in Co: Pearman 1993.								
2037	**Beryl-spangled Tanager** *Tangara nigroviridis*	4	cyanescens (W Ec, N&W Co, N Ve) lozanoana * (W Ve) nigroviridis (E Ec, E Co)	T-Te	*Ssp. nov.: Aveledo & Perez 1994.								
2038	**Blue-and-black Tanager** *Tangara vassorii*	3	vassorii (Andes: Ec, Co & Ve)	Te-P									
2039	**Black-capped Tanager** *Tangara heinei*	M	(E Ec, N&W Co, NW Ve)	T-S									
2040	**Silvery Tanager** *Tangara viridicollis*	2	fulvigula (S Ec)	T-S									
2041	**Straw-backed Tanager** *Tangara argyrofenges*	2	caeruleigularis (S Ec)	T-S	Recorded in Ec: RG&G.								
2042	**Black-headed Tanager** *Tangara cyanoptera*	2	cyanoptera (N Co, NW Ve) whitelyi (S Ve, Gu)	T-S									
2043	**Opal-rumped Tanager** *Tangara velia*	4	iridina (E Ec, SE Co, S Ve) velia (E Ve, Gu Su, FG)	T									
2044	**Opal-crowned Tanager** *Tangara callophrys*	M	(E Ec, SE Co)	T									
2045	**Golden-collared Honeycreeper** *Iridophanes pulcherrima*	2	aureinucha (W Ec) pulcherrima (E Ec, C Co)	T-S	Formerly *Tangara*								
2046	**Turquoise Dacnis-Tanager** *Pseudodacnis hartlaubi*	M	(W Co)	T-S	Formerly *Dacnis* **Endemic**								
2047	**White-bellied Dacnis** *Dacnis albiventris*	M	(E Ec, E Co, S Ve)	T									
2048	**Black-faced Dacnis** *Dacnis lineata*	3	aequatorialis (W Ec) egregia (C Co) lineata (E Ec, E Co, S Ve, Gu, Su, FG)	T	egregia may be a sep. sp. (Yellow-tufted Dacnis): Ridgely & Tudor 1989.								
2049	**Yellow-bellied Dacnis** *Dacnis flaviventer*	M	(E Ec, SE Co, SC Ve)	T									
2050	**Scarlet-thighed Dacnis** *Dacnis venusta*	2	fuliginata (NW Ec, W Co)	T									
2051	**Blue Dacnis** *Dacnis cayana*	8	baudoana (W Ec, W Co) cayana (E Co, Ve, Tr, Gu, Su, FG) coerebicolor (C Co) glaucogularis (S Co) napea (N Co) ultramarina (NW Co)	T									
2052	**Viridian Dacnis** *Dacnis viguieri*	M	(NW Co)	T									
2053	**Scarlet-breasted Dacnis** *Dacnis berlepschi*	M	(NW Ec, SW Co)	T									

No.	Species	Ssp. Total	Subspecies in Northern South America	Altitude Range	References and Comments	Ec	Co	Ve	Ar Cu Bo	Tr To	Gu	Su	FG
2054	**Green Honeycreeper** *Chlorophanes spiza*	7	*caerulescens* (E Ec, SE Co) *exsul* (W Ec, SW Co) *spiza* (E Co, Ve, Tr, Gu, Su, FG) *subtropicalis* (Co, W Ve)	S									
2055	**Short-billed Honeycreeper** *Cyanerpes nitidus*	M	(E Ec, Co, S Ve)	T									
2056	**Shining Honeycreeper** *Cyanerpes lucidus*	2	*isthmicus* (NW Co)	T									
2057	**Purple Honeycreeper** *Cyanerpes caeruleus*	5	*caeruleus* (Co, Ve, Su, FG) *chocoanus* (W Ec, W Co) *hollmayri* (Gu) *longirostris* (Tr) *microrhynchus* (E Ec, Co, W&S Ve)	T									
2058	**Red-legged Honeycreeper** *Cyanerpes cyaneus*	10	*carneipes* (NW Co) *cyaneus* (SE Ve, Tr, Gu, Su, FG) *dispar* (Co, S Ve) *eximius* (N Co, N Ve, Bo) *gemmeus* (NE Co) *gigas* (Co: Gorgona Is.) *pacificus* (W Ec, W Co) *tobagensis* (To)	T									
2059	**Tit-like Dacnis** *Xenodacnis parina*	3	*bella* ? (S Ec)	T-P	Sight records in Ec: SFP&M.	?							
2060	**Swallow Tanager** *Tersina viridis*	3	*grisescens* (Co: Sta Marta) *occidentalis* (Ec, Co, Ve, Tr, Gu, Su, FG)	S									
2061	**Plush-capped Finch** *Catamblyrhynchus diadema*	3	*diadema* (Ec, Co & Ve: Andes) *federalis* (Ve: Coastal Range)	S-P									
2062	**Tanager Finch** *Oreothraupis arremonops*	M	(NW Ec, SW Co)	S									
2063	**Black-backed Bush-Tanager** *Urothraupis stolzmanni*	M	(C Ec, C&S Co)	P									
2064	**Rusty Flower-piercer** *Diglossa sittoides*	6	*coelestis* (Ve: Perijá) *decorata* (Ec) *dorbignyi* (C Co, W Ve) *hyperythra* (NE Co, N Ve) *mandeli* (NE Ve)	S-P									
2065	**Venezuelan Flower-piercer** *Diglossa venezuelensis*	M	(NE Ve)	S-P	**Endemic**								
2066	**Black-throated Flower-piercer** *Diglossa brunneiventris*	2	*vuilleumieri* (W Co)		Graves 1980								
2067	**White-sided Flower-piercer** *Diglossa albilatera*	4	*albilatera* (Ec, Co, W Ve) *federalis* (N Ve) *schistacea* (SW Ec)	S-Te									
2068	**Chestnut-bellied Flower-piercer** *Diglossa gloriosissima*	2	*gloriosissima* (Co: Cauca) *boyley* * (Co: Antioquía)	Te-P	* Ssp nov.. Graves 1990 **Endemic**								
2069	**Glossy Flower-piercer** *Diglossa lafresnayii*	5	*lafresnayii* (Ec, C Co, W Ve)	S-P									
2070	**Coal-black Flower-piercer** *Diglossa gloriosa*	M	(Ve: Andes)	P	Formerly *D. carbonaria gloriosa* **Endemic**								

No.	Species	Ssp. Total	Subspecies in Northern South America	Altitude Range	References and Comments	Ec	Co	Ve	Ar Cu Bo	Tr To	Gu	Su	FG
2071	**Black Flower-piercer** *Diglossa humeralis*	3	*aterrima* (Ec, S Co) *humeralis* (N&C Co: E Andes, SW Ve) *nocticolor* (Co: Sta Marta & W Ve: Perijá)	S-P	Vuilleumier 1984								
2072	**Scaled Flower-piercer** *Diglossa duidae*	3	*diudae* (Ve: C Amazonas) *georgebarrowcloughi* * (SW Ve) *hitchcocki* (Ve: N Amazonas)	S	* Ssp. nov.: Dickerman 1987								
2073	**Greater Flower-piercer** *Diglossa major*	4	*chimantae* (Ve: Chimanta) *disjuncta* (Ve: tepuis of C, S & W Bolivar) *gilliardi* (Ve: Auyantepui) *major* (SE Ve: SE tepuis)	S									
2074	**Indigo Flower-piercer** *Diglossa indigotica*	M	(W Ec, SW Co)	T-S									
2075	**Deep-blue Flower-piercer** *Diglossa glauca*	2	*tyrianthina* (E Ec)	S									
2076	**Bluish Flower-piercer** *Diglossa caerulescens*	6	*caerulescens* (N Ve) *ginesi* (NW Ve) *media* (S Ec) *saturata* (Co, SW Ve)	S-Te									
2077	**Masked Flower-piercer** *Diglossa cyanea*	5	*cyanea* (Ec, Co, W Ve) *dispar* (SW Ec) *obscura* (NW Ve) *tovarensis* (NC Ve)	S-P									
2078	**Blue-winged Warbler** *Vermivora pinus*	M	(Boreal migrant: winters to N Co, NW Ve; occasionally to Cu, Ar, Bo)	T-LS	Formerly *Dendroica*								
2079	**Golden-winged Warbler** *Vermivora chrysoptera*	M	(Boreal migrant: winters to N Co, NW Ve; occasionally to Cu, Ar, Bo)	S-Te	Sight records in Ec: RG&G.								
2080	**Tennessee Warbler** *Vermivora peregrina*	M	(Boreal migrant: winters to N Co, NW Ve; occasionally to Cu, Ar, Bo)	T-Te									
2081	**Northern Parula** *Parula americana*	M ?	(Boreal migrant: winters to C & S Am.)	T-LS	Possibly comprises 2 ssp: *ludoviciana* (wintering in C Am.) & *americana* (wintering in the West Indies): Dunn & Garrett 1997.								
2082	**Tropical Parula** *Parula pitiayumi*	14	*alarum* (E Ec) *elegans* (Co,Ve: N & Marg, Tr, To) *nana* (NW Co) *pacifica* (SW Co, W Ec) *roraimae* (S Ve, Gu, W Su)	T-S									
2083	**Yellow Warbler** *Dendroica petechia*	43	N S.Am. ssp. fall into 3 groups, treated separately below.		Sometimes regarded as 3 sep. sp. (e.g. RG&G), but maintained as a single species in 3 groups in AOU 1998.								
a.	**[Northern Yellow Warbler]** *aestiva* group	9	*aestiva* (Ec, Co, Ve) *amnicola* (Ec, Co, Ve, FG) *morcomi* (Ec, Co, Ve, FG) *sonorana* (Ec, Co) Unidentified ssp. * (Ar, Cu, Bo, Tr, To, Gu, Su, FG)	T-Te	Boreal migrants. * SFP&M								

No.	Species	Ssp. Total	Subspecies in Northern South America	Altitude Range	References and Comments	Ec	Co	Ve	Ar Cu Bo	Tr To	Gu	Su	FG
b.	[Golden Warbler] *petechia* group	18	*aurifrons* (NE Ve) / *cienagae* (N&NW Ve) / *obscura* (Ve: C offshore islands) / *rufopileata* (Ve: E offshore islands, Ar, Cu, Bo) / Unidentified ssp.* (Co)	LT	Residents, primarily Caribbean. Considerable plumage variation in *obscura* suggests possibility of inter-island movements. SFP&M.								
c.	[Mangrove Warbler] *erithachorides* group	16	*chrysendeta* (NE Co, NW Ve) / *erithachorides* (Co) / *jubaris* (W Co) / *paraguanae* (NW Ve) / *peruviana* (W Ec, SW Co)	LT	Residents.								
2084	Chestnut-sided Warbler *Dendroica pennsylvanica*	M	(Boreal migrant: winters to Ec, Co, Cu, Bo, Ar, Ve, Tr)	T-LS									
2085	Magnolia Warbler *Dendroica magnolia*	M	(Boreal migrant: winters to N Co, Ve, Tr, To)	T-LS	Sight records in Ve, Tr, To: Dunn & Garrett 1997			?		?			
2086	Cape May Warbler *Dendroica tigrina*	M	(Boreal migrant: winters to Co, Cu, Bo, Ar, Ve, Tr)	T-LS	Records in Co, Ar/Bo/Cu, Ve, Tr: SFP&M.								
2087	Black-throated Blue Warbler *Dendroica caerulescens*	2	*caerulescens* (Boreal migrant: winters to Co, Ve) / *cairnsi* ? (Boreal migrant: winters to Ar, Cu, Bo, Tr, To?)	T-S									
2088	Yellow-rumped Warbler *Dendroica coronata*	4	*coronata* group (Boreal migrant: winters to Co, Ve, To, Ar, Cu, Bo)	Te-P	*coronata* group = Myrtle Warbler								
2089	Townsend's Warbler *Dendroica townsendi*	M	(Boreal migrant: winters rarely to N Co)	T-Te									
2090	Black-throated Green Warbler *Dendroica virens*	M	(Boreal migrant: winters rarely to N Co, Cu, Bo, Ar, N Ve, Tr)	T-Te									
2091	Blackburnian Warbler *Dendroica fusca*	M	(Boreal migrant: winters to all N S.Am.)	T-Te									
2092	Yellow-throated Warbler *Dendroica dominica*	4	*albilora* (Boreal migrant: winters rarely to Co, Tr, To)	LT									
2093	Prairie Warbler *Dendroica discolor*	2	*discolor* (boreal migrant through C.Am.: winters Co?) / *paludicola* (boreal migrant through West Indies: winters rarely to Cu, Ar, Bo, Tr?)	T-LS									
2094	Palm Warbler *Dendroica palmarum*	2	*palmarum* (boreal migrant: winters to Co, Cu, Bo, Ar, Ve)	T-LS	Recorded in Ve: Rodriguez & Lentino 1997								
2095	Bay-breasted Warbler *Dendroica castanea*	M	(Boreal migrant: winters to Ec, Co, Cu, Bo, Ar, Ve: N&W & Tortuga Is., Tr)	T									
2096	Blackpoll Warbler *Dendroica striata*	M	(Boreal migrant: winters to E Ec, E Co, Cu, Bo, Ar, S Ve, Tr, Gu, Su, FG)	T									
2097	Cerulean Warbler *Dendroica cerulea*	M	(Boreal migrant: winters to E Ec, E Co, W Ve, Cu, Ar, Bo)	UT-S									
2098	Black-and-white Warbler *Mniotilta varia*	M	(Boreal migrant: winters Ec, Co, Cu, Bo, Ar, N&E Ve, Tr)	T-S									
2099	American Redstart *Setophaga ruticilla*	M	(Boreal migrant: winters to Ec, Co, Cu, Bo, Ar, Ve, Tr, Gu, Su, FG)	T-LS									
2100	Prothonotary Warbler *Protonotaria citrea*	M	(Boreal migrant: winters to N Ec, Co, Cu, Bo, Ar, N Ve, Tr, To, Gu, Su)	LT									

No.	Species	Ssp. Total	Subspecies in Northern South America	Altitude Range	References and Comments	Ec	Co	Ve	Ar Cu Bo	Tr To	Gu	Su	F
2101	**Worm-eating Warbler** *Helmitheros vermivorus*	M	(Boreal migrant: winters very rarely to Co, Ve)	T-LS	Recorded in Ve: Dunn & Garrett 1997. Sight records in Co: SFP&M.		?						
2102	**Swainson´s Warbler** *Limnothlypis swainsonii*	M	(Boreal migrant: winters very rarely to NW Ve)	LT	Recorded in Ve: Casler & Esté 1997								
2103	**Ovenbird** *Seiurus aurocapillus*	M	(Boreal migrant: winters to Co, Cu, Bo, Ar, Ve, Tr)	T-LS									
2104	**Northern Waterthrush** *Seiurus noveboracensis*	M	(Boreal migrant: winters to N Ec, Co, Cu, Bo, Ar, Ve, Tr, Gu, Su, FG)	T-S									
2105	**Louisiana Waterthrush** *Seiurus motacilla*	M	(Boreal migrant: winters to C Co, W Ve, Cu, Ar, Bo, Tr)	T-S									
2106	**Kentucky Warbler** *Oporornis formosus*	M	(Boreal migrant: winters to N Co, NW Ve; occasionally to Cu; Ar, Bo)	T	Formerly *Geothlypis*								
2107	**Connecticut Warbler** *Oporornis agilis*	M	(Boreal migrant: winters to Co, Ve; occasionally to Cu; Ar & Bo?)	LT	Formerly *Geothlypis*								
2108	**Mourning Warbler** *Oporornis philadephia*	M	(Boreal migrant: winters to Ec, Co, Ve; occasionally to Cu, Ar, Bo)	T	Formerly *Geothlypis*								
2109	**Common Yellowthroat** *Geothlypis trichas*	13	*trichas* group (boreal migrant: winters to Co, Cu, Bo, Ar; dubious for Ve, Tr)	T-Te									
2110	**Olive-crowned Yellowthroat** *Geothlypis semiflava*	2	*semiflava* (W Ec, W Co)	T-S									
2111	**Masked Yellowthroat** *Geothlypis aequinoctialis*	4	*aequinoctialis* (NE Co, Ve, Tr, Gu, Su, FG) *auricularis* (W Ec)	T-S									
2112	**Hooded Warbler** *Wilsonia citrina*	M	(Boreal migrant: winters occasionally to N Co, N Ve, Cu, Bo, Ar, Tr)	T									
2113	**Canada Warbler** *Wilsonia canadensis*	M	(Boreal migrant: winters to Ec, Co, Ve)	T-Te									
2114	**Slate-throated Whitestart** *Myioborus miniatus*	12	*ballux* (Ec, Co: N & Andes, Ve: NW & Andes) *pallidiventris* (Ve: Coastal Range) *sanctaemartae* (Co: Sta Marta) *subsimilis* (SW Ec) *verticalis* (SE Ec, S&SE Ve, W Gu)	T-Te									
2115	**Tepui Whitestart** *Myioborus castaneocapillus*	3	*castaneocapillus* (S Ve: Gran Sabana, W Gu) *duidae* (S Ve: Amazonas tepuis) *maguirei* (S Ve: Neblina)	S	All 3 ssp. formerly conspecific with *M. brunniceps*: R&T.								
2116	**Yellow-faced Whitestart** *Myioborus pariae*	M	(NE Ve: Paria)	UT	**Endemic**								
2117	**White-faced Whitestart** *Myioborus albifacies*	M	(S Ve: Tepuis of N Amazonas)	UT-S	**Endemic**								
2118	**Saffron-breasted Whitestart** *Myioborus cardonai*	M	(SE Ve: Tepuis of N Amazonas)	UT-LS	**Endemic**								
2119	**Spectacled Whitestart** *Myioborus melanocephalus*	5	*ruficoronatus* (Ec, SW Co)	US-P									
2120	**Golden-fronted Whitestart** *Myioborus ornatus*	2	*chrysops* (Co: W&C Andes) *ornatus* (C Co, SW Ve: Tachira)	S-P									

No.	Species	Ssp. Total	Subspecies in Northern South America	Altitude Range	References and Comments	Ec	Co	Ve	Ar Cu Bo	Tr To	Gu	Su	FG
2121	**White-fronted Whitestart** *Myioborus albifrons*	M	(Ve: Andes)	Te-P	**Endemic**			X					
2122	**Yellow-crowned Whitestart** *Myioborus flavivertex*	M	(Co: Sta Marta)	S-Te	**Endemic**		X						
2123	**Grey-and-gold Warbler** *Basileuterus fraseri*	2	fraseri (C&S Ec) ochraceicrista (W Ec)	T		X							
2124	**Two-banded Warbler** *Basileuterus bivittatus*	3	roraimae (SE Ve)	T-LS				X			X		
2125	**Golden-bellied Warbler** *Basileuterus chrysogaster*	2	chlorophrys (NW Ec, SW Co)	T		X	X						
2126	**Pale-legged Warbler** *Basileuterus signatus*	2	signatus ? (Co: Cundinamarca)	S-Te			X						
2127	**Citrine Warbler** *Basileuterus luteoviridis*	5	luteoviridis (E Ec, E Co, SW Ve) quindianus (Co: C Andes) richardsoni (Co: W Andes)	Te-P		X	X	X					
2128	**Black-crested Warbler** *Basileuterus nigrocristatus*	M	(E Ec, Co, SW Ve)	S-P		X	X	X					
2129	**Grey-headed Warbler** *Basileuterus griseiceps*	M	(NE Ve: E Coastal Range)	S	**Endemic**			X					
2130	**Santa Marta Warbler** *Basileuterus basilicus*	M	(NE Co: Sta Marta)	US-Te	**Endemic**		X						
2131	**Grey-throated Warbler** *Basileuterus cinereicollis*	3	cinereicollis (Co: E Andes) pallidulus (NE Co, NW Ve) zuliensis * (Ve: Perijá)	UT-S	* Ssp nov.: Aveledo & Perez 1994		X	X					
2132	**White-lored Warbler** *Basileuterus conspicillatus*	M	(Co: Sta Marta)	T-S	**Endemic**		X						
2133	**Russet-crowned Warbler** *Basileuterus coronatus*	8	castaneiceps (SW Ec) elatus (W Ec, SW Co) orientalis (E Ec regulus (CW Ve)	S-Te		X	X	X					
2134	**Golden-crowned Warbler** *Basileuterus culicivorus*	13	austerus (C Co) cabanisi (NE Co, NW Ve) indignus (Co: Sta Marta) occultus (W&NC Co) olivascens (E Co, NE Ve, Tr) segrex (SE Ve & W Gu)	T-S			X	X	X	X	X		
2135	**Three-banded Warbler** *Basileuterus trifasciatus*	2	nitidior (SW Ec)	S-Te		X							
2136	**Rufous-capped Warbler** *Basileuterus rufifrons*	8	mesochrysus (N Co, W Ve)	T-Te			X	X					
2137	**Pirre Warbler** *Basileuterus ignotus*	M	(Extreme NW Co: Cerro Tacarcuna)	S			X						
2138	**Three-striped Warbler** *Basileuterus tristriatus*	12	auricularis (Co: E &SW Andes, Ve: Tachira) baezae (E Ec) bessereri (N Ve: Coastal Range) daedalus (W Ec, W Co) meridanus (W Ve) pariae (NE Ve: Paria) tacarcunae (NW Co)	UT-S		X	X	X					
2139	**Flavescent Warbler** *Basileuterus flaveolus*	M	(NE Co, W&NC Ve)	T			X	X					
2140	**Buff-rumped Warbler** *Basileuterus fulvicauda*	6	motacilla (CW Co) fulvicauda (E Ec) semicervin (E&W Ec, W Co)	T	Formerly *Phaeothlypis*	X	X						
2141	**River Warbler** *Basileuterus rivularis*	3	mesoleuca (NE Ve, Gu, Su, FG)	T	Formerly *Phaeothlypis*			X			X	X	X

113

No.	Species	Ssp. Total	Subspecies in Northern South America	Altitude Range	References and Comments	Ec	Co	Ve	Ar Cu Bo	Tr To	Gu	Su	FG
2142	**Rose-breasted Chat** *Granatellus pelzelni*	2	*pelzelni* (SE Ve, Gu, Su)	T									
2143	**Chestnut-vented Conebill** *Conirostrum speciosum*	3	*amazonum* (E Ec, E Co, SW Ve, Gu, FG) *guaricola* (C Ve)	T									
2144	**White-eared Conebill** *Conirostrum leucogenys*	3	*leucogenys* (N Co, NW Ve) *panamense* (NW Co)	T									
2145	**Bicolored Conebill** *Conirostrum bicolor*	2	*bicolor* (N Co, N Ve, Gu, Su, FG) *minor* (E Ec)	LT	Sight records in Ec: RG&G.	?							
2146	**Cinereous Conebill** *Conirostrum cinereum*	3	*fraseri* (Ec, SW Co)	T-P									
2147	**Rufous-browed Conebill** *Conirostrum rufum*	M	(N Co, W Ve)	Te-P									
2148	**Blue-backed Conebill** *Conirostrum sitticolor*	3	*intermedium* (W Ve) *pallidus* (Ve: Perijá) *sitticolor* (Ec, Co)	Te-P									
2149	**Capped Conebill** *Conirostrum albifrons*	6	*albifrons* (E Co, SW Ve) *atrocyaneum* (Ec, SW Co) *centralandium* (C Co) *cyanotum* (N Ve)	UT-Te									
2150	**Giant Conebill** *Oreomanes fraseri*	3	*fraseri* (Ec, SW Co)	Te-P									
2151	**Rufous-browed Peppershrike** *Cyclarhis gujanensis*	21	*canticus* (N&E Co) *flavipectus* (Ve: Paria, Tr) *gujanensis* (extreme E Co, S Ve, Gu, Su, FG) *parvus* (Co: E Andes, N&C Ve) *virenticeps* (SW&E Ec)	T-Te									
2152	**Black-billed Peppershrike** *Cyclarhis nigrirostris*	2	*atrirostris* (W Ec, SW Co) *nigrirostris* (C&W Co, E Ec)	S-Te									
2153	**Yellow-browed Shrike-Vireo** *Vireolanius eximius*	2	*eximius* (NE Co, NW Ve) *mutabilis* (NW Co)	T									
2154	**Slaty-capped Shrike-Vireo** *Vireolanius leucotis*	4	*leucotis* (E Ec, SW Co, S Ve, Gu, Su, FG) *mikettae* (NW Ec, Co)	T-S									
2155	**Yellow-throated Vireo** *Vireo flavifrons*	M	(Boreal migrant: winters to Co, N&W Ve, Cu, Bo, Ar, Tr)	T-S									
2156	**Philadelphia Vireo** *Vireo philadelphicus*	M	(Boreal migrant: winters to Co: Chocó & Bogota)	T-S									
2157	**Red-eyed Vireo** *Vireo olivaceus*	13	*diversus* & *chivi* (residents in all S.Am.; southern birds are austral migrants to N S.Am.) *forreri* & *insulanus* (resident in C.Am., migrants to N S.Am.) *olivaceus* (resident N.Am., boreal migrant to N S.Am.) *griseobarbatus* (W Ec) *caucae* (W Co) *solimoensis* (E Ec) *vividor* (NE Co, Ve, Tr, Gu, Su, FG) *tobagensis* (To)	T	Johnson & Zink 1985 Johnson *et al.* 1988								
2158	**Yellow-green Vireo** *Vireo flavoviridis*	M	(Resident in Florida, West Indies & N Ve; migrant to N S.Am.)	T-S	Johnson & Zink 1985 Johnson *et al.* 1988								

No.	Species	Ssp. Total	Subspecies in Northern South America	Altitude Range	References and Comments	Ec	Co	Ve	Ar Cu Bo	Tr To	Gu	Su	FG
2159	**Choco Vireo** *Vireo masteri*	M	(C Co)		Sp. nov.: Salaman & Stiles 1996								
2160	**Black-whiskered Vireo** *Vireo altiloquus*	6	*altiloquus* (boreal migrant: winters to Co, Ve, Gu) *barbadensis* (resident in Tr) *barbatulus* (boreal migrant: in transit through Co, Ve) *bonairensis* (resident in Ar, Cu, Bo, Ve: Marg & Los Roques)	T									
2161	**Brown-capped Vireo** *Vireo leucophrys*	7	*disjunctus* (N Co: C & W Andes) *dissors* C&S Co, C & W Andes) *josephae* (W Ec, SW Co: Nariño) *leucophrys* (E Ec, E Co: E Andes) *mirandae* (Co: Sta Marta, Ve: Perijá, Andes & Coastal Range)	T-S	Formerly all ssp. were included in Warbling Vireo *V. gilvus*.								
2162	**Lemon-chested Greenlet** *Hylophilus thoracicus*	2	*aemulus* (E Ec, Co: Andes) *griseiventris* (E Ve, Gu, Su, FG)	T	Uncertain in Co: SFP&M.		?						
2163	**Grey-chested Greenlet** *Hylophilus semicinereus*	3	*viridiceps* (S Ve, FG)	T									
2164	**Ashy-headed Greenlet** *Hylophilus pectoralis*	M	(E Ve, Gu, Su, FG)	T									
2165	**Tepui Greenlet** *Hylophilus sclateri*	M	(S Ve, W Gu)	T-S									
2166	**Buff-cheeked Greenlet** *Hylophilus muscicapinus*	2	*muscicapinus* (S Ve, Gu, Su, FG)	T									
2167	**Brown-headed Greenlet** *Hylophilus brunneiceps*	2	*brunneiceps* (E Co, S Ve)	T									
2168	**Dusky-capped Greenlet** *Hylophilus hypoxanthus*	5	*fuscicapillus* (E Ec) *hypoxanthus* (SE Co, extreme S Ve)	T									
2169	**Rufous-naped Greenlet** *Hylophilus semibrunneus*	M	(E Ec, Co, NW Ve: Zulia & Perijá)	T-S									
2170	**Golden-fronted Greenlet** *Hylophilus aurantiifrons*	3	*aurantiifrons* (Co: N coast) *helvinus* (W Ve) *saturatus* (E Co, NC & NE Ve, Tr)	T									
2171	**Scrub Greenlet** *Hylophilus flavipes*	7	*acuticauda* (Ve: N&E & Marg) *flavipes* (N Co) *galbanus* (W&NW Ve) *insularis* (To) *melleus* (Co: Guajira)	T	C.Am. ssp. sometimes considered a sep. sp. (Yellow-green Greenlet): AOU 1998.								
2172	**Olivaceous Greenlet** *Hylophilus olivaceus*	M	(CE Ec)	T	Formerly *H. flavipes olivaceus*: S&M.								
2173	**Tawny-crowned Greenlet** *Hylophilus ochraceiceps*	9	*bulunensis* (W Ec, W Co) *ferrugineifrons* (E Ec, SE Co, S Ve, W Gu) *luteifrons* (extreme E Ve, Gu, Su, FG)	T									
2174	**Lesser Greenlet** *Hylophilus decurtatus*	3	*darienensis* (W Co) *minor* (W Ec, SW Co: Nariño)	T	Nominate ssp., of C.Am., sometimes considered to be a sep. sp. (Grey-headed Greenlet): AOU 1998.								

No.	Species	Ssp. Total	Subspecies in Northern South America	Altitude Range	References and Comments	Ec	Co	Ve	Ar Cu Bo	Tr To	Gu	Su	F
2175	**Casqued Oropendola** *Psarocolius oseryi*	M	(E Ec)	T									
2176	**Crested Oropendola** *Psarocolius decumanus*	4	*decumanus* (E Ec, E Co, Ve) *insularis* (Tr, To) *melanterus* (NW Co)	T									
2177	**Green Oropendola** *Psarocolius viridis*	M	(E Ec, extreme E Co, S&E Ve, Gu, Su, FG)	T									
2178	**Russet-backed Oropendola** *Psarocolius angustifrons*	7	*alfredi* (SE Ec) *angustifrons* (E Ec, SE Co) *atrocastaneus* (W Ec) *neglectus* (W Ve, Co: E Andes, E slope) *oleaginus* (NC Ve) *salmoni* (Co: W & C Andes) *sincipitalis* (Co: E Andes)	T-S									
2179	**Chestnut-headed Oropendola** *Psarocolius wagleri*	2	*ridgwayi* (W Co, W Ec)	T									
2180	**Band-tailed Oropendola** *Ocyalus latirostris*	M	(E Ec, SW Co)	T	Formerly *Psarocolius*								
2181	**Baudo Oropendola** *Gymnostinops cassini*	M	(NW Co: Chocó)	T	Formerly *Psarocolius* **Endemic**								
2182	**Olive Oropendola** *Gymnostinops yuracares*	M	(E Co, S Ve)	T	Formerly *Psarocolius bifasciatus yuracares*								
2183	**Black Oropendola** *Gymnostinops guatimozinos*	M	(NW Co)	T	Formerly *Psarocolius*								
2184	**Yellow-rumped Cacique** *Cacicus cela*	3	*cela* (Tr, all N S.Am. E of Andes) *flavicrissum* (W Ec) *vitellinus* (N Co)	T									
2185	**Red-rumped Cacique** *Cacicus haemarrhous*	2	*haemarrhous* (E Ec, SE Co, S Ve, Gu, Su, FG)	T									
2186	**Subtropical Cacique** *Cacicus uropygialis*	M	(E Ec, Co: W & E Andes, NW Ve)	T									
2187	**Scarlet-rumped Cacique** *Cacicus microrhynchus*	2	*pacificus* (W Co, W Ec)	S	Formerly *C. uropygialis microrhynchus*								
2188	**Northern Mountain Cacique** *Cacicus leucoramphus*	2	*leucoramphus* (E Ec, Co: Andes, Ve: Táchira)	S-Te									
2189	**Ecuadorean Cacique** *Cacicus sclateri*	M	(E Ec, Co)	T									
2190	**Solitary Black Cacique** *Cacicus solitarius*	M	(E Ec, E Co, NW Ve)	T									
2191	**Yellow-billed Cacique** *Amblycercus holosericeus*	3	*australis* (E Ec, Co, NW Ve) *flavirostris* (W Co, W Ec) *holosericeus* (N Co)	T-Te	Formerly *Cacicus*								
2192	**Moriche Oriole** *Icterus chrysocephalus*	M	(E Ec, E Co, S&E Ve, Tr, Gu, Su, FG)	T	Formerly *I. cayanensis chrysocephalus*								
2193	**Epaulet Oriole** *Icterus cayanensis*	5	*cayanensis* (Su, FG)	T									
2194	**Yellow-backed Oriole** *Icterus chrysater*	4	*giraudii* (NE Co, NW&N Ve) *hondae* (W&C Co)	T-S									
2195	**Yellow Oriole** *Icterus nigrogularis*	4	*curasoensis* (Ar, Bo, Cu) *heliodes* (Ve: Marg.) *nigrogularis* (N Co, N&C Ve, Gu, Su, FG) *trinitatis* (Tr, Ve: Paria)	T									
2196	**Yellow-tailed Oriole** *Icterus mesomelas*	4	*carrikeri* (N&W Co, NW Ve) *taczanowskii* (W Ec)	T-S									
2197	**Orange-crowned Oriole** *Icterus auricapillus*	M	(N Co, N&C Ve)	T									

No.	Species	Ssp. Total	Subspecies in Northern South America	Altitude Range	References and Comments	Ec	Co	Ve	Ar Cu Bo	Tr To	Gu	Su	FG
2198	White-edged Oriole *Icterus graceannae*	M	(SW Ec)	T		■							
2199	Troupial *Icterus icterus*	3	*icterus* (E Co, N Ve) *metae* (Co & Ve: Meta River) *ridgwayi* (N Co, Ve: NW & Marg, Ar, Cu)	T	AOU 1998		■	■	■				
2200	Orange-backed Oriole *Icterus croconotus*	2	*croconotus* (E Ec, SE Co, Gu)	T	Formerly *I. icterus croconotus*, but considered to be a sep. sp. by Freeman & Zink 1995, fide AOU 1998.	■	■				■		
2201	Baltimore Oriole *Icterus galbula*	4	*galbula* (boreal migrant to N Co & extreme NW Ve)	T-S			■	■					
2202	Orchard Oriole *Icterus spurius*	3	*spurius* (boreal migrant to N Co & extreme NW Ve)	T-S			■	■					
2203	Oriole Blackbird *Gymnomystax mexicanus*	M	(E Ec, E Co, N&C Ve, Gu, Su, FG)	T		■	■	■			■	■	■
2204	Pale-eyed Blackbird *Agelaius xanthophthalmus*	M	(Boreal migrant: winters to Ec)	T	Formerly *Xanthocephalus*	■							
2205	Red-winged Blackbird *Agelaius phoeniceus*	23	Several boreal migrant ssp. in the '*phoeniceus*' group are possible.	T-Te	Casual to Tr: AOU 1998. Sight records in Tr: SFP&M.					?			
2206	Yellow-hooded Blackbird *Agelaius icterocephalus*	2	*bogotensis* (EC Co) *icterocephalus* (N&E Co, N&C Ve, Tr, Gu, Su, FG)	T			■	■		■	■	■	■
2207	Chestnut-capped Blackbird *Agelaius ruficapillus*	2	*frontalis* (FG)	T									■
2208	Red-breasted Blackbird *Sturnella militaris*	2	*militaris* (N&E Co, Ve, Tr, To, Gu, Su, FG)	T-S	Formerly *Leistes*		■	■		■	■	■	■
2209	Peruvian Meadowlark *Sturnella bellicosa*	M	(W Ec)	T-S	Formerly *Pezites militaris bellicosa*	■							
2210	Eastern Meadowlark *Sturnella magna*	14	*meridionalis* (C Co, NW Ve) *paralios* (N Co, C Ve) *praticola* (E Co, SE Ve, Gu, Su, FG)	T-P			■	■			■	■	■
2211	Red-bellied Grackle *Hypopyrrhus pyrohypogaster*	M	(Co: W Andes & southernmost E & C Andes)	T-S	Endemic		■						
2212	Velvet-fronted Grackle *Lampropsar tanagrinus*	5	*guianiensis* (E Ve, Gu) *tanagrinus* (E Ec, Co)	T		■	■	■			■		
2213	Golden-tufted Grackle *Macroagelaius imthurni*	M	(Ve & Gu: Pantepui)	T-S	Sometimes considered to be conspecific with *M. subalaris*.			■			■		
2214	Mountain Grackle *Macroagelaius subalaris*	M	(Co: W Andes)	S-Te	Endemic		■						
2215	Scrub Blackbird *Dives warszewiczi*	2	*warszewiczi* (W Ec)	T-S		■							
2216	Great-tailed Grackle *Quiscalus mexicanus*	8	*peruvianus* (W Ec, Co: N coast, NW Ve)	T-S		■	■	■					
2217	Carib Grackle *Quiscalus lugubris*	8	*insularis* (Ve: Marg & Frailes Is.) *lugubris* (Co, N Ve, Tr, Gu, Su, FG) *luminosus* (Ve: Testigos Is.) *orquillensis* (Ve: Hermanos Is.)	T			■	■		■	■	■	■

No.	Species	Ssp. Total	Subspecies in Northern South America	Altitude Range	References and Comments	Ec	Co	Ve	Ar Cu Bo	Tr To	Gu	Su	F
2218	**Shiny Cowbird** *Molothrus bonariensis*	7	*aequatorialis* (SW Co, W Ec) *cabanisii* (NW,W&C Co) *minimus* (Tr, To; Gu, Su, FG) *occidentalis* (SW Ec) *venezuelensis* (E Co, Ve,)	T-S	Recorded in Cu: Debrot & Prins 1992								
2219	**Bronzed Cowbird** *Molothrus aeneus*	4	*armenti* (Co: N coast & SE lowlands)	T-S									
2220	**Giant Cowbird** *Scaphidura oryzivora*	2	*oryzivora* (Ec, Co, Ve, Gu, Su, FG)	I-S									
2221	**Bobolink** *Dolichonyx oryzivorus*	M	(Boreal migrant: in transit through N S.Am., winters to S S.Am.)	T									
2222	**Andean Siskin** *Carduelis spinescens*	3	*spinescens* (N&W Ve, Co: E Andes, Sta Marta) *nigricauda* (Co: C&W Andes)	S-P	Birds from N Ec may be a sep. ssp. *capitanea* synonymous with *spinescens*: Robbins et al. 1994.								
2223	**Yellow-faced Siskin** *Carduelis yarrelli*	M		T	Uncertain in Ve & Gu.			?			?		
2224	**Red Siskin** *Carduelis cucullata*	M	(N Ve, NE Co)	T-LS	Introduced in Tr: J.C. Eitniear pers. comm.								
2225	**Hooded Siskin** *Carduelis magellanica*	11	*capitalis* (C&S Co, Ec) *longirostris* (S&SE Ve, Gu) *paula* (S Ec)	T-P									
2226	**Saffron Siskin** *Carduelis siemiradzkii*	M		T									
2227	**Olivaceous Siskin** *Carduelis olivacea*	M	(SE Ec)	T-Te									
2228	**Yellow-bellied Siskin** *Carduelis xanthogastra*	2	*xanthogastra* (W Ec, Co, Ve)	S-Te									
2229	**Lesser Goldfinch** *Carduelis psaltria*	5	*columbiana* (N Ve, N&C Co, N&W Ec)	T-Te									
2230	**Common Waxbill** *Estrilda astrild*	13	Ssp. not identified (Tr)	T	Introduced								
2231	**Tricolored Munia** *Lonchura malacca*	M	(Ve: NW Llanos)	T	Restall 1995 Introduced								
2232	**Java Sparrow** *Lonchura oryzivora*	M	(Ve: NW Llanos)	T	Formerly *Padda*: Restall 1996 Introduced								
2233	**Village Weaver** *Ploceus cucullatus*	8	Ssp. uncertain (N Ve)	T	Introduced								
2234	**Southern Masked Weaver** *Ploceus velatus*	7	Ssp. uncertain.	T	Sight records in N Ve: K. Castelain & D. Lauten pers. comm. Introduced			?					
2235	**House Sparrow** *Passer domesticus*	13	Ssp. uncertain.	T-S	Sight records in Ve: C. Sharpe pers. comm. Summers-Smith 1963. Introduced			?					
2236	**European Starling** *Sturnus vulgaris*	12	*vulgaris*? (Ar/Cu/Bo)	T-S	Introduced N.Am. Accidental Ar/Cu/Bo: A&S.				?				
2237	**Black-collared Jay** *Cyanolyca armillata*	3	*armillata* (SW Ve, Co) *meridana* (W Ve) *quindiuna* (Co)	S-P									
2238	**Turquoise Jay** *Cyanolyca turcosa*	M	(S Co, Ec)	Te-P									
2239	**Beautiful Jay** *Cyanolyca pulchra*	M	(W Co)	T-Te									

No.	Species	Ssp. Total	Subspecies in Northern South America	Altitude Range	References and Comments	Ec	Co	Ve	Ar Cu Bo	Tr To	Gu	Su	FG
2240	**Violaceous Jay** *Cyanocorax violaceus*	2	*pallidus* (NC Ve) *violaceus* (E Ec, E Co, W&S Ve, S Gu)	T		X	X	X			X		
2241	**Azure-naped Jay** *Cyanocorax heilprini*	M	(SE Co, S Ve)	T			X	X					
2242	**Cayenne Jay** *Cyanocorax cayanus*	M	(SE Ve, Gu, Su, FG)	T				X			X	X	X
2243	**Black-chested Jay** *Cyanocorax affinis*	2	*affinis* (N Co, NW Ve)	T			X	X					
2244	**White-tailed Jay** *Cyanocorax mystacalis*	M	(SW Ec)	T		X							
2245	**Green Jay** *Cyanocorax yncas*	11	*cyanodorsalis* (C&E Co, NW Ve) *galeatus* (W Co) *guatemalensis* (N Ve) *yncas* (SW Co, E Ec)	T-Te	Ssp. divided into 2 groups: '*luxuosus*' group = Green Jay: 6 ssp. in Central America, '*yncas*' group = Yncas Jay: 5 ssp. in Andes; perhaps 2 sep. sp.: S&M.	X	X	X					

BIBLIOGRAPHY

ALTMAN, A. & B. SWIFT. 1993. *Checklist of the Birds of South America.* (3rd edn.) Privately published.

AMADON, D. 1982. A revision of the sub-buteonine hawks (Accipitridae: Aves). *Amer. Mus. Novit.* 2741: 1-20.

AMADON, D. & J. BULL. 1988. Hawks and Owls of the World: A Distributional and Taxonomic List. *Proc. Western Found. Vert. Zool.* 3: 294-357.

AMES, P.L., M.A., HEIMERDINGER & S.L. WALTER. 1968. The anatomy and systematic position of the antpipits *Conopophaga* and *Corythopis. Postilla* 114: 1-32.

AGRO, D.J. & R.S. RIDGELY. 1998. First record of Striped Manakin *Machaeropterus regulus* in Guyana. *Bull. Brit. Orn. Club* 118: 122-123.

A.O.U. 1983. *Checklist of North American Birds.* (6th edn.) American Ornithologists' Union, Washington, D.C.

A.O.U. 1998. *Checklist of North American Birds.* (7th edn.) American Ornithologists' Union, Washington, D.C.

ARMANI, G. C. 1985. *Guide des Passereaux Granivores.* Soc. Nouvelle des Editions Boubée, Bruxelles.

ARNDT, T. 1990-1996. *Lexicon of Parrots.* 4 Vols. Arndt-Verlag, Bretten.

AVELEDO, R. 1997. Nueva subespecie de la familia Picidae del Estado Lara. *Bol. Soc. Ven. Cien. Nat.* 46 (150): 46 : 3-8.

AVELEDO, R. & R.H. GINES. 1950. Descripción de cuatro aves nuevas de Venezuela. *Mem. Soc. Cien. Nat. La Salle* 10 (26): 59-71.

AVELEDO, R. & A.R. PONS. 1952. Aves nuevas y extensiones de distribución a Venezuela. *Nov. Cien. Ser. Zool.* 7: 1-25.

AVELEDO, R. & PEREZ-CH., L. 1991. Dos nuevas subespecies de aves (Trochilidae, Formicariidae) de la región oriental y occidental de Venezuela. *Bol. Soc. Ven. Cien. Nat.* 44 (147): 15-25.

AVELEDO, R. & PEREZ-CH., L. 1994. Descripción de nueve subespecies nuevas y comentarios sobre dos espécies de aves de Venezuela. *Bol. Soc. Ven. Cien. Nat.* 44 (148): 229-257.

BANKS, R. & C. DOVE. 1992. The generic name for Crested Caracara (Aves: Falconidae). *Proc. Biol. Soc. Wash.* 105: 420-425.

BANKS, R.C. 1997. The name of Lawrence's Flycatcher. Pp. 21-24 in R.W. DICKERMAN (compiler) *The Era of Allan R. Phillips: a festschrift.* Horizon Communications, Albuquerque, New Mexico.

BARROWCLOUGH, G., M. LENTINO & P. SWEET. 1997. New records of birds from Auyan-tepui, Estado Bolivar, Venezuela. *Bull. Brit. Orn. Club* 117: 194-198.

BATES, J.M. 1997. Distribution & geographic variation in three South American grassquits (Emberizinae, *Tiaris*). In J.V. REMSEN JR. (ed.) *Studies in Neotropical Ornithology honoring Ted Parker. Ornith. Monogr.* 48: 91-110.

BIERREGAARD JR., R.O., M. COHN-HAFT & D.F. STOTZ. 1997. Cryptic biodiversity: an overlooked species and new subspecies of antbird (Aves: Formicariidae) with revision of *Cercomacra tyrannina* in north-eastern South America. In J.V. REMSEN JR. (ed.) *Studies in Neotropical Ornithology honoring Ted Parker. Ornith. Monogr.* 48: 111-128.

BOCK, W. 1994. History and nomenclature of avian family-group names. *Bull. Am. Mus. Nat. Hist.* 222: 1-281.

BROOKE, R.K. 1974. Nomenclatural notes on the type localities of some taxa in the Apodidae and Hirundinidae (Aves). *Durban Mus. Novitates* 10: 127-137.

BROWNING, M.R. 1989. The correct name for the Olivaceus Cormorant, "Maiague" of Piso (1685). *Wilson Bull.* 101: 101-106.

BRUMFIELD, R.T. & J.V. REMSEN. 1996. Geographic variation and species limits in *Cinnycerthia* wrens of the Andes. *Wilson Bull.* 108: 205-227.

CAPPARELLA, A.P., G.H. ROSENBERG & S.W. CARDIFF. 1997. A new subspecies of *Percnostola rufifrons* (Formicariidae) from northeastern Amazonian Peru, with a revision of the *rufifrons* complex. In J.V. REMSEN JR. (ed.) *Studies in Neotropical Ornithology honoring Ted Parker. Ornith. Monogr.* 48: 165-170.

CARPENTER, F.L. 1976. Ecology and evolution of an Andean hummingbird (*Oreotrochilus estella*). *Univ. Calif. Publ. Zool.* 106: 1-74.

CARRIKER, M.A. 1954. Additions to the avifauna of Colombia. *Novedades Colombianas* 1: 14-19.

CASLER, C.L. 1996. First record of the Great Black-backed Gull (*Larus marinus*) in Venezuela. *Bol. Ctr. Invest. Biol. Univ. del Zulia* 30: 1-8.

CASLER, C.L. & E.E. ESTÉ. 1997. Record of Swainson´s Warbler (*Limnothlypis swainsonii*) in Northern South America. *Bol. Ctr. Invest. Biol. Univ. del Zulia* 31: 95-98.

CHANTLER, P. & G. DRIESSENS. 1995. *Swifts: A Guide to the Swifts and Treeswifts of the World.* Pica Press, Sussex.

CHESSER, R.T. 1994. Migration in South America: an Overview of the Austral System. *Bird Conservation International* 4: 91-107.

CLARK, W.S. & R.C. BANKS. 1992. The taxonomic status of the White-tailed Kite. *Wilson Bull.* 104: 571-579.

CLEERE, N. & D. NURNEY. 1998. *Nightjars: A Guide to the Nightjars and Related Nightbirds.* Pica Press. Sussex.

CLEMENT, P., A. HARRIS & J. DAVIS. 1993. *Finches & Sparrows: An Identification Guide.* Christopher Helm, London.

CLEMENTS, J.F. 1991. *Birds of the World: A Checklist.* (4th edn.) Ibis Publishing, Vista, California.

COHN-HAFT, M. 1993. Rediscovery of the White-winged Potoo (*Nyctibius leucopterus*). *Auk* 110: 391-394.

COLVEE, J. 1999. First report on the Rose-ringed Parakeet (*Psittacula krameri*) in Venezuela and preliminary observations on its behavior. *Orn. Neotropical* 10: 115-117.

COLLAR, N.J., M.J. CROSBY & A.J. STATTERSFIELD. 1994. *Birds to Watch: The World List of Threatened Birds.* BirdLife Conserv. Series 4. BirdLife International, Cambridge.

COLLAR, N.J., L.P. GONZAGA, N. KRABBE, A. MADROÑO NIETO, L.G. NARANJO, T.A. PARKER & D.C. WEGE. 1992. *Threatened Birds of the Americas.* International Council for Bird Preservation, Cambridge.

CORY, C.B. & C.E. HELLMAYR. 1925. Catalogue of Birds of the Americas and Adjacent Islands, Part IV: Furnariidae – Dendrocolaptidae. *FMNH Pub.* 234, *Zool. Series* XIII.

CURSON, J., D. QUINN & D. BEADLE. 1994. *New World Warblers.* Christopher Helm, London.

DEBROT, A. & T. PRINS. 1992. First record and establishment of the Shiny Cowbird in Curaçao. *Carib. Jour. Sci.* 28: 104-105.

DEL HOYO, J., A. ELLIOTT & J. SARGATAL, eds. 1992-1997. *Handbook of the Birds of the World,* Vols. I, II, III, IV, V. Lynx Edicions, Barcelona.

DELGADO, F. & S. FRANCISCO. 1985. A new subspecies of the Painted Parakeet (*Pyrrhura picta*) from Panamá. In P.A. BUCKLEY, M.S. FOSTER, E.S. MORTON, R.S. RIDGELY & F.G. BUCKLEY (eds.) *Neotropical Ornithology. Ornith. Monogr.* 36: 17-22.

DEMASTES, J.W., & J.V. REMSEN JR. 1994. The genus *Caryothraustes* (Cardinalinae) is not monophyletic. *Wilson Bull.* 106: 733-738.

DICKERMAN, R.W. 1988. An unnamed subspecies of *Euphonia rufiventris* from Venezuela and northern Brazil. *Bull. Brit. Orn. Club* 108: 20-22.

DICKERMAN, R.W. 1987. Notes on the plumages of *Diglossa duidae* with the description of a new subspecies. *Bull. Brit. Orn. Club* 107: 42-44.

DICKERMAN, R.W., G.F. BARROWCLOUGH, P.F. CANNELL, W.H. PHELPS JR. & D.E. WILLARD. 1986. *Phylidor hylobius* Wetmore & Phelps, is a synonym of *Automolus roraimae* Hellmayr. *Auk* 103: 431-432.

DUNN, J. & K. GARRETT. 1997. *Warblers.* Houghton Mifflin, Boston.

EISENMANN, E. 1958. The spelling of *Notharcus macrorhychos hyperrhynchus. Auk* 75: 101.

ELEY, J.W. 1982. Systematic relationships and zoogeography of the White-winged Guan (*Penelope albipennis*) and related forms. *Wilson Bull.* 94: 241-432.

ESCALANTE-P., P. & A.T. PETERSON. 1992. Geographic variation and species limits in Middle American woodnymphs (*Thalurania*). *Wilson Bull.* 104: 205-338.

FARQUHAR, C.C. 1998. *Buteo polyosoma* and *B. poecilochrous,* the "red-backed buzzards" of South America, are conspecific. *Condor* 100: 27-43.

FFRENCH, R. 1991. *A Guide to the Birds of Trinidad and Tobago.* (2nd edn.). Cornell University Press, Ithaca, New York.

FISHER, D. 1998. The first record of Spotted Redshank *Tringa erythropus* for South America. *Cotinga* 9: 21.

FITZPATRICK, J.W. & D.E.WILLARD. 1982. Twenty one bird species new or little known from the Republic of Colombia. *Bull. Brit. Orn. Club* 102: 153-158.

FITZPATRICK, J.W. & J. P. O'NEILL. 1979. A new Tody-Tyrant from Peru. *Auk* 96: 443-447.

FJELDSÅ, J. 1985. Origin, evolution and status of the avifauna of Andean wetlands. In P.A. BUCKLEY, M.S. FOSTER, E.S. MORTON, R.S. RIDGELY & F.G. BUCKLEY (eds.) *Neotropical Ornithology. Ornith. Monogr.* 36: 85-112.

FJELDSÅ, J. & N. KRABBE. 1990. *Birds of the High Andes.* Zoological Museum, Univ. of Copenhagen and Apollo Books.

FRY, C.H., K. FRY & A. HARRIS. 1992. *Kingfishers, Bee-eaters and Rollers.* Christopher Helm, London.

GARCIA-M., J. & J. FJELDSÅ. 1999. Re-evaluation of species limits in the genus *Atlapetes* based on mtDNA sequence data. *Ibis* 141: 199-207.

GARRIDO, O.H., A.T. PETERSON & O. KOMAR. 1999. Geographic variation and taxonomy of the Cave Swallow (*Petrochelidon fulva*) complex, with the description of a new sub-species from Puerto Rico. *Bull. Brit. Orn. Club* 119: 80-90.

GARRIDO, O.H. & J.V. REMSEN JR. 1996. A new subspecies of the Pearly-eyed Thrasher *Margarops fuscatus* (Mimidae) from the island of St. Lucia, Lesser Antilles. *Bull. Brit. Orn. Club* 116: 75-80.

GOCHFELD, M., S. KEITH & P. DONAHUE. 1980. Records of rare or previously unrecorded birds from Colombia. *Bull. Brit. Orn. Club* 100: 196-201.

GRAVES, G. & D. URIBE. 1989. A new allopatric taxon in the *Hapalopsittaca amazonina* (Psittacidae) superspecies from Colombia. *Wilson Bull.* 101: 369-376.

GRAVES, G.R. 1980a. A new species of Metaltail hummingbird from northern Peru. *Wilson Bull.* 92:1-148.

GRAVES, G.R. 1980b. A new subspecies of *Diglossa* (*carbonaria*) *brunneiventris. Bull. Brit. Orn. Club* 100: 230-232.

GRAVES, G.R. 1986a. Geographic variation in the White-mantled Barbet (*Capito hypoleucos*) of Colombia (Aves: Capitonidae). *Proc. Biol. Soc. Wash.* 99: 61-64.

GRAVES, G.R. 1986b. Systematics of the Gorgeted Woodstars (Aves: Trochilidae: *Acestrura*). *Proc. Biol. Soc. Wash.* 99: 218-224.

GRAVES, G.R. 1987. A new subspecies of *Siptornis striaticollis* (Aves: Furnariidae) from the eastern slope of the Andes. *Proc. Biol. Soc. Wash.* 100: 121-124.

GRAVES, G.R. 1988. *Phylloscartes lanyoni,* a new species of Bristle-tyrant (Tyrannidae) from the lower Cauca Valley of Colombia. *Wilson Bull.* 100: 529-534.

GRAVES, G.R. 1990. A new subspecies of *Diglossa gloriosissima* (Aves: Thraupinae) from the western Andes of Colombia. *Proc. Biol. Soc. Wash.* 103: 962-965.

GRAVES, G.R. 1992. Diagnosis of a hybrid antbird (*Phlegopsis nigromaculata* x *Phlegopsis erythroptera*) and the rarity of hybridization among suboscines. *Proc. Biol. Soc. Wash.* 105: 834-840.

GRAVES, G.R. 1993. Relic of a lost world: A new species of Sun-angel (Trochilidae: *Heliangelus*) from "Bogota". *Auk* 110: 1-8.

GRAVES, G.R. 1997. Colorimetric and morphometric gradients in Colombian populations of Dusky Antbirds (*Cercomacra tyrannina*), with a description of a new species *Cercomacra parkeri.* In: J.V. REMSEN JR (ed.) *Studies in Neotropical Ornithology honoring Ted Parker. Ornith. Monogr.* 48: 21-36.

HACKETT, S.J. 1993. Phylogenetic and biogeographic relation-ships in the Neotropical genus *Gymnopithys* (Formicariidae). *Wilson Bull.* 105: 301-315.

HAFFER, J. 1974. Avian Speciation in Tropical South America. *Publ. Nuttall Ornith. Club* 14: 1-390.

HAFFER, J. 1975. Avifauna of northwestern Colombia, South America. *Bonn Zool. Monogr.* 7: 5-182.

HAFFER, J. 1997. Contact zones between birds of southern Amazonia. In: J.V. REMSEN JR (ed.) *Studies in Neotropical Ornithology honoring Ted Parker Ornith. Monogr.* 48: 281-305.

HARRISON, P. 1983. *Seabirds: An Identification Guide.* Croom Helm, Beckenham, Kent.

HAVERSCHMIDT, F., & G.F. MEES. 1994. *Birds of Surinam.* Vaco. Paramaribo.

HAYMAN, P., J. MARCHANT & T. PRATER. 1986. *Shorebirds: An Identification Guide.* Croom Helm, London & Sydney.

HEIDRICH, P., C. KÖNIG & M. WINK. 1995. Molecular phylo-geny of South American Screech Owls of the *Otus atricapillus* complex (Aves: Strigidae), inferred from nucleotide seq-uences of the mitochondrial cytochrome b gene. *Zeitschrift für Naturforschung, Section C, Biosciences* 50 (3-4): 294-302.

HELLMAYR, C.E. 1927. Catalogue of the Birds of the Americas and the Adjacent Islands. Part 5, Tyrannidae. *Zool. Ser. Field Mus. Nat. Hist.* 13 (11 parts).

HERKLOTS, G.A.C. 1961. *The Birds of Trinidad & Tobago.* Collins, London.

HILTY, S. 1999. Three new species in Venezuela and notes on the behaviour and distribution of other poorly known species. *Bull. Brit. Orn. Club.* 119: 220-234.

HILTY, S. In prep. *Birds of Venezuela.* Princeton Univ. Press, Princeton.

HILTY, S.L. & W.L. BROWN. 1986. *A Guide to the Birds of Colombia.* Princeton Univ. Press, Princeton.

HINKELMANN, C. 1996. Systematics and geographic variation in long-tailed hermit hummingbirds, the *Phaetornis superciliosus-malaris-longirostris* species group (Trochilidae), with notes on their biogeography. *Orn. Neotropical* 7: 119-148.

HINKELMANN, C. & K.-L. SCHUCHMANN. 1997. Phylogeny of the Hermit Hummingbirds (Trochilidae: Phaethornithinae). *Stud. Neotrop. Fauna & Environm.* 32: 142-163.

HOWELL, S.N.G. 1994. The specific status of Black-faced Antthrushes in Middle America. *Cotinga* 1: 20-25.

HOWELL, S.N.G. & M. ROBBINS. 1995. Species limits of the Least Pigmy-Owl (*Glaucidium minutissimum*) complex. *Wilson Bull.* 107: 7-25.

ISLER, M.L. & P.R. ISLER. 1987. *The Tanagers: Natural History, Distribution and Identification.* Smithsonian Inst. Press, Washington, DC.

ISLER, M.L., P.R. ISLER. & B.M. WHITNEY. 1997. Biogeography and Systematics of the *Thamnophilus punctatus* (*Thamnophilidae*) complex. In J.V. REMSEN JR. (ed.) *Studies in Neotropical Ornithology honoring Ted Parker. Ornith. Monogr.* 48: 355-381.

ISLER, M.L., P.R. ISLER. & B.M. WHITNEY. 1999. Species limits in Antbirds: The *Myrmotherula surinamensis* complex. *Auk* 116: 83-96.

JAMES, C. & C. HISLOP. 1988. Status and conservation of two cracid species – the Trinidad Piping Guan (*Pipile pipile*) and the Cocrico (*Ortalis ruficauda*) in Trinidad & Tobago. *Proc. II International Cracid Symposium*, Caracas.

JOHNSGARD, P.A. 1988. *The Quails, Partridges and Francolins of the World.* Oxford Univ. Press, Oxford.

JOHNSON, N.K. & R.M. ZINK. 1985. Genetic evidence for relationships in the Avian family Vireonidae. *Condor* 90: 428-445.

JOHNSON, N.K., R.M. ZINK & J.A. MAARTEN. 1988. Genetic evidence for relationships among the Red-eyed, Yellow-green, and Chivi Vireos. *Wilson Bull.* 97: 421-435.

JUNIPER, T. & M. PARR. 1998. *Parrots: A Guide to the Parrots of the World.* Pica Press, Sussex.

KÖNIG, C. 1991. Zur Taxonomie und Ökologie der Sperlingskäuze (*Glaucidium* spp.) des Andenraumes. *Ökol. Vögel* 13: 15-76.

KÖNIG, C. 1994. Biological patterns in owl taxonomy, with emphasis on bioacustical studies on Neotropical pygmy (*Glaucidium*) and screech (*Otus*) owls. In MEYBURG, B.U. & R.D. CHANCELLOR (eds.) *Raptor Conservation Today*, Pica Press, Sussex.

KÖNIG, C., F. WEICK & J-H. BECKING. 1999. *Owls: A Guide to the Owls of the World.* Pica Press, Sussex.

KRABBE, N. 1992. A new subspecies of the Slender-billed Miner *Geositta tenuirostris* (Furnariidae) from Ecuador. *Bull. Brit. Orn. Club* 112: 166 169.

KRABBE, N. 1992. Notes on distribution and natural history of some poorly known Ecuadorian birds. *Bull. Brit. Orn. Club* 112: 169-174.

KRABBE, N. & T.S. SCHULENBERG. 1997. Species limits and natural history of *Scytalopus* tapaculos (Rhinocryptidae), with descriptions of the Ecuadorian taxa, including three new species. In J.V. REMSEN JR. (ed.) *Studies in Neotropical Ornithology honoring Ted Parker. Ornith. Monogr.* 48: 47-88.

KRABBE, N., D.J. AGRO, N.H. RICE, M. JACOMAI, L. NAVARRETE & F. SORNOZA-M. 1999. A new species of antpitta (Formicariidae: *Grallaria*) from southern Ecuadorian Andes. *Auk* 116: 882-890.

KRABBE, N., M. ISLER, P. ISLER, B. WHITNEY, J. ALVAREZ & P. GREENFIELD. 1999. A new species in the *Myrmotherula haematonota* superspecies (Aves: Thamnophilidae) from the western Amazonian lowlands of Ecuador and Peru. *Wilson Bull.* 111: 157-302.

LANE, D.F. 1999. A Phylogenetic Analysis of the American Barbets using Plumage and Vocal Characters (Aves; Family Ramphastidae; Subfamily Capitonidae). M.Sc. Thesis, Louisiana State Univ.

LANYON, W.E. 1978. Revision of the *Myiarchus* flycatchers of South America. *Bull. Amer. Mus. Nat. Hist.* 161: 427-627.

LANYON, W.E. 1984. A phylogeny of the kingbirds and their allies. *Am. Mus. Novit.* 2797: 1-28.

LANYON, W.E. 1986. A phylogeny of the thirty-three genera in the *Empidonax* assemblage of Tyrant Flycatchers. *Am. Mus. Novit.* 2846: 1-64.

LANYON, W.E. 1988. A phylogeny of the thirty-two genera in the *Elaenia* assemblage of Tyrant Flycatchers. *Am. Mus. Novit.* 2914: 1-64.

LENTINO R., M. 1988. *Notiochelidon flavipes*, a swallow new to Venezuela. *Bull. Brit. Orn. Club* 108: 70-71.

LENTINO R., M. 1997. Lista Actualizada de las Aves de Venezuela. Pp: 145-202 in E. LA MARCA (ed.) *Vertebrados Actuales y Fósiles de Venezuela.* Mus. de Cienc. y Tec. de Mérida.

LIGON, J. 1967. Relationships of the Cathartid vultures. *Occ. Papers Mus. Zool. Univ. Michigan* 651: 1-26.

LIVEZEY, B.C. 1991. A phylogenetic analysis and classification of recent dabbling ducks (Tribe Anatini) based on comparative morphology. *Auk* 108: 471-507.

LIVEZY, B.C. 1995. Phylogeny and comparative ecology of stiff-tailed ducks (Anatidae: Oxyurini). *Wilson Bull.* 107: 214-234.

LOWERY, G.H. & D.A. TALLMAN. 1976. A new genus and subspecies of nine-primaried oscine of uncertain affinities from Peru. *Auk* 93: 415-428.

LOWERY, G.H. & J.P. O'NEILL. 1969. A new species of Antpitta from Peru and a revision of the subfamily Grallariinae. *Auk* 86: 1-12.

MADGE, S. & H. BURN. 1988. *Wildfowl: An Identification Guide to the Ducks, Geese and Swans of the World.* Christopher Helm, London.

MADGE, S. & H. BURN. 1993. *Crows and Jays: A Guide to The Crows, Jays and Magpies of the World.* Christopher Helm, London.

MARANTZ, C.A. 1997. Geographic variation of plumage patterns in the woodcreeper genus *Dendrocolaptes*. In J.V. REMSEN JR. (ed.) *Studies in Neotropical Ornithology honoring Ted Parker. Ornith. Monogr.* 48: 399-429.

MARANTZ, C.A. & J.V. REMSEN. 1991. Seasonal distribution of the Slaty Elaenia, a little-known austral migrant of South America. *J. Field Ornith.* 62:162-172.

MARCHANT, S. 1960. The breeding of some southwestern Ecuadorian birds. *Ibis* 102: 349-382 & 584-599.

MARIN, M. 1997. Species limits and distribution of some New World spinetail swifts (*Chaetura* spp.). In J.V. REMSEN JR. (ed.) *Studies in Neotropical Ornithology honoring Ted Parker. Ornith. Monogr.* 48. 431-444.

MARIN, M. & F.G. STILES. 1992. On the biology of five species of swifts (Apodidae, Cypseloidinae) in Costa Rica. *Proc. Western Found. Vert. Zool.* 4: 287-351.

MAYR, E. & F. VUILLEUMIER. 1983. New species of birds described from 1966 to 1975. *J. Orn.* 124: 217-232.

MEES, G.F. 1974. Additions to the avifauna of Suriname. *Zool. Meded.* 48: 55-67.

MEES, G.F. 1985. Nomenclature and systematics of birds from Suriname. *Proc. K. Acad. Wet. Series C*, 88: 75-91.

MEYER DE SCHAUENSEE, R. 1948-1952. *The Species of Bird of South America and their Distribution.* Philadelphia Academy of Nat. Sciences.

MEYER DE SCHAUENSEE, R. 1966. The birds of the Republic of Colombia: their distribution, and keys for their identification. *Caldasia* 5: 251-1223.

MEYER DE SCHAUENSEE, R. 1967. *Eriocnemis mirabili*, a new species of hummingbird from Colombia. *Not. Naturae* 402: 1-2.

MOBLEY, J.A. & R.O. PRUM. 1995. Phylogenetic relationships of the Cinnamon Tyrant, *Neopipo cinnamomea*, to the Tyrant Flycatchers (Tyrannidae). *Condor* 97: 650-662.

MONROE, B.L. & M.R. BROWNING. 1992. A re-analysis of *Butorides*. *Bull. Brit. Orn. Club* 112: 81-85.

MONROE, B.L. & C.G. SIBLEY. 1993. *Checklist of Birds of the World*. Yale Univ. Press, New Haven.

O'NEILL, J.P. 1966. Notes on the distribution of *Conothraupis speculigera* (Gould). *Condor* 68: 598-600.

O'NEILL, J.P. & T.A. PARKER. 1977. Taxonomy and range of *Pionus "seniloides"* in Peru. *Condor* 79: 274.

O'NEILL, J.P. & T.A. PARKER. 1981. New subspecies of *Pipriola riefferii* and *Chlorospingus ophthalmicus* from Peru. *Bull. Brit. Orn. Club* 101: 294-299.

O'NEILL, J.P. & T.A. PARKER. 1997. New subspecies of *Myrmoborus leucophrys* (Formicaridae) and *Phrygilus alaudinus* (Emberizidae) from the upper Huallaga Valley, Peru. In J.V. REMSEN JR. (ed.) *Studies in Neotropical Ornithology honoring Ted Parker. Ornithol. Monog.* 48: 485-492.

OLROG, C. C. 1968. *Las Aves Sudamericanas: una guia de campo.* Fundación Instituto Miguel Lillo, Tucuman.

OLSEN, K.M. & H. LARSSON. 1997. *Skuas and Jaegers: A Guide to the Skuas and Jaegers of the World.* Pica Press, Sussex.

OLSON, S.L. 1981a. Interaction between the two subspecies groups of the Seed-Finch *Sporophila angolensis* in the Magdalena Valley, Colombia. *Auk* 98: 379-38.

OLSON, S.L. 1981B. A revision of the northern forms of *Euphonia xanthogaster. Proc. Biol. Soc. Wash.* 94: 101-106.

OLSON, S.L. 1981c. The nature and variability in the Variable Seedeater of Panamá (*Sporophila americana*, Emberizinae). *Proc. Biol. Soc. Wash.* 94: 380-390.

OLSON, S.L. 1983. Geographic variation in *Chlorospingus ophthalmicus* in Colombia and Venezuela (Aves: Thraupidae). *Proc. Biol. Soc. Wash.* 96: 103-109.

ORTIZ-VON HALLE, B. 1990. Adiciones a la avifauna de Colombia, de especies arribadas a la Isla Gorgona. *Caldasia* 16: 209-214.

OUELLET, H. 1993. Bicknell's Thrush: taxonomic status and distribution. *Wilson Bull.* 105: 545-572.

PARKER, T.A. & J.L. O'NEILL. 1985. A new species and a new subspecies of *Thryothorus* wren from Peru. In P.A. BUCKLEY, M.S. FOSTER, E.S. MORTON, R.S. RIDGELY & F.G. BUCKLEY (eds.) *Neotropical Ornithology. Ornith. Monogr.* 36: 9-15.

PARKER, T.A. & J.V. REMSEN JR. 1987. Fifty-two Amazonian bird species new to Bolivia. *Bull. Brit. Orn. Club* 107: 94-107.

PARKER, T.A., S.A. PARKER & M.A. PLENGE. 1982. *An Annotated Checklist of Peruvian Birds.* Buteo, S. Dakota.

PAYNTER, R.A. 1978. Biology and evolution of the avian genus *Atlapetes* (Emberizinae). *Bull. Amer. Mus. Comp. Zool.* 148: 323-369.

DE LA PEÑA, M.R. & M. RUMBOLL. 1998. *Birds of Southern South America and Antarctica.* HarperCollins, London.

PEARMAN, M. 1993. Some range extensions and five species new to Colombia, with notes on some scarce or little known species. *Bull. Brit. Orn. Club* 113: 66-75.

PETERS, J.L., M.A. TRAYLOR JR., E. MAYR, J.C. GREENWAY JR., R.A. PAYNTER JR. & G.W. COTTRELL (eds.). 1931-1986. *Check-list of Birds of the World.* Vols. 1-15. Harvard Univ. Press & Mus. Comp. Zool., Cambridge.

PHELPS, W.H. & W.H. PHELPS JR. 1950. Lista de las aves de Venezuela con su distribución, Parte 2, Passeriformes. *Bol. Soc. Ven. Cienc. Nat.* 12: 1-427.

PHELPS, W.H. & W.H. PHELPS JR. 1952. Nine new subspecies of birds from Venezuela. *Proc. Biol. Soc. Wash.* 65: 46- 54.

PHELPS, W.H. & W.H. PHELPS JR. 1954. Notes on Venezuelan birds and descriptions of six new subspecies. *Proc. Biol. Soc. Wash.* 67: 103-114.

PHELPS, W.H. & W.H. PHELPS JR. 1955. Five new Venezuelan birds and nine extensions of ranges to Colombia. *Proc. Biol. Soc. Wash.* 68: 47-580.

PHELPS, W.H. & W.H. PHELPS JR. 1956. Three new birds from Cerro El Teteo, Venezuela, and extensions of ranges to Venezuela and Colombia. *Proc. Biol. Soc. Wash.* 69: 127-134.

PHELPS, W.H. & W.H. PHELPS JR. 1956. Five new birds from Rio Chiquito, Táchira, Venezuela, and two extensions of ranges from Colombia. *Proc. Biol. Soc. Wash.* 69: 157-166.

PHELPS, W.H. & W.H. PHELPS JR. 1958. Descriptions of two new Venezuelan birds and distributional notes. *Proc. Biol. Soc. Wash.* 71: 119-124.

PHELPS, W.H. & W.H. PHELPS JR. 1958. Lista de las aves de Venezuela con su distribución, Tomo 2, Parte 1, No-Passeriformes. *Bol. Soc. Ven. Cienc. Nat.* 19: 1-317.

PHELPS, W.H. & W.H. PHELPS JR. 1962. Two new subspecies of birds from Venezuela. *Proc. Biol. Soc. Wash.* 75: 199-203.

PHELPS, W.H. & W.H. PHELPS JR. 1963. Lista de las aves de Venezuela con su distribución. Tomo 1, Parte 2 Passeriformes, (2 ed.). *Bol. Soc. Ven. Cienc. Nat.* 24: 1-479.

PHELPS, W.H., JR. 1973. Adiciones a las listas de aves de Sur América, Brasil y Venezuela y notas sobre aves venezolanas. *Bol. Soc. Ven. Cienc. Nat.* 30: 23-40.

PHELPS, W.H., JR. 1976. Descripción de una raza geográfica de *Crypturellus obsoletus* (Aves: Tinamidae) de Los Andes de Venezuela. *Bol. Soc. Ven. Cienc. Nat.* 32: 15-22.

PHELPS, W.H., JR. 1977a. Aves colectadas en las mesetas de Sarisariñama y Jaua durante tres expediciones al Macizo de Jaua, Estado Bolívar. Descripciones de dos nuevas subespecies. *Bol. Soc. Ven. Cienc. Nat.* 33: 15-42.

PHELPS, W.H., JR. 1977b. Una nueva especie y dos nuevas subespecies de aves (Psittacidae, Furnariidae) de la Sierra de Perijá cerca de la divisoria colombo-venezolana. *Bol. Soc. Ven. Cienc. Nat.* 33(134): 43-53.

PHELPS JR., W.H. & R.W. DICKERMAN. 1980. Cuatro subespecies nuevas de aves (Furnariidae, Formicariidae) de la región de Pantepui, Estado Bolivar y territorio Amazonas, Venezuela. *Bol. Soc. Ven. Cienc. Nat.* 138: 139-147.

PHELPS JR., W.H. & R. AVELEDO. 1984. Dos nuevas subespecies de aves (Troglodytidae, Fringillidae) del Cerro Marahuaca, Territorio Amazonas, Venezuela. *Bol. Soc. Ven. Cienc. Nat.* 39: 5-10.

PHELPS JR., W.H. & R. AVELEDO. 1987. Cinco nuevas subespecies de aves (Rallidae, Trochilidae, Picidae, Furnariidae) y tres extensiones de distribucion para Venezuela. *Bol. Soc. Ven Cienc. Nat.* 41: 7-26

PHELPS W.H., JR. & R.M. DE SCHAUENSEE. 1994. *Una Guia de las Aves de Venezuela* (2 ed.). Ex Libris, Caracas.

PHILLIPS, A.R. 1994. A review of the northern *Pheucticus* grosbeaks. *Bull. Brit. Orn. Club* 114: 162-170.

PITMAN, R.L. & J.R. JEHL. 1998. Geographic variation and reassessment of species limits in the "Masked Boobies" of the eastern Pacific Ocean. *Wilson Bull.* 110: 155-170.

PRUM, R.O. 1992. Syringeal morphology, phylogeny, and evolution of the Neotropical Manakins (Aves: Pipridae). *Amer. Mus. Nov.* 3043: 1-65.

PRUM, R.O. 1994. Species status of the White-fronted Manakin *Lepidothrix serena* (Pipridae), with comments on conservation biology. *Condor* 96: 692-702.

REMSEN JR., J.V. 1997. A new genus for the Yellow-shouldered Grosbeak. In J.V. REMSEN JR. (ed.) *Studies in Neotropical Ornithology honoring Ted Parker. Ornith. Monogr.* 48: 89-90.

REMSEN JR., J.V. & W.S. GRAVES IV. 1995. Distribution patterns and zoogeography of *Atlapetes* Brush-Finches (Emberizinae) of the Andes. *Auk* 112: 210-224.

REMSEN JR., J.V. & W.S. GRAVES IV. 1995. Distribution patterns of *Buarremon* Brush-Finches (Emberizinae) and interspecific competition in Andean birds. *Auk* 112: 225-236.

RESTALL, R.L. 1995. Proposed additions to the genus *Lonchura* (Estrildidae). *Bull. Brit. Orn. Club* 115: 140-157.

RESTALL, R.L. 1996. *Munias and Mannikins.* Pica Press, Sussex.

RESTALL, R.L. In press. A comment on the status of *Sporophila insularis* (Emberizidae) of Trinidad and Venezuela.

RIDGELY, R.S. & D.J. AGRO. 1997. *The Birds of Iwokrama.* Website of the Phil. Acad. Nat. Sciences.

RIDGELY, R.S. & G. TUDOR. 1989. *The Birds of South America, Vol. I: The Oscine Passerines.* Univ. of Texas Press, Austin.

RIDGELY, R.S. & G. TUDOR. 1994. *The Birds of South America, Vol, II: The Suboscine Passerines.* Univ. of Texas Press, Austin.

RIDGELY, R.S. & M.B. ROBBINS. 1988. *Pyrrhura orcesi*, a new parakeet from southwestern Ecuador, with systematic notes on the *Pyrrhura melanura* complex. *Wilson Bull.* 100: 173-182.

RIDGELY, R.S., P.J. GREENFIELD & M. GUERRERO. 1998. *Una Lista Anotada de las Aves de Ecuador Continental Continental.* Fund. Ornitologica del Ecuador, CECIA, Quito.

ROBBINS, M.B. & R.S. RIDGELY. 1991. *Sipia rosenbergi* (Formicariidae) is a synonym of *Myrmeciza* (*laemosticta*) *nigricauda*, with comments on the validity of the genus *Sipia. Bull. Brit. Orn. Club* 111: 11-18.

ROBBINS, M.B. & R.S. RIDGELY. 1992. Taxonomy and natural history of *Nyctiphrynus rosenbergi* (Caprimulgidae). *Condor* 94: 984-987.

ROBBINS, M.B. & R.S. RIDGELY. 1993. A new name for *Myrmeciza immaculata berlepschi* (Formicariidae). *Bull. Brit. Orn. Club* 113: 190.

ROBBINS, M.B. & S.N.G. HOWELL. 1995. A new species of Pygmy-owl (Strigidae: *Glaucidium*) from the Eastern Andes. *Wilson Bull.* 107:1-6.

ROBBINS, M.B. & T.A. PARKER III. 1997. Voices and taxonomy of *Caprimulgus* (*rufus*) *otiosus* (Caprimulgidae), with a re-evaluation of the *Caprimulgus rufus* subspecies. In J.V. REMSEN JR. (ed.) *Studies in Neotropical Ornithology honoring Ted Parker. Ornith. Monogr.* 48: 601-608.

ROBBINS, M.B., N. KRABBE, G.H. ROSENBERG & F. SONORZA M. 1994. Geographic variation in the Andean Siskin *Carduelis spinescens* with comments on its status in Ecuador. *Orn. Neotropical* 5: 61-63.

ROBBINS, M.B. & F.G. STILES. 1999. A new species of Pygmy-Owl (Strigidae: *Glaucidium*) from the Pacific slope of the northern Andes. *Auk* 116: 305-315.

RODRIGUEZ, G. AND M. LENTINO. 1997. Range expansion and summering of Palm Warbler *Dendroica palmarum* in Venezuela. *Bull. Brit. Orn. Club* 117: 76-77.

ROJAS, R., W. PIRAGUA, F. G. STILES & T. MCNEISH. 1997. Primeros registros para Colombia de cuatro taxones de la familia Tyrannidae. *Caldasia* 19(3): 523-525.

ROMERO-Z., H. 1977. Status taxonómico de *Catamenia oreophila* Todd. *Lozania* 23:1-7.

ROMERO-Z., H. 1980. Una nueva subespecie colombiana de *Campylorhamphus pusillus. Lozania* 31:1-4.

ROMERO-Z., H. & J.E. MORALES-SANCHEZ. 1981. Descripción de una nueva subespecie de *Leptotila verreauxi* Bonaparte, 1855 (Aves: Columbidae) del sureste de Colombia. *Caldasia* 13: 291-296.

ROMERO-Z., H. & J. HERNÁNDEZ-CAMACHO. 1979. Una nueva subespecie colombiana de *Haplophaedia aureliae. Lozania* 30: 1-6.

ROMERO-Z., H. & J.V. RODRIGUEZ. 1980. Hallazgo de *Oncostoma cinereigulare* (Sclater) (Aves: Tyrannidae) en Colombia. *Lozania* 31: 5-6.

SALAMAN, P.G. & F.G. STILES. 1996. A distinctive new species of vireo (Passeriformes: Vireonidae) from the western Andes of Colombia. *Ibis* 138: 610-619.

SALAMAN, P.G. & L.A. MAZARIEGOS. 1998. The hummingbirds of Colombia. *Cotinga* 10: 30-36.

SCHUCHMANN, K.-L. & K. DUFFNER. 1993. Geographical variation and speciation patterns in the Andean hummingbird genus *Aglaicercus* Zimmer 1930. *Mitt. Zool. Mus. Berl.* 69 Suppl.: *Ann. Orn.* 17: 75-92.

SCHULENBERG, T.S. & M.D. WILLIAMS. 1982. A new species of Antpitta (*Grallaria*) from northern Peru. *Wilson Bull.* 94 : 105-240.

SCHULENBERG, T.S. & T.A. PARKER III. 1997. A new species of tyrant flycatcher (Tyrannidae: *Tolmomyias*) from the western Amazon basin. In J.V. REMSEN JR. (ed.) *Studies in Neotropical Ornithology honoring Ted Parker. Ornith. Monogr.* 48: 723-731.

SCHWARTZ, P. 1972. On the taxonomic rank of the Yellow-billed Toucanet (*Aulacorhynchus calorhynchus*). *Bol. Soc. Ven. Cienc. Nat.* 29: 459-476.

SCHWARTZ, P. 1972. *Micrastur gilvicollis*, a valid species sympatric with *M. ruficollis* in Amazonia. *Condor* 74: 399-415.

SCHWARTZ, P. 1975. Solved and unsolved problems in the *Sporophila lineola / S. bouvronides* complex (Aves: Emberizidae). *Ann. Carnegie Mus.* 45: 277-285.

SCHWARTZ, P. 1977. Some clarifications about *Ramphastos "aurantiirostris". Auk* 94: 775-777.

SCHWARTZ, P. & M. LENTINO. 1984. Relaciones de los Tinamidos venezolanos del grupo *Crypturellus noctivagus*, indicadas por su voz (Aves: Tinamidae). *Serie Informes Cientificos.* DGSIIA/IC-23, MARNR, Caracas.

SEUTIN, G., J. BRAWN, R.E. RICKLEFS & E. BERMINGHAM. 1993. Genetic divergence among populations of a tropical passerine, the Streaked Saltator (*Saltator albicollis*). *Auk* 104: 97-108.

SHORT, L. 1982. Woodpeckers of the World. *Delaware Mus. Nat. Hist. Monogr.* 4.

SIBLEY, C.G. & B.L. MONROE, JR. 1990. *Distribution and Taxonomy of Birds of the World.* Yale Univ. Press, New Haven.

SIBLEY, C.G. & B.L. MONROE, JR. 1993. *A Supplement to Distribution and Taxonomy of Birds of the World.* Yale Univ. Press, New Haven.

SICK, H. 1993. *Birds in Brazil: A Natural History.* Princeton Univ. Press, Princeton.

SNOW, D.W. 1973. The classification of the Cotingidae (Aves). *Breviora* 409: 1-27.

SNOW, D.W. 1975. *Laniisoma elegans* in Peru. *Auk* 92: 583-584.

SNOW, D.W. 1975. The classification of the Manakins. *Bull. Brit. Orn. Club* 95: 20-27.

SNOW, D.W. 1985. Systematics of the *Turdus fumigatus / hauxwelli* group of thrushes. *Bull. Brit. Orn. Club* 105: 30-37.

STILES, F.G. 1981. The taxonomy of Rough-winged Swallows (*Stelgidopteryx*; Hirundinidae) in southern Central America. *Auk* 98: 282-293.

STILES, F.G. 1983. The taxonomy of *Microcerculus* wrens (Troglodytidae) in Central America. *Wilson Bull.* 95: 169-183.

STILES, F.G. 1992. A new species of antpitta (Formicariidae: *Grallaria*) from the eastern Andes of Colombia. *Wilson Bull.* 104: 389-399.

STILES, F.G. 1995a. La situación del Tororoi Pechicanela (*Grallaria haplonota*, Formicariidae) en Colombia. *Caldasia* 17: 607-610.

STILES, F.G. 1995b. Distribución y variación en el Hermitaño Carinegro (*Phaethornis anthophilus*) en Colombia. *Caldasia* 18: 119-129.

STILES, F.G. 1996. A new species of Emerald Hummingbird (Trochilidae, *Chlorostilbon*) from the Sierra de Chiribiquete, southeastern Colombia, with a review of the *C. mellisugus* complex. *Wilson Bull.* 108: 1-27.

STILES, F.G. 1996. When black plus white equals grey: the nature of variation in the Variable Seedeater complex (Emberizinae: *Sporophila*). *Orn. Neotropical* 7: 75-107.

STOTZ, D.F., J.W. FITZPATRICK, T.A. PARKER III & D.K. MOSKOVITZ. 1996. *Neotropical Birds: Ecology and Conservation.* Univ. of Chicago Press, Chicago.

SUMMERS-SMITH, J.D. 1963. *The House Sparrow.* Collins, London.

TAYLOR, B. & B. VAN PERLO. 1998. *Rails. A Guide to the Rails, Crakes, Gallinules and Coots of the World.* Pica Press, Sussex.

TOSTAIN, O., J.L. DUJARDIN, CH. ERARD & J.M. THIOLLAY. 1992. *Oiseaux de Guyane.* Societe d'Etudes Ornithologiques, Cayenne.

TRAYLOR JR., M.A. 1977. A Classification of the Tyrant Flycatchers. *Bull. Mus. Comp. Zool.* 148: 129-184.

TRAYLOR JR., M.A. 1985. Species limits in the *Ochthoeca diadema* species-group (Tyrannidae). In P.A. BUCKLEY, M.S. FOSTER, E.S. MORTON, R.S. RIDGELY & F.G. BUCKLEY (eds.) *Neotropical Ornithology. Ornith. Monogr.* 36: 430-442.

TURNER, A. & C. ROSE. 1989. *A Handbook to the Swallows and Martins of the World.* Christopher Helm, London.

VAURIE, C. 1967. Systematic notes on the bird family Cracidae. No. 10: The genera *Mitu* and *Pauxi*, and the generic relationships of the Cracini. *Amer. Mus. Novit.* 2307: 1-20.

VAURIE, C. 1968. Taxonomy of the Cracidae (Aves). *Bull. Amer. Mus. Nat. Hist.* 138: 131-260.

VAURIE, C. 1980. Taxonomy and geographical distribution of the Furnariidae (Aves: Passeriformes). *Bull. Amer. Mus. Nat. Hist.* 166: 1-357.

VAURIE, C. & P. SCHWARTZ. 1972. Morphology and vocalizations of *Synallaxis unirufa* and *Synallaxis castanea* (Furnariidae, Aves), with comments on other *Synallaxis. Amer. Mus. Novit.* 2483: 1-13

VIELLIARD, J. 1989. Una nova especie de *Glaucidium* (Aves: Strigidae) da Amazonia. *Revista Bras. Zool.* 6: 685-693.

VOOUS, K.H. 1982. Straggling to islands: South American birds in the islands of Aruba, Curaçao and Bonaire, South Caribbean. *J. Yamashina Inst. Ornith.* 14: 171-178.

VOOUS, K.H. 1985. Additions to the avifauna of Aruba, Curaçao and Bonaire, South Caribbean. In P.A. BUCKLEY, M.S. FOSTER, E.S. MORTON, R.S. RIDGELY & F.G. BUCKLEY (eds.) *Neotropical Ornithology. Ornith. Monogr.* 36: 247-254.

VOOUS, K.H. 1986. Striated or Green Herons in the South Caribbean islands? *Aus. Naturhist. Mus. Wien* 88/89: 101-106.

VUILLEUMIER, F. 1984. Zoogeography of Andean birds: two major barriers; and speciation and taxonomy of the *Diglossa carbonaria* superspecies. *Nat. Geo. Soc. Res. Rep.* 16: 713-731.

VUILLEUMIER, F. & E. MAYR. 1987. New species of birds described from 1976 to 1980. *J. Ornith.* 128: 137-150.

WATTEL, J. 1973. Geographical differentiation in the genus *Accipiter. Publ. Nuttall Ornith. Club* 13: 1-231.

WELLER, A.A. & K-L. SCHUCHMANN. 1999. Geographical variation in the southern distributional range of the Rufous-tailed Hummingbird, *Amazilia tzacatl* De la Llave, 1832: a new subspecies from Nariño, southwestern Colombia. *J. Orn.* 140: 457-466.

WESKE, J.S. 1985. A new subspecies of Collared Inca Hummingbird (*Coeligena torquata*) from Peru. In P.A. BUCKLEY, M.S. FOSTER, E.S. MORTON, R.S. RIDGELY & F.G. BUCKLEY (eds.) *Neotropical Ornithology. Ornith. Monogr.* 36: 41-46.

WESKE, J.S. & J.W. TERBORGH. 1981. *Otus marshalli,* a new species of Screech Owl from Peru. *Auk* 98: 1-7.

WETMORE, A. 1946. New birds from Colombia. *Smithsonian Misc. Coll.* 106: 1-14

WETMORE, A. 1953. Further additions to the birds of Panamá & Colombia. *Smithsonian Misc. Coll.* 122: 1-12.

WETMORE, A. 1965. Additions to the list of birds of the Republic of Colombia. *L'Oiseau* 35: 156-162.

WETMORE, A. 1968. The birds of the Republic of Panamá. Columbidae (Pigeons) to Picidae (Woodpeckers). *Smithsonian Misc. Coll.* 150, Part 2: 1-605.

WETMORE, A. 1970. Descriptions of additional forms of birds from Panamá and Colombia. *Proc. Biol. Soc. Wash.* 82: 767-776.

WETMORE, A. 1972. The birds of the Republic of Panamá. Passeriformes: Dendrocolaptidae (Woodcreepers) to Oxyruncidae (Sharpbills). *Smithsonian Misc. Coll.* 150, Part 3: 1-631.

WETMORE, A., & W.H. PHELPS. 1956. Further additions to the list of birds of Venezuela. *Proc. Biol. Soc. Wash.* 69: 1-12.

WETMORE, A., R.F. PASQUIER & S.L. OLSON. 1984. The Birds of the Republic of Panamá. Passeriformes: Hirundinidae (Swallows) to Fringillidae (Finches). *Smithsonian Misc. Coll.* 150, Part 4: 1-670.

WHITNEY, B.M. 1992. Observations on the systematics, behaviour and vocalizations of *"Thamnomanes" occidentalis* (Formicariidae). *Auk* 109: 302-308.

WHITNEY, B.M. & J.A. ALONSO. 1998. A new *Herpsilochmus* antwren (Aves: Thamnophilidae) from northern Amazonian Peru and adjacent Ecuador: the role of edaphic heterogeneity of terra firme forests. *Auk* 115: 559-576.

WILLIS, E.O. 1969. On the behaviour of 5 species of *Rhegmatorhina,* ant-following antbirds of the Amazon basin. *Wilson Bull.* 81: 363-395.

WILLIS, E.O. 1984. Antshrikes (Formicariidae) as army ant followers. *Pap. Avuls. Zool.* 35: 177-182.

WILLIS, E.O. 1992. Three *Chamaeza* antthrushes in eastern Brazil (Formicariidae). *Condor* 94: 110-116.

WILLIS, E.O. 1992. Comportamento e ecologia do Arapaçu Barrado *Dendrocolaptes certhia* (Aves, Dendrocolaptidae). *Bol. Mus. Paraense Emilio Goeldi, Ser Zool.* 8: 151-216.

WINKLER, H., D.A. CHRISTIE & D. NURNEY. 1995. *Woodpeckers: A Guide to the Woodpeckers, Piculets and Wrynecks of the World.* Pica Press, Sussex.

ZIMMER, J.T. 1936. Studies of Peruvian Birds No. 19: Notes on the genera *Geositta, Furnarius, Phleocryptes, Certhiaxis, Cranioleuca* and *Asthenes. Amer. Mus. Novit.* 860: 1-17.

ZIMMER, J.T. 1939. Studies of Peruvian Birds No. 33: The genera *Tolmomyias* and *Rhynchocyclus,* with further notes on *Ramphotrigon. Amer. Mus. Novit.* 1045: 1-23..

ZIMMER, J.T. 1948. Studies of Peruvian Birds No. 53: The family Trogonidae. *Amer. Mus. Novit.* 1380: 1-56.

ZIMMER, J.T. 1951. Studies of Peruvian Birds No. 61: The genera *Aglaeactis, Lafresnaya, Pterophanes, Boissonneaua, Heliangelus, Eriocnemis, Haplophaedia, Ocreatus, Lesbia. Amer. Mus. Novit.* 1540: 1-55.

ZIMMER, J.T. 1955. Studies of Peruvian Birds No. 66: The Swallows (Hirundinidae). *Amer. Mus. Novit.* 1723: 1-35.

ZIMMER, K.J. 1997. Species limits in *Cranioleuca vulpina.* In: J.V. REMSEN JR. (ed.) *Studies in Neotropical Ornithology honoring Ted Parker. Ornith. Monogr.* 48: 849-864.

ZIMMER, J.T. & W.H. PHELPS. 1950. Three new Venezuelan birds. *Amer. Mus. Novit.* 1455: 1-7.

ZIMMER, J.T. & W.H. PHELPS. 1955. Three new subspecies of birds from Venezuela. *Amer. Mus. Novit.* 1709: 1-6.

INDEX OF GENERA

Graydidascalus 24
Griseo-tyrannus 82
Guira 25
Guiraca 101
Gygis 19
Gymnocichla 63
Gymnoderus 87
Gymnomystax 117
Gymnopithys 64
Gymnostinops 116

Habia 103
Haematoderus 87
Haematopus 16
Halocyptena 3
Hapalopsittaca 24
Hapaloptila 44
Haplophaedia 38
Haplospiza 96
Harpagus 8
Harpia 9
Harpyhaliaetus 9
Heliactin 40
Heliangelus 38
Helicolestes 7
Heliodoxa 36
Heliomaster 40
Heliornis 14
Heliothryx 40
Hellmayrea 54
Helmitheros 112
Hemispingus 102
Hemithraupis 102, 103
Hemitriccus 70
Henicorhina 94
Herpetotheres 10
Herpsilochmus 61, 62
Heterocercus 85
Heteroscelus 15
Heterospingus 103
Heterospizias 9
Himantopus 16
Hirundinea 77
Hirundo 89
Hoploxypterus 17
Hydranassa 5, 6
Hydroprogne 18
Hydropsalis 29
Hylexetastes 50
Hylocharis 34

Hylocichla 90
Hylocryptus 57
Hyloctistes 56
Hylomanes 42
Hylonympha 36
Hylopezus 66, 67
Hylophilus 115, 116
Hylophylax 64, 65
Hypnelus 43
Hypocnemis 63
Hypocnemoides 63
Hypopyrrhus 117

Icterus 116, 117
Ictinia 8
Idioptilon 70
Inezia 73, 74
Iodopleura 86, 87
Ionolaima 36
Iridophanes 108
Iridosornis 105, 106
Ixobrychus 6

Jabiru 7
Jacamerops 43
Jacana 14

Klais 33
Knipolegus 79, 80

Lafresnaya 37
Lampropsar 117
Lamprospiza 101
Laniisoma 86
Lanio 103
Laniocera 80
Larosterna 18
Larus 17, 18
Laterallus 12, 13
Lathrotriccus 77, 78
Legatus 82
Leistes 117
Lepidocolaptes 52
Lepidopyga 34
Lepidothrix 84
Leptasthenura 53
Leptodon 7
Leptopogon 69
Leptosittaca 22
Leptotila 20, 21

Lesbia 39
Leucippus 35
Leucopternis 8
Limnodromus 15
Limnothlypis 112
Limosa 14
Liosceles 67
Lipaugus 87
Lochmias 58
Loddigesia 40
Lonchura 118
Lophornis 33
Lophostrix 27
Lophotriccus 75
Lurocalis 28
Lysurus 99

Machaeropterus 85
Machetornis 80
Macroagelaius 117
Malacoptila 43, 44
Manacus 85
Margarops 89
Margarornis 55
Masius 84
Mecocerculus 73
Megaceryle 42
Megarhynchus 82
Megastictus 59
Melanerpes 47
Melanopareia 67
Melospiza 95
Merganetta 5
Mesembrinibis 7
Metallura 39
Metopothrix 55
Metriopelia 20
Micrastur 10
Microbates 94
Microcerculus 94
Micromonacha 44
Micropalama 16
Micropanyptila 31
Micropygia 12
Microrhopias 62
Milvago 10
Mimus 89
Mitrephanes 78
Mitrospingus 103
Mitu 11

INDEX OF ENGLISH NAMES

The Phelps Ornithological Collection (COP) in Caracas has the largest collection of Venezuelan birds in the world. It was started by W.H. Phelps in 1939 and continued by his son W.H. Phelps, Jr. Today, as a foundation presided over by Kathy Phelps, it exists to further the knowledge and conservation of the birds of Venezuela.

Since its inception, the Phelps family and members of the staff of the COP have described some 276 species and subspecies new to science. When it first appeared in 1978, *A Guide to the Birds of Venezuela* was the first of the modern field guides in South America. In the same spirit of fresh contribution to the ornithology of the region, the present volume and the accompanying fully illustrated field guide, due for publication next year, is the work of members of the COP team.

Clemencia Rodner is a volunteer Research Assistant at the COP. She is an active environmentalist and conservationist with Board positions on several key NGOs, and is currently President of the Venezuela Audubon Society. She co-ordinates the management programme for wintering Dickcissels, in co-operation with a number of US and local institutions and government agencies.

Miguel Lentino is the Director/Curator of the COP. He is a senior consultant ornithologist to the Venezuela Audubon Society and a respected authority on the taxonomy and distribution of Venezuelan species. Miguel set up and directs the migrant banding station at the Porchuelo Pass, in the Henri Pittier National Park. He is an active field ornithologist, presently working on a number of systematic studies.

Robin Restall is a Research Associate at the COP and an accomplished writer and illustrator. His book *Munias and Mannikins* was published by Pica Press in 1996. In addition to various field projects, including an in-depth study of the Tri-colored Munia, an Indian bird now established in Venezuela, Robin is working on a book about New World seedeaters, and is painting all the illustrations for the *Field Guide to the Birds of Northern South America*.